Women Swindlers
in America,
1860–1920

ALSO BY KERRY SEGRAVE
AND FROM MCFARLAND

Ticket Scalping: An American History, 1850–2005 (2007)

America on Foot: Walking and Pedestrianism in the 20th Century (2006)

Drive-in Theaters: A History from Their Inception in 1933 (2006 [1992])

Suntanning in 20th Century America (2005)

Endorsements in Advertising: A Social History (2005)

Women and Smoking in America, 1880 to 1950 (2005)

Foreign Films in America: A History (2004)

Lie Detectors: A Social History (2004)

Product Placement in Hollywood Films: A History (2004)

Piracy in the Motion Picture Industry (2003)

Jukeboxes: An American Social History (2002)

Vending Machines: An American Social History (2002)

Age Discrimination by Employers (2001)

Shoplifting: A Social History (2001)

Movies at Home: How Hollywood Came to Television (1999)

American Television Abroad: Hollywood's Attempt to Dominate World Television (1998)

Tipping: An American Social History of Gratuities (1998)

American Films Abroad: Hollywood's Domination of the World's Movie Screens from the 1890s to the Present (1997)

Baldness: A Social History (1996)

Policewomen: A History (1995)

Payola in the Music Industry: A History, 1880–1991 (1994)

The Sexual Harassment of Women in the Workplace, 1600 to 1993 (1994)

Women Serial and Mass Murderers: A Worldwide Reference, 1580 through 1990 (1992)

BY KERRY SEGRAVE AND LINDA MARTIN
AND FROM MCFARLAND

The Continental Actress: European Film Stars of the Postwar Era; Biographies, Criticism, Filmographies, Bibliographies (1990)

The Post Feminist Hollywood Actress: Biographies and Filmographies of Stars Born After 1939 (1990)

Women Swindlers in America, 1860–1920

Kerry Segrave

McFarland & Company, Inc., Publishers
Jefferson, North Carolina, and London

LIBRARY OF CONGRESS CATALOGUING-IN-PUBLICATION DATA

Segrave, Kerry, 1944–
  Women swindlers in America, 1860–1920 / Kerry Segrave.
    p.   cm.
  Includes bibliographical references and index.

    ISBN-13: 978-0-7864-3039-0
    (softcover : 50# alkaline paper) ∞

  1. Swindlers and swindling — United States — Case studies.
2. Fraud — United States — Case studies.   3. Female offenders —
United States — Case studies   4. United States — History —
1865–1921.   I. Title.
HV6695.S44 2007
364.16'3092273 — dc22
                                                      2007007482

British Library cataloguing data are available

©2007 Kerry Segrave. All rights reserved

No part of this book may be reproduced or transmitted in any form or by any means, electronic or mechanical, including photocopying or recording, or by any information storage and retrieval system, without permission in writing from the publisher.

On the cover: Bottle and lamp *(PhotoSpin)*; palm reading model *(Brand X Pictures)*

Manufactured in the United States of America

McFarland & Company, Inc., Publishers
  Box 611, Jefferson, North Carolina 28640
    www.mcfarlandpub.com

Contents

Preface 1

1. Spiritualism 7
2. Spiritualism — Ann O'Delia Diss Debar 20
3. Love and Marriage 35
4. Sob Stories 45
5. Passing Bad Paper 76
6. Passing Bad Paper — Mabel Parker 110
7. Commercial Interests 115
8. Commercial Interests — Marion La Touche 128
9. Faking Wealth 136
10. Faking Wealth — Sarah Casselman 151
11. Faking Wealth — Bertha Heyman 157
12. Faking Wealth — Cassie Chadwick 163
13. Pension Fraud and Imposters 176
14. Various Frauds 186
15. Various Frauds — Ellen Peck 210

Chapter Notes 219
Bibliography 227
Index 235

Preface

Women who engaged in any sort of crime in this period, relative to men, were very much underrepresented in the statistics. The numbers for female arrest rates and for females incarcerated in prisons generally hovered at around five percent of the overall total. If the crimes of prostitution and shoplifting were eliminated, the proportion of women criminals would have fallen still further. Indicating how divorced the image of women and crime was in that time was how society dealt with female involvement in shoplifting, an activity growing rapidly in the era. For the first time women of middle and upper economic backgrounds — with no previous involvement with the police — were being arrested for shoplifting. Rather than accept the idea that such women could be criminals, society, for a time, denied the fact and invented a non-existent condition — kleptomania — in order to deal with such females, but at the same time pretend they were not criminals.

Violent crimes were barred to most women for the simple reason that they lacked the physical size and strength to be as effective in physical confrontations as were men. When females murdered they usually did so "non-violently" with poisoning being the preferred method. But they were as well suited as men to engage in fraud and various larcenous acts. Those frauds ranged from behaviors that netted millions of dollars down to ones that earned the women little more than pennies. They ranged from elaborate and sophisticated scams down to ill-advised and ill-conceived plots that almost guaranteed the women would be caught. Some of the women profiled in this book were well-off financially and apparently were motivated by greed. However, a large number were impoverished women struggling to survive in an unforgiving and ruthless capitalist system in which something like a "social safety net" was a dream at best.

In the profiles of women fraud artists in this book, many of the details are sketchy and many of the details unknown. While a woman many have received some media coverage at the time of her crime and/or arrest, the outcomes of cases were often never followed up by the media. Names of the perpetrators were never discovered in some cases, while in others the name the woman gave and by which she was identified in media accounts (and in this book) was almost certainly false. Police science and methods were still rudimentary in this period. An accused woman could go through a trial under a certain name and only later, coincidentally, would it be discovered she had a criminal record in another jurisdiction either under the current name or a different one.

Chapters 1 and 2 are concerned with women who were scam artists in the field of spiritualism. Mediums of both sexes were very popular in this period with most dealing in the standard materializing séance, with sub-specialties such as spirit photographs and spirit writing. One of these was Elsie Reynolds, who was dramatically exposed as a fraud on a regular basis yet, despite the widespread media attention to her as a clear fraud, she continued to attract large numbers of followers. Prosecutions of such people were rare with authorities being reluctant to touch them, declaring it was difficult in such cases to prove there was an "intent" to defraud. So often were mediums exposed that they routinely had bodyguards ("sluggers") on hand during their séances and shows to prevent the irate non-believers from switching on the lights, storming the stage and tearing off the ghostly sheet, and so on. Some bilked the same person over a long period of time with repeated private sessions. Mary Ann Scannell used her prowess as a spiritualist to produce a marriage with one of the socially and financially prominent Vanderbilt clan.

None made as much of a splash in the spiritualism world as did Ann O'Delia Diss Debar. She became so prominent that reporters and authorities took to using her name as a marker for others, as in something being "another Diss Debar case." While she started as a spiritualist, her fraudulent activities soon moved on to other areas and became more depraved and violent. Debar served jail time and became notorious enough that she was hired at a huge salary to headline a vaudeville bill in New York City, albeit for a brief time, to tell her tale as celebrity television insinuated itself into the entertainment world long before television arrived.

Chapter 3 revolves around the theme of love and marriage. Women were very active in the old marriage racket. They answered ads from men that appeared in lovelorn columns, or placed ads of their own. The object, of course, was never matrimony but to increase their bank balance, which they often managed to do. Ida Macumber ran one of these successful matrimonial scams for over a year while, all the time, being incarcerated in a state asylum for the insane. Elizabeth Young, "sixty years old, fat and shabby," reportedly enjoyed repeated success in bilking old farmers who vied for her hand.

Chapter 4 is about women who used sob stories — sad but usually false tales — to get money from dupes, in a variety of circumstances and situations. Recurring themes were that all such begging females were liars, that many were well-off financially, and that most were "unworthy." It was an age wherein the destitute fell into either the "worthy" or "unworthy" category and woe be to those in the latter group. Organized charities pursued such women vigorously; they did not like anyone intruding on their turf. Babies and young children were often part of the props used by these women to elicit sympathy and to separate people from their money. Some played a small organ, or similar instrument, on the street to try and avoid a vagrancy charge. All that gave rise to the sarcastic media response that these women were part of the "rent the baby, grind the organ" brigade. As far as the media was concerned these women with the sob stories typically rented the babies from other women and later split the money. And all the women spent all the money they scammed on alcohol. But the reality was much different. This section illustrates the difficulties of being a poor woman with limited resources and skills caught in a patriarchal system and the desperate measures so many were driven to take in order to try and survive. One of those more impoverished than larcenous was Elizabeth Hennery. She was described as about 65, no more than 4' 6" tall and weighing no more than 80 pounds. For begging door-to-door with a fraudulent sob story she was sent to jail for six months.

Chapters 5 and 6 are about women who passed bad paper, checks and drafts. They swindled financial institutions, retailers, and individuals for amounts ranging from a few dollars to perhaps over $100,000. A few of the profiled women apparently committed fraud to get cash for a man; some got away with forgeries for years because family members made good on losses. In some cases juries refused to convict even when the evidence was overwhelming and the accused had admitted in court to the crime. Some were poor, some were wealthy; they ranged from young to old. A few stood out as having strong powers of persuasion. Notable among the check passers was Mabel Parker, who actively led and directed a small gang of men in a fairly elaborate scheme.

Chapters 7 and 8 are about commercial interest crimes. All the frauds involved businesses of some sort ranging from a simple affair of a woman going door-to-door soliciting work for a supposed at-home sewing business to more elaborate affairs wherein a woman opened an office and held herself out as an investment dealer. In the commercial area none was as active for such a long period of time and so successful as Marion La Touche. During a career in larceny that spanned some fifty years, La Touche was arrested many times, served about four prison terms and bilked victims out of untold amounts of money. At the age of 85 she was still criminally active.

Chapters 9 through 12 involve women who faked wealth as a background to their larcenous ways, although their fraudulent schemes had little else in common. The women who enjoyed the most successful and notorious careers as swindlers did so by using fake wealth as part of their set-up. Once they had convinced others that they themselves were rich or had access to a lot of money, it seemed to make it easier to commit fraud; listeners to their tales became victims much more quickly, as their own greed blinded them to reality. Lying was so much a part of the lives of some of these women that they conned victims even when no money was involved. In addition, some of these females were name-droppers, mentioning people who were rich and famous as being a part of their circle. Notable among these women were Sarah Casselman, who specialized in bilking landladies, and Bertha Heyman, who earned the nickname "the Confidence Queen." Even when she was in prison serving time for fraud Heyman managed to bilk one of her visitors out of a substantial sum of money. Reportedly, she used that money to buy favored treatment from the prison warden. Most notorious of all was Cassie Chadwick. She likely scammed more money than any other woman profiled in this book (the total was never determined) and she did it by using as background a story of her incredible wealth that was ridiculously and outrageously unbelievable. Her activities could have been stopped early and easily if someone had written a letter or made a single phone call. But no one did. Chadwick ruined the careers of many supposedly shrewd and hard-headed bankers. Single-handedly she caused one bank to suddenly close its doors and go out of business.

Chapter 13 deals with pension frauds and the few women who acted fraudulently as imposters. The problems of women who became widows (from the Civil War) and the difficulties of obtaining pensions from the U.S. Army were illustrated by these women as they struggled with the rules for receiving a paltry pension. These women, too, seemed more impoverished than larcenous.

Finally, Chapters 14 and 15 deal with various types of fraud not easy to classify anywhere else. They ranged from sharp horse traders to investment swindlers to "professional" damage claimants. Oddest of all was Ellis Glenn, whose masquerading as a man was more fascinating and drew more media attention than did her larcenous ways. So successful was she in passing as a man that she was engaged, at different times and places, to two young women and, amazingly, spent some six weeks in a city jail holding cell with her real gender going undetected.

Another notorious fraud artist of long standing was Ellen Peck, who pulled a variety of scams over some 35 years. For no apparent reason (or one never reported) she turned to crime suddenly at about the age of 50, having led a nondescript but crime-free existence until then. However, having turned to larceny she remained a fraudster until at least the year before she died at the age of 85. She served several stints in jail and had one sentence commuted by a state governor very early in the term when Peck was 82. The governor thought she was then too old to be a menace to society any longer. He was wrong.

Almost all of the women profiled in this book operated alone, that is, they were not led or directed by a man. They took the initiative, albeit a criminal one. A few had men involved in their scams but in such cases the females seemed to have been at least equal partners. Another missing component in most cases was sexuality. Few of these women were aided in their schemes by their great beauty. Many were older and many were described in media accounts in unflattering ways as being quite unattractive and even repulsive. Notorious women such as Heyman, Chadwick, Reynolds, Peck, and others all fell into that category. What they did apparently have was personality, a presence, a strong persuasive ability.

The period covered by this book marked a time when women were still not people — in the sense that men were. Many dates could be chosen to mark the occasion, symbolically, of the arrival of personhood. One would be 1920 when women in the U.S.A. received the right to vote federally — suffrage had been achieved in some lesser jurisdictions before that time. Thus, in the period 1860 to 1920 American women were not yet people. Despite that handicap they could still, on occasion, be criminals.

Spiritualism

Mrs. L. Carter

Fake spiritualism was a popular and staple scam operated all over the nation in this period. According to an 1880 news report, "spiritualistic mediums" were the hot fraud of the time, especially in Los Angeles, which was home to all kinds of them, such as healing mediums, clairvoyants, materializing mediums, and so on. A reporter for the *Los Angeles Times* had his attention caught that year by the following ad running in local papers. It read: "PERSONAL—SPIRIT PHOTOGRAPHS taken at 173 N. Workman st., East Los Angeles by Mrs. L. Carter. Cut this out."[1]

When the reporter arrived at the address he found a rundown hovel—apparently a recently converted barn—with the number 173 written above the door in chalk. Among the "junky furniture" was found Mrs. Carter and a male aide, described as "low-class people." Getting down to business, the newsman asked the price of spirit photos and was told $3.50 a sitting was the rate, and 50 cents for each picture over the six that were part of the base price. "No special preparation was necessary," said the journalist as he explained the process. "You merely sat down, as in an ordinary gallery, and the pictures were taken. The faces of departed friends would be recognized [in the developed photos] if they were by, but if they were attending to other business in the spirit world they would send substitutes. No, she never had a failure." If the spirit of the departed person did not show up the first time, she kept trying until it did. According to Carter, she had been about the only spirit photographer in the U.S. for 10 years. After the reporter said $3.50 seemed a high price, Carter paused for a moment and then declared that her "control" (from the spirit world) had just informed her she could charge the gentleman $2.50. Then the reporter made an appointment for another day and left, never intending to return. Concluded the journalist, "Of course Mrs. Carter is a fraud, as the so-called spirit photography is only a trick well known to every photographer, but so far she has done but little in this city, if appearances are to be believed, nor is she likely to increase her bank account to any very great extent." Carter was likely at the low end of the profession, working out of shabby quarters and making little or no money from her attempted scam. Others, though, did better, at least for a time.[2]

Elsie Reynolds

Elsie Reynolds operated her spirit world scam in various parts of America in the 1880s, with a concentration in California. An account from Los Angeles in April 1887 smugly declared, "The spiritualistic fraud and humbug has been exposed once more. True she is a woman, and many will say that her sex should protect her from the scorn and contempt which follows such exposures when made public to the world" but because Elsie had caused such harm that was a reason "for giving her sharp tricks to the public."[3]

Less than a year or two earlier she had been exposed as a charlatan in San Francisco, her apparent first stop in California. While there, and before she was exposed, she reportedly had a great many followers who firmly believed Reynolds could bring them into contact with their dead relatives. But after the San Francisco *Examiner* proved beyond a doubt that she was a "fraud of the first magnitude" her followers left her and she took up residence in Los Angeles, renting a house, and once again her materializing séances were going "full blast." Rounding up a number of dupes she did well financially in Los Angeles and, noted an account, "the golden shekels poured into her bottomless pocket at the rate of $20 to $30 a night. Her wonderful tricks were the talk of the city, and people who were noted for their good common horse-sense, fell down and almost worshipped this gigantic female fraud." She conducted a standard-style séance that included a dark room and a circle of believers. Reynolds and her chair moved mysteriously into a cabinet, from which ghost-like figures (representing different people) appeared. For one of these performances each male member of the circle was charged $1; each woman paid 50 cents. Most séances were held at Reynolds's residence, but not all.[4]

Then came the dramatic Los Angeles exposure at the Flower Street home of a prominent bank executive (who was not identified at his request, as he was too embarrassed to have his name used); it took place on April 21, 1887. He insisted on anonymity because several members of his family were becoming stronger and stronger believers in Reynolds. Pretending to be a believer, over the course of a month the banker attended several séances at her home. Convincing Reynolds he was indeed a true believer, he arranged with her to hold a séance at his home in the presence of his family and a few friends. During that séance the banker suddenly flooded the room with light while a ghost (spirit) was cavorting about. It turned out to be Reynolds herself, decked out in a sheet. Many other such props were found in the cabinet which was always part of a séance whether in her home or on the road. According to a reporter, "The woman is evidently a good elocutionist for she changes her voice from a little child's to a rough man's in a second, and almost any one would think there were two or three persons in the cabinet." Generally, it was said she used three or four bodyguards at her séances to take care of hecklers and people who tried to expose her, but that night she was only accompanied by one. (Mediums were so regularly the victims of dramatic exposures such as the one involving Reynolds that almost all of them used bodyguards, or thugs, who regularly beat up the people who had turned on the lights, tried to pull the sheet off the ghost, and so forth. So common were they that one generic term that evolved at this time to describe them was "sluggers.") After Reynolds was exposed as a swindler that night it was said, "She admitted having been exposed time and time before, but brazenly denied that she was a humbug." The banker declined to press criminal charges but he ignored Reynolds's pleas to not take the story to the press.[5]

After the exposure of Reynolds appeared in the Los Angeles newspapers, a number of people who knew her in the past came forward to tell what they knew of her background. Seven years earlier (around 1880) she was living on 62nd Street in New York City and was known as Mrs. Elsie Crandall. Her husband lived with her and was part of the operation, with Elsie holding regular séances and making a good deal of money. Then she moved to a house on 32nd Street in New York, owned by a Mrs. Decker. Continuing to hold séances, she soon counted Decker and her family among her firm believers. However, one day Decker entered

Elsie's room to clean it while she was absent. The landlady stumbled upon the trick cabinet so integral to Reynolds's séances, and the fake props it contained such as sheets and wigs, and became so angry that she exposed her tenant as a fraud. As a result, Reynolds left the area; she also separated from her husband around the same time. The next stop for her was Brooklyn, where she was suckered into holding a séance in the home of a prominent physician. Unbeknownst to her he was a nonbeliever and turned up the lights in mid séance, exposing Reynolds prancing about in her ghost apparel. Several reporters were also present and spread the news to the public. Things became so unpleasant for Elsie that she left for Ohio and settled in a small place called Clyde. Again she enjoyed success for a time before, yet again, skeptics dramatically exposed her. Reportedly, she was arrested and incarcerated that time, along with her son Harry Crandall, who then worked with her. Apparently they were soon released, for Elsie made her way to the Southern states "where she swindled people right and left." Around 1883 she found herself in Kansas City, where she enjoyed success with her fraudulent séances for a time until a group of reporters exposed her once again. From there it was on to San Francisco, where in time reporters exposed her again, and then on to Los Angeles.[6]

Fleeing Los Angeles after exposure Elsie did not go too far, settling in San Diego. She and Harry Crandall were arrested there in September 1888, charged with obtaining money under false pretenses and conspiracy to cheat and defraud. That came in the wake of her exposure in San Diego by B. L. Boaz, a skeptic who had spent some four months on a plan to expose the medium. Several months earlier he had joined the Reynolds's group of friends and he and his wife gained the confidence of Elsie, becoming special confidants. When Elsie conducted séances at home she had a special trapdoor beneath her cabinet. It was there that her props were hidden so that a search of the cabinet — as some skeptics insisted on — revealed it to be empty. On the road, though, special arrangements had to be undertaken to get the props to Reynolds as the cabinet was also regularly scrutinized. Oft times the medium allowed even herself to be searched, along with the cabinet, to quiet the non-believers. Those road difficulties were obviated by a confederate who hid the props for the soon-to-be-materialized spirit on her person and, in response to cues from Reynolds when the lights were dimmed, delivered the props to the medium. In San Diego Mrs. Boaz filled that role. In private conversations with Boaz, he asserted, Reynolds told him she was a fraud as were all spiritualists. She told him she had been exposed as a fraud five separate times but always got away without suffering imprisonment. Also, she explained to him how a number of spiritualism tricks were done.[7]

The trial of the pair in San Diego was said to have created a considerable sensation in the city with the courtroom "thronged" all the time by both men and women eager to hear the testimony. Much of the last day or two of the trial hinged on the word "materializing" and whether or not Elsie used the word — she insisted she never did. On October 23 the trial came to an end. Judge Monroe then rendered the following decision: "While the court is individually and personally satisfied that the so-called séance was one of the flimsiest frauds ever perpetrated on a good-natured public, still there is a doubt, from the evidence, as to the intention to misrepresent, and the Court is inclined to give the defendant the benefit of that doubt. The Court therefore holds that the defendant be discharged and all bail exonerated."[8]

For at least the next fifteen years, Reynolds would hold her sessions and be regularly exposed as a fraud in the same dramatic fashion as in the past. For the same period of time the newspapers would report those exposures and describe Reynolds in scathingly negative terms. Yet the public continued to patronize her and her sessions. In November 1888, she held a session at a hall in Los Angeles. "The usual price of admission to these kind of Sunday night fakes [meaning other mediums] is 10 cents," noted an account, but Reynolds charged 50 cents a head and drew about 100 people. "Mrs. Reynolds looked very well," wrote a journalist. "She wore a large black hat something like a Gainsborough, a beaded black wrap and a brown silk dress. She appears about 40 years old, and is not bad looking. She has black hair and dull gray eyes."[9]

Early in 1889, she was working her scam in the area of Azusa, California, and charging those who wished to contact the spirit world $1 each. During the summer of 1901 she was holding her séances in Sycamore Grove, California. "For the past month [Reynolds] has been gathering a rich harvest at Sycamore Grove. People have flocked to the camp every day of the week to sit at her feet; and it costs each a dollar a sitting," noted an observer. At one session the lights were suddenly turned on by the non-believers in attendance and Elsie was once again pulled from her cabinet in her spirit clothing and her props displayed. At a séance she held in Los Angeles in October 1903 Reynolds was again exposed dramatically as a fake.[10]

Apparently she stayed away from Los Angeles then for a couple of years but re-established herself there early in 1906, taking rooms at the Grand Pacific hotel. Just prior to that, said an account, "She was at Sawtelle for months and did a thriving business among the old soldiers, some of whom, it is said, she bled for $5 or more for a sitting." When she held a séance at the Grand Pacific in March she charged 50 cents a head and yet again was exposed dramatically as a fake, in the same way as she had been revealed so many times in the past. So raucous did that exposure become that police had to attend to restore order. But no arrest of Reynolds was made then or, for that matter, at any time since her court discharge so many years earlier. On this occasion Prosecutor Frederickson explained that it was hard to make a case stick against a fake medium.[11]

Amanda Cowan

On a Wednesday evening in April 1888 some 25 people were present at the séance given by Amanda Cowan at the Hotel Van Renssalaer in Boston, among them a party of men and women convinced she was a fraud and who intended to unmask her. After several spirit forms had been seen, a point was reached when three forms appeared at once. One of them was grabbed by one of the skeptics and her cry was the signal for turning on the lights. The spirit caught proved to be a woman in the employ of Cowan and, declared an account, "At once all was confusion, and the husband of Mrs. Cowan and three or four sluggers in their employ assaulted the party and John D. Dunbar [one of the skeptics] was struck with a billy." Police arrived and found Mrs. Cowan partly disrobed behind the cabinet curtain along with a man and a girl found in the cabinet. Cowan and his wife were taken to the police station with Mr. Cowan held for assault and battery, while Amanda was released.[12]

Lizzie Bangs and May Bangs

At the same time, in Chicago, sisters Lizzie and May Bangs were said to "conduct the leading spiritualistic establishment in Chicago, and in their capacity cater to a large element in the community. Their elegant parlors have been crowded by day as well as by night and money flowed into their coffers in large streams." One of their customers was an unnamed Chicago photographer who was a regular patron of the séances conducted by the Bangs. He was an admirer of the anarchist August Spies who had been executed several months earlier. Thus, the sisters, observed a reporter, "furnished the photographer, among things usually furnished by professional mediums, the slate writing of the dead Anarchist," with the result that he neglected his work and instead, "all his time and money was given to the sisters." Soon the photographer was in an insane asylum and the sisters out on bail to answer charges of obtaining money under false pretenses and keeping a place of amusement without the necessary license. "The arrest was made while a séance was in full bloom and the paraphernalia confiscated. These women are frauds of the first water," asserted a reporter.[13]

In the midst of the arrest of the sisters the seven-year-old daughter of Lizzie Bangs died and at the funeral Mrs. Cora Richmond conducted the services, entirely of a spiritualistic nature. For a number of years Richmond had posed in public as a trance speaker, and as such gave scientific, philosophical and spiritualistic lectures while under the controlling influence, as she claimed, of some long dead scientist or philosopher. During the funeral for the child, Richmond went into her trance condition and delivered a discourse that lasted almost an hour. Lizzie Bangs blamed the police for the death of her daughter Maude, explaining she got a cold when taken to the police station and passed it on to Maude. In the child it developed into diphtheria and she was dead within a week. Of the funeral for the Bangs's child it was said, "A large crowd was present during the sad, though somewhat novel ceremonies." The specialty of the pair was slate writing wherein the medium, purportedly in a trance, put messages on a slate, with those messages coming from dead people in the spirit world temporarily taking control of the medium's body. One of the Bangs's customers was a Mr. Jestram and, whenever he had the money, he got the Bangs to call up the spirits of his dead children and display to him letters written by them since their deaths. All of that stretched the bounds of credibility more than usual because one of his offspring had lived only 24 hours, the other just four months. That is, they were not able to write during their very brief lives.[14]

Various

An 1891 article in the *Los Angeles Times* discussed the status of mediums in general, in the wake of all the publicity showered on the by-this-time notorious Mme. Diss Debar (see Chapter 2). So common had spirit photographs (photos taken by mediums supposedly of dead people, spirits, after they were dead) become as part of the stock in trade of spiritualists that they had received their own generic descriptor in the media — "spook pictures." Mrs. Tobias Stryker had secured the confidence of a wealthy New York merchant and produced a spook picture of his dead son and a spook photo of his wedding — on the "other side" in the spirit world — to an Indian wife called "Bright Eyes." With a straight face Stryker told the merchant a heavenly child was to be born to this spirit world union. Upon its alleged arrival Stryker declared that a christening was just as much in order for a child born in the spirit world as on earth and that the dead parents had determined to have their child baptized at Niagara Falls. A carload of folks went to the Falls and took part in the ceremony, conducted by Stryker under trance conditions. Since that time Stryker had dropped out of sight. Mme. Stoddard Gray flourished for a while in New York City and brought under her influence a merchant mourning the loss of his wife. Gray got him to several of her séances and provided him with several so-called interviews with the spirit of his wife. However, the merchant's friends decided a fraud was being perpetrated and decided to step in. At one séance they grabbed the spirit of the dead wife and turned on the lights; it turned out to be Gray's adult son. A similar exposure terminated the career of Eliza A. Wills, who enjoyed success for a brief time in New York City. Anna Eva Fay came to grief in Boston after an exposure at one of her séances and the Fog sisters came forward, partly out of a sense of duty to the public and partly for their own peace of mind, to confess that their lives as spiritualists had been lives of deception and fraud.[15]

Matilda Chadwick

Dr. Henry R. Rogers, the promoter of spirits, and Mrs. Matilda Chadwick, "the spook of the show," were arraigned before Magistrate Crane in Yorkville Police Court in New York on a November day in 1895. They had been arrested the evening before in a raid on an apartment where an alleged spiritualistic manifestation took place, on the complaint of Neal Girard that the pair had swindled him out of $1 by reason of a fake manifestation. Items seized in the raid included a blond wig, a soiled shroud, a black sweater, some yards of mosquito netting, and several pairs of soiled white kid gloves. Facing the magistrate, Rogers put forward the argument that Chadwick had not been impersonating a spirit, but that the spirit had materialized into Chadwick when touched by the hands of unbelievers. But, remarked a reporter, Chadwick, "the personator of the spirits, who is over fifty years old, and who looks as though she had had many sorrows, made a full statement of the whole deception." She explained, "I was paid $5 a séance by Dr. Rogers for impersonating materialized spirits. I had to do something, as my husband abandoned me six years ago, and does not support me, and I have three children to take care of. It was either this or dishonor." According to her testimony she entered the cabinet through a door in the back of it and, "I would dress myself in different costumes and come to the curtains, personating the various spirit friends of the believers present.... The messages I, of course, would invent as I went along." Chadwick had worked for Rogers for about two months. In conclusion she declared of her involvement in the scam, "I was sick and weak, and was glad to do anything almost for a living. I know I was committing a moral wrong in posing as a spirit, but I didn't think I was doing anything criminally wrong."[16]

Mary Ann Scannell

Mary Ann Scannell's notorious career figured largely in court proceedings brought by the daughter and other relatives of Edward Ward Vanderbilt in June 1907, to save the Vanderbilt estate from the hands of the self-styled spiritualistic bishop. Max Arnstein, a lawyer representing Vanderbilt's relatives declared, citing a then very famous person involved in a scam of her own, "This is another Diss Debar case." Relatives had taken an action to pronounce a commission in lunacy for the old man who took the advice of Mary Ann Scannell's spirit guide "Little Bright Eyes" to give her money, a house, and eventually to make the Pepper woman Mrs. Vanderbilt.[17]

Mary Ann was the daughter of a New England broom maker named Scannell. Her first matchmaking spirit guide appeared in the form of a Dublin ghost when the young woman worked as a servant girl in the household of a Mrs. Kenyon. In those days Mary Ann was deeply interested in marriage and Kenyon said her servant used to write letters to herself proposing marriage. The ghost of the dead Irishman tried to get Scannell married to the nephew of Father Finnegan, a Catholic priest in

Providence, Rhode Island, apparently without success. The next spirit to come along was Little Bright Eyes, the spirit of an Indian woman that used to live near New Bedford. (Either that was a remarkable coincidence or Scannell "borrowed" material from the above-mentioned Stryker.) Mary Ann "hired" Little Bright Eyes as a spirit control while she was living in that city. She persuaded George William Pepper to leave his wife and children and devote his $40 a week salary to the needs of Mary Ann.[18]

Later she and George relocated to Brooklyn. Although the couple was never legally married, she took his name and posed as his wife. It was while she was in Brooklyn that Mary Ann set up her Spiritualist Church and got involved with Vanderbilt, making many visits to his country home where Little Bright Eyes took over. Supposedly the spirit wrote letters to Vanderbilt in which she asked him to send checks for large amounts of money to Mary Ann. He usually complied. It was not the first time she had used a spirit to try and get what she wanted. One day, at an earlier time, she wanted a nice white dress that belonged to her friend, Mrs. Sawyer. The dress was a present to Sawyer from Mrs. William Tinkman, a believer in spiritualism who had recently died. During a séance Mary Ann was giving at Sawyer's house, she announced that Tinkman's spirit had just appeared to her and, said Mary Ann, "She wants you to give me that white dress she gave you." Sawyer wanted to keep the dress but did not want to offend the spirit of her dead friend. She would have gotten the dress if Mrs. J. P. Monroe, another spirit medium, had not advised her Mary Ann's message was a fake. Minerva Vanderbilt, the daughter, maintained Little Bright Eyes persuaded her father to buy a fine house and give it to Mary Ann. Edward Vanderbilt was described as "perfectly normal mentally, except for his belief in astrology, spiritualism, and a few other things of metaphysical character." The feature of the spiritualistic campaign to woo Vanderbilt that his relatives reportedly most resented was the use of letters to him purported to be from the spirit of his wife, who had been dead only a short time.[19]

Mary Ann was able to play upon Vanderbilt's love of his recently deceased wife and sent him letters, supposedly from the spirit of his dead wife, urging Vanderbilt to be generous to Mary Ann as Bright Eyes had been so helpful to her in the spirit world. Those letters were all written in Mary Ann's handwriting and sent through the regular U.S. postal service. One had been mailed to him postmarked from Germany, during the time Mary Ann was in that country on a brief holiday.[20]

At one point during the competency hearing on Vanderbilt, Mary Ann agreed the letters were in her handwriting but that her own earthly self had not been responsible; she was in a trance at the time. She told the Sheriff's jury she had been born in Mansfield, Massachusetts in 1867 and resided there until she was eight years old, whereupon her family moved to Providence. According to her she was the Reverend Mary Ann, pastor of the First Spiritualist Church of Brooklyn.[21]

Later in 1907 she was arrested on the complaint of Minerva Vanderbilt and charged with larceny in connection with her receipt of the house from Minerva's father. Soon after that, Mary Ann conveyed the house back to the Vanderbilt family. In the following year the larceny charge was stayed. Also in 1907, the sheriff's jury declared Vanderbilt to be incompetent. However, that verdict was later set aside by a higher court.[22]

Carrie Sawyer and Adella Carnahan

Officials of the League of Justice, composed of a group of business and professional men and women, declared, in April 1912, a "war of extermination" on fake spiritualism in Los Angeles. According to the results of their investigations, there were no less than 300 mediums in the city then actively engaged in the business of separating people from their money "by the boldest and most transparent of fraudulent séances." The opening shot in that war was fired the same day with the issuing by the League of formal complaints against Mrs. Carrie M. Sawyer, a "famous medium" who was caught faking a materialization that week, and Mrs. Adella B. Carnahan, an alleged assistant who "viciously assaulted" one of the investigators at that séance in an apparent effort to prevent the exposure. Both women were charged with conspiracy to defraud.[23]

Another effort to be made by the League of Justice in its campaign was its plan to ask the city of Los Angeles for an ordinance to prohibit such practices. Explained F. M. Hall, the League's Assistant Secretary, "The idea of pulling off our expose of the other night was to furnish concrete evidence of the things we charge.... We hope that the evidence will take root in the minds of the Council and an ordinance will be passed.... Los Angeles is getting to be too big a city to stand this country-fair fakerism." Assistant City Prosecutor Nimmo issued the complaints for the arrests; specifically the charge was conspiring to defraud J. J. Biszant of $45 by means of fake spiritualistic séances and manifestations. It was alleged the women accepted $30 from Biszant under the promise that they would produce before him the spirit of his dead wife Lily. The other $15 was spent by Biszant for séance tickets. Biszant, a wealthy retired lumber merchant, appeared before Nimmo and admitted he had been deceived. He told of his meeting with the women and the séances that followed, and stated that one of the women, after learning he had considerable property, wanted him to marry one of the members of the spiritualist circle. "But if I do this," he replied, "I can no longer attend the séances, for the spirit of my dead wife would then be angry." After that, the idea of marriage was dropped. As well, he admitted to the police that he had been paying the board bills of Sawyer and Carnahan for the past few weeks because he said he felt sorry for the women after their tales of woe regarding large financial outlays involved in trying to bring spirits to earth. Some 20 witnesses appeared before Nimmo who had been to various séances (for different spirits). However, apparently Sawyer was not a good elocutionist because all of them declared to Nimmo that regardless of the spirit supposedly conjured up, they recognized the voice and form to be that of Sawyer.[24]

The League of Justice was an organization formed, according to itself, to promote justice to all classes of people, to enforce honesty in public offices and to protect the taxpayer from burdens of dishonesty. It wanted to see all forms of spiritualism banned in the city because the existence of "no fewer than 300 mediums" operating in Los Angeles produced "a blot upon the good name of an otherwise charming city."[25]

Los Angeles City Prosecutor Eddie declared in May 1912 that he was not going to prosecute Sawyer and Carnahan, ordering the charges against them dropped and the defendants discharged. Eddie gave as his reason that complaining witness Biszant had left the jurisdiction of the city of Los Angles; he was then in St. Louis. When Eddie discovered his absence he wrote to Biszant, asking him to return and appear against the two "confessed fakers," but the latter refused. In her confession, it was said, Sawyer admitted she had no power to summon up spirits and that it was she who represented herself to be the spirit of the late Mrs. Biszant. Carnahan corroborated Sawyer's confession. Unable to raise bail, the two women were held in jail from their April 3 arrest until May 9. One account observed, "They had the moral support of other alleged mediums and spiritualists in the city, some of whom made the open boast that the defendants would never be brought to trial." When arraigned the pair begged that they be given an opportunity to converse with Biszant, declaring if they could see him for a few minutes they would be able to clear the whole matter up. However, it was reported, "The request was denied because it was feared the women had such control or influence over the contractor that they would be able to induce him to drop the prosecution or leave the city."[26]

None of the mediums made as much of a splash in America as did the notorious Diss Debar. She ran a variety of scams but first came to notice for her work as a medium. So famous was she for a time that she regularly became mentioned as a marker for other cases, as in "This is another Diss Debar case." Every conceivable spelling of the woman's name was used (De Bar, de Bar, Debar, and so on) in print, and each variation seemed to appear as often as any other. For consistency her name will be rendered herein as Debar.

Spiritualism — Ann O'Delia Diss Debar

Ann O'Delia (née Saloman) Diss Debar first achieved notoriety in the spring of 1888. On the last day of March in that year U.S. Senator Leland Stanford felt compelled to issue a public statement that there was no truth in the statement made in the New York newspapers by Mme. Diss Debar to the effect that he was willing to pay her a large sum of money if she would produce a spirit portrait for him. "I have no knowledge of her," fumed the Senator, "except that derived from the newspaper." Likely Diss Debar had simply invented the idea, for if nothing else she was a relentless self-promoter.[1]

On April 11, 1888 Mme. Diss Debar (she used many aliases over the years), her husband "General" Diss Debar (actually a painter named Joseph with whom she lived for a time and whose name she took, although she was never legally married to him), Benjamin Lawrence and his son Frank Lawrence were all arrested for conspiracy to defraud an elderly lawyer, Luther R. Marsh, through fake spiritual manifestations. Marsh was both wealthy and prestigious as he had once been a partner in a law firm with Chester A. Arthur (U.S. President 1881–1885). Spirits from the other side, conjured up by Diss Debar, had suggested he treat the medium generously. He complied by giving her money and deeding a luxurious house to her, which she promptly mortgaged to the maximum. Marsh was said to have been rendered a laughingstock in the high society circles in which he moved, due to the nature of the confidence trick played on him. During a brief court appearance the day after her arrest William F. Howe, a lawyer who appeared on behalf of the friends and relatives of Marsh, told the court he was there "in the interest of public morality and also to protect the heretofore-respected citizen, Luther R. Marsh, from the delusion under which he is now held by this adventuress and swindler, who calls herself the daughter of the Princess Editha Lolita Montez and Countess of Langfeldt, but who was no more that person than he was."[2]

Even before the trial was held people were using the publicity generated to their own advantage. Dr. Benjamin Lawrence (arrested with Diss Debar but apparently not put on trial) announced he felt compelled to make a full public statement of many "startling" facts and that he would do so at a lecture he gave on May 13 at the People's Theatre. At his lecture he promised to answer such questions as "Is Mrs. Diss Debar a gigantic fraud?" and "Is Luther Marsh a deluded dupe?" by means of a talk in support of spiritualism. Reportedly 175 people attended that lecture with 150 of them described as spiritualists, 19 "were boys, who giggled and snickered at brief intervals, and the remainder were reporters." One of those six reporters summed up the talk as containing nothing new and being simply a rehash of the oft-told old story "as to the manner in which spirit hands, holding a material brush and working with spiritual paints, produced first-class oil paintings on canvas held over the heads of sitters, through the mediumship of Mme. Diss Debar."[3]

One of Diss Debar's scams was the production of spirit paintings, which were different from spirit photographs as the former were oil paintings. It was Marsh himself who brought about the investigation of the "spirit pictures"—and inadvertently triggered the beginnings of a probe that undid Diss Debar—by writing to the newspapers about them. He declared that through some mysterious agency, which he felt certain was spirit power, the medium of which was Mme. Edith Diss Debar, daughter of King Louis of Bavaria and Lola Montez, he had been presented with seventy-five oil paintings, adding, "As a lawyer occupied in trying cause to hard facts for 52 years, I have no hesitation in saying that I have been able to discover no other way in which these phenomena can be produced than by the way claimed. The theory of fraud or collusion is out of the question." Such statements sent reporters out to discover that Marsh had deeded a house at 166 Madison Avenue to Diss Debar and that she had promptly mortgaged it for almost its full value. Also discovered by the journalists was how she did the painting trick. She had got all 75 of those paintings from well-known New York art collector Samuel Loewenhertz on the pretense of selling them on commission.

Then she covered a painting with a coating of chalk, making it look like a clean canvas. Presenting that "blank" canvas before Marsh, in a dim light, she would make mysterious passes before this supposedly clean canvas with her right hand; the left hand held a concealed sponge containing a cleaning fluid that she used to surreptitiously remove the chalk and reveal a spirit painting.[4]

At her trial in June 1888, Diss Debar took the stand and said the mortgage placed on the house Marsh had given her had been placed there at the suggestion of Marsh. Before the trial began she had reconveyed the house at 166 Madison Avenue to Marsh, reportedly after pressure from the New York Bar Association, although when she was on the stand she insisted the house had been returned because of a "spirit communication." At one point in the trial Judge Gildersleeve suggested it might improve her case if she would produce by spirit power some pictures in the courtroom. To that suggestion she said she had thought that very thing herself and if a spirit moved her she would act on the judge's suggestion. None did. A man by the name of David W. Crane testified he had visited a spiritual camp near Boston where Diss Debar produced a picture of his father on a card he had picked from the table. Being skeptical, he returned the next day with a marked card purchased from a photographer. However, she told him what he had been thinking and told him he had a purchased card under his vest.[5]

On June 18, 1888 Diss Debar and her husband were each sentenced to six months imprisonment. As he passed sentence Judge Gildersleeve "severely criticized the effrontery and audacity of the Madame's conduct during the trial."[6]

She served her time at the penitentiary on Blackwell's Island where she was kept at work as a seamstress. A reporter visited her on the first allowable visiting day, early in July, and when Diss Debar met the reporter in the visiting area, "She was at first inclined to angry silence, and when she first spoke at all it was to berate all newspaper men as enemies of herself and her cause." But then she became loquacious and explained to her visitor that she was constantly in the company of the same band of spirit guides who had controlled her at the residence of Marsh and that they consisted of six ancient Greeks, two Indians, an American, and a Spaniard. They had promised to continue their backing of her and to make her proposed spiritual enterprises, after she got out of prison, successful. Although she allowed as it was doubtful whether those spirits would produce any more pictures for her and it was likelier that her séances would be devoted to materializations, still, she "expected to go a great way beyond anything in that line that had been achieved by other mediums."[7]

Diss Debar told the newsman she calculated that her punishment would make her a martyr in the eyes of spiritualists while even to unbelievers it would recommend her as a famous medium. On her release from prison she planned to open a house in New York for the purpose of holding séances. In fact, an agent had leased for her a house at 151 West 49th Street, and she would convert the premises into what she would call a Temple of the Spirits. A bureau of spiritual investigation existed in New York and was mandated to undertake investigations of mediums, with a view to exposing fraud and endorsing honesty. However, membership in that bureau consisted of "leading spiritualists." When the reporter read the report they had prepared on Diss Debar, he said, "It tacitly, although not expressly, admits that the woman may have resorted to trickery to some extent, and that her business dealings with Marsh were wrong." With respect to her spirit paintings that report "asserted at great length and with much positiveness that the portraits produced by her are made by spirit hands, and that her séances for the materialization of spirits have been as wonderful as anything involved by spiritualism." In the opinion of the reporter such an "official" endorsement was "bound to make the woman accepted as a medium by all spiritualists."[8]

In conjunction with that visit the reporter called on New York District Attorney Fellows and asked him whether or not he would deem it his duty to indict and prosecute Diss Debar if she resumed her spiritualism business when released. He said it would depend upon whether anybody complained of being swindled by her. If she simply gave séances, with an admission fee of a dollar, she would only be doing what two or three dozen other mediums then did in New York, and he did not feel it was his duty to interfere. Rather, it rested with the police to raid such concerns if they thought best. Superintendent Murray, of the New York Police Department, told the journalist "that spiritual mediumship, as ordinarily practiced, was hardly the sort of evil for the police to try to abate." Anyhow, he added, it was a religious matter and he felt sure that the Diss Debars would not be molested by the police if they were giving "ordinary exhibitions." All those comments caused the newsman to conclude, "Thus it looks as though the woman will soon make as much of a fortune as the one which she schemed to get out of Marsh, and this time in safety."[9]

Exactly six months after her sentencing Diss Debar was released from prison, on December 18, 1888. "She looked as happy as ever and proposes to go upon the lecture platform," wrote one observer.[10]

Apparently she did give exhibitions of "spirit painting" on the stage right after her release from prison but they proved a failure. Whatever else she may have tried in those first six months or so after release was almost certainly unsuccessful for in July 1889 she was in court over her debts. One claim against her was from the firm of Ryerson & Brown in the amount of $254.51 for carriage hire. At her examination in those proceedings she claimed that most of her property was still in the hands of the New York Police Department — having been seized at the time of her April 1888 arrest. She told the court she was then living at 138 Waverly Place where she rented two floors furnished and that she had no property in her possession. As far as she was concerned those possessions held by the police, including the spirit paintings, were worth at least $20,000. Trying to turn the proceedings to her advantage she declared, "This examination will be a godsend to me because now I shall in all probability be able to get my property which was taken from me by Inspector Byres and others." She promised the court to submit an inventory of all her property when the proceedings continued the following week. A reporter, who apparently did not believe Diss Debar's story about having no possessions, made the point indirectly by writing, of her court appearance, "Madame Diss Debar was richly clad in black silk and black lace."[11]

When the hearing resumed she produced no inventory list. The Ryerson judgment was entered and the last legal screw was turned when Judge Leicaster Holmes assigned a receiver to the case. That meant her spiritual paintings, furniture, surplus clothing, and so forth, would be turned over to the police (if they could be found) and sold to satisfy the demands of her creditors. At this session of the hearing Diss Debar claimed most of her property was in the hands of a Mary Gilbert Deane of Brockton, Chautagua, New York.[12]

She was born Ann O'Delia Saloman, daughter of George Saloman, who lived in Louisville, Kentucky, where he was a music teacher at the time of her birth. Her birth date was unstated but she likely was born in the late 1840s. One account estimated her age at almost 70 in 1909 while a second account guessed, in 1913, that she was past 60. Through much of her life she insisted she was the offspring of King Louis of Bavaria and actor Lola Montez (very famous in her day). Such a claim was particularly impossible as her real parents were both alive long after she started making such claims. King Louis I and Lola Montez did have an affair that ran, approximately, from 1846 to 1848 and the bad public reaction to the illicit union was one of the reasons Louis abdicated the throne. Perhaps Ann O'Delia was born in that time period. Reportedly before she was 15 she had run away from home several times and was gone for days and weeks at a time, coming back home with some impossible romance to account for her absence on each occasion. At the age of 15 she was gone from home for a year. Her family finally heard from her when she wrote them a letter from France wherein she told them she was living with a Frenchman whom she had met and married in New York. When she returned to Louisville sometime thereafter she told her parents her husband was dead but refused to tell them his name. Next she made her way to New York again where she styled herself Edith Lola Montez. While there she made the acquaintance of Joseph Diss Debar, a naturalized Frenchman whose home was in Philadelphia and who left his family to live with her in New York.[13]

Once her bankruptcy proceedings were finished in New York after her release from jail, she may or may not have made a trip to Europe before returning to America and settling briefly in the Chicago area, where she practiced her spiritualism frauds. One small news item from Chicago, dated September 18, 1891, stated the identity of Vera P. Ava, who mysteriously disappeared on September 9 and was so sensationally found two days later in Cincinnati, had been settled to the satisfaction of the Chicago Police Department. Upon receipt of a photo a number of officers identified Ava as Diss Debar. No charges were contemplated with respect to the incident, but no details were given. Another very brief item dated Quincy, Illinois, October 21, 1892, noted the "notorious" Ann O'Delia Diss Debar was arrested there on that date on the complaint of a woman at Elgin, Illinois, for defrauding her out of $1,000. Later accounts giving background information on the woman said she was sent to the penitentiary at Joliet, Illinois for two years at this time for a fraud conviction.[14]

Upon her release from Joliet she ventured again to Europe, around 1892–1893, when she was arrested in Rome, accused of swindling in the American colony there on an extended scale as a spiritualistic medium. The Italian authorities decided the best way to handle the situation was simply to order her out of the country. She was reported to have married a wealthy man named William J. McGowan in 1895 in Chicago. In

1899 she came to the attention of the police in New Orleans keeping company with Theodore Jackson, "a cheap gambler and crook" much younger than herself, and who she presented as her husband. While in New Orleans Diss Debar organized some kind of mystic organization she labeled the Colony of the Order of the Crystal Sea, under the cover of which she and her husband did a blackmailing business based on fortune telling. She and Jackson were sentenced to 30 days each for the offense of fortune telling, and ordered to leave town after the sentences were served.[15]

A 1900 news account reported that news had been cabled to the U.S. recently that Diss Debar, the "obese spiritualistic medium" (she weighed a reported 300 pounds), was then flourishing financially in Capetown, South Africa. This article gave a slightly different account of her whereabouts in the 1890s. While she was in Chicago, around 1891, according to this story, she "set up quite a dazzling establishment and had a royal time of it for a year or so. Then her money gave out, and she appeared for a big weekly stipend in a Clark street museum for a number of weeks. After that she gradually went to the bad in a financial sense, seeming to have lost her cunning in entrapping elderly victims with sizeable bank rolls." From there she moved on to Washington, D.C., for a few months in 1893 where she lived "in squalor" on E Street, between Ninth and Tenth. Unavailingly, she tried to work her spiritualistic painting scam in the nation's capital. Failing dismally, she traveled to New Orleans. When the couple were run out of New Orleans they went to Florida "where she picked up a good thing here and there, and continued to enjoy the comforts without being compelled to strive very hard for them."[16]

One year later, in 1900, they turned up in Capetown, South Africa, where Diss Debar established a spirit painting racket and where occultism and hypnotic performances were the order of the day. One of her South African dupes, a wealthy contractor, gave a good deal of money to her to establish a colony of brotherly love. Mrs. Jackson rechristened herself there Mme. Swami Viva Amanda. She advertised herself in Capetown as a "qualified lady doctor, who believing the spirit greater than the body, had laid aside all medicine and trusts to faith and the power of the spirit to cure her patients." Then the pair moved to London, England, around 1900, to establish that league of brotherly love.[17]

Detective Inspector Kane of the London police had two prisoners in custody as of October 1901, Theodore Jackson and Laura Horos, on a charge of conspiring to defraud women of jewelry and money by fortune telling. Kane told news people there was no doubt Laura Horos was the former wife of General Diss Debar though she was then married to Jackson, with whom she had been living for some time in England and on the continent. "There is no doubt that they are both mesmerists," Kane added. "They could not otherwise have obtained the influence they had over their English victims."[18]

When the hearing began in October 1901 in London with the pair facing charges of immorality and fraud, Laura Jackson acted as lawyer for the pair. That caused a courtroom observer to remark on "the shrewdness the woman defendant displayed in cross-examining the witnesses. She was very theatrical, and became so violent once that it seemed as if she would have to be removed from the court." At the end of one day when the judge announced the case was to be adjourned for a few weeks and the pair remanded in custody Laura snarled, "That suits us precisely." Whereupon the large crowd present in the packed courtroom "hissed the pair heartily" as they were led out of court. Outside more crowds of people waited patiently in hopes of catching a glimpse of the pair "but in vain for a chance of hooting the prisoners. The police are taking special precautions, fearing that the prisoners might be lynched if the mob ever got hold of them."[19]

A few weeks later, as the hearing continued, a minor named Daisy Adams, 16, was "sharply" cross-examined by Laura with a view to showing her alleged intimacy with Theodore was not her first experience with vice. Photos of Laura were presented to the court by the prosecution. Obtained from the Chicago Police Department, one had been taken at the Joliet penitentiary; those photos bore the name Ann O'Delia Diss Debar. Interrupting the proceedings during the introduction of the photos, an angry Laura shouted that she had never been there. At the end of the hearing the magistrate announced he would commit her for trial on the charge of swindling and that he would commit him for trial on the charge of "unnatural" acts. Both were committed on the charge of committing criminal assaults on a girl under 16.[20]

Vera Croysdale arrived in London on a summer day in 1901 on a train from the northern reaches of Yorkshire. She had come to London in response to an advertisement in a Leeds newspaper that read: "Foreign gentleman of 35, educated, attractive, of independent means, desires to meet lady of means with a view to matrimony." Responding to the ad after some reticence, she had received a reply from the man's mother "couched in refined and friendly terms," asking her to pay them a visit in London. The letter was written on the note paper of Claridge's Hotel, which the country girl knew to be "one of the smartest in London...." That letter stated the writer was the widow of a U.S. senator who was traveling with her son for pleasure, and that herself being of English birth, she wanted her son — "who had been much sought after by American heiresses"— to find an English wife. "Lady of means" had appeared in the ad, said the letter, because to have left those words out would have subjected the advertiser "to the wiles of adventuresses." The letter was signed "Caroline Shaw."[21]

Thirty-year-old Vera was anxious to marry but saw little opportunity to do so in the small village where she lived and was employed as governess in the family of a local manufacturer. Thus, one day she told her employer she had received an invitation from friends in London to visit them and, having secured a week's holiday, took the train to London. Upon her arrival there she was met by the advertiser, Theodore Shaw, who was accompanied by a liveried footman. From the station they traveled to a handsome house in the fashionable district of Eaton Square — Caroline Shaw had rented furnished the house of one of London's stock exchange millionaires, who had suddenly fallen on hard times.[22]

According to the description provided by reporter Frank White, with respect to the latest incarnation of Diss Debar, "She was not much more than 5 feet in height, and literally as broad as she was high, weighing something like 300 pounds. Her face was masculine, and her manner at once masterful and kindly." Croysdale took to her right away and soon the pair was exchanging confidences. Vera explained to Shaw she was the daughter of a solicitor from Leeds who had died five years earlier, leaving her a fortune of 5,000 pounds Sterling invested in stocks and bonds that yielded her an income of about 200 pounds Sterling annually. She had accepted a position as governess more to occupy her time than for the additional 50 pounds Sterling per year it brought in as salary. Her mother had died when Vera was a child and she had no near relatives. For her part Shaw told Vera that it would cause a great sensation in America when it became known that she and her son had determined to devote the wealth of the late senator, estimated to be many millions of dollars, to the service of humanity. Indeed, they had already lived among the holy men of Tibet and under the auspices of the Dalai Lama himself Shaw had founded the Theocratic Unity and Purity League, of which she was the swami, or teacher, and her son Theodore

Shaw, the "perfect man." The sole purpose of the League (to be headquartered at the Eaton Square house) she declared was "the uplifting of mankind." Shaw requested her guest to call her swami in their daily intercourse and promised to permit her to join the League very soon.[23]

Within a week of her arrival in London, Vera was initiated into the League by the swami and the perfect man. She was taken into a small room and blindfolded; then a rope was tied about her waist and she was led to a door, which opened after a series of measured knocks. Following that the swami declared, "Child of Earth, I consecrate thee with water; child of earth I consecrate thee with fire." A wet finger then made a cross on her forehead and her hand was held over a lamp. Vera then had to recite the following bizarre and ominous oath:

> In the presence of the Lord of the Universe and of the Hall of Neophytes of the Order of the Golden Dawn in the Outer, regularly assembled under warrant of the great high chiefs of the second order. I do hereby most solemnly pledge myself to keep secret this order, its name, the names of its members, and the proceedings that take place at its meetings from all and every person in the whole world who is outside the pale of the order, and not even to discuss these with initiates unless he or they are in possession of the password for the time being, nor yet with any person who has resigned, demitted, or been expelled, and I undertake to maintain a kindly and benevolent relation with zeal for the occult sciences, and not to seek to obtain any writings or ritual relating to the Order of the Golden Dawn in the Outer without authorization from the Praemonstrator, the penalty of breaking any part of this oath being expulsion from the order as a wilful perjured wretch, void of all moral worth, and unfit for the society of all upright and true persons, and in addition, under the awful penalty of voluntarily submitting myself to a deadly and hostile current of will set in motion by the chief of the order, by which I shall fall slain or paralyzed without visible weapon, as if blighted by the lightning flash.[24]

While Caroline told Vera her son had been proclaimed by the holy men of Tibet to be physically, mentally and morally the most perfect man on the planet at the time, the issue of marriage no longer was discussed. However, Shaw did say to Vera it was a shame to leave her money where it earned such a low rate of return (four percent) when the swami was willing to place it in some of her own enterprises in America that would pay 20 percent. Mother and son repeatedly discussed high finance in Vera's presence and she had seen checks supposedly drawn on Shaw's accounts for sums such as $250,000 and $500,000. Theodore had a habit of flashing 100-pound notes around in Croysdale's presence. Dutifully Vera sent home for her stocks and bonds and when they arrived she turned them over to Caroline. Other young women who also seemed to be guests of the swami were to be found in the Eaton Square house during Vera's time there, but Vera only met them in the dining room or occasionally in the halls. Apparently those young women never conversed with each other. Most of the time she was not with her hostess, Vera spent alone in her room. Neither the swami nor the perfect man left the house very often, and never at the same time. Theodore did pay some attention to Vera "but his manners were too free and easy for the country girl, and she had to repulse him more than once when he had attempted to take liberties."[25]

On the day after Vera turned over her stocks to Shaw, the swami came to her to say, excitedly, that a cable from the U.S. had come with news that required her and her son to go to America immediately for a few weeks. They had decided to close the house for that period and it would be best if Vera returned to Yorkshire until their return. Off she went. She had been back home for one month when she read of the arrests in London of Mr. and Mrs. Theodore Jackson. On reading about Theodore and Laura Jackson's activities Croysdale realized the pair were the swami and the perfect man. Reporter Frank White revealed the scam operated in London was based on matrimonial advertising with the plan of the Jacksons being to get women with small fortunes under their control and then rob them as they did Croysdale. Their advertisements were always placed in newspapers some distance from London, in order that the victims might be as far away as possible from relatives and friends when they fond themselves stripped of money. The Jacksons were very careful in selecting the letters in response to their ads that they answered, for women with only a little knowledge of the world would be less likely to see through their scheme. It was only those who, after the Jacksons had made their acquaintance, seemed to be guileless or ignorant enough to fall for the swindle whom it was attempted to victimize, but the police found that during the year they had been in London they had secured the money of scores of dupes, including many women in positions similar to that of Croysdale — provincial women with small fortunes.[26]

Only women and girls with money were initiated into the League with different ruses used to get their money. Sometimes Laura would say that her American remittances were overdue, and ask for a loan until their arrival; sometimes they borrowed a victim's jewelry and pawned it. In some cases new members of the League were informed it was a communal institution, and that all were expected to put what they had into a common purse. Nothing was ever given back by the Jacksons, of course, and women who refused to part with their money were soon gotten rid of, as were those who did part with it. White believed it spoke well for the ingenuity of Laura that she often had half a dozen or so women and girls in the house at once, each believing that she was the prospective fiancée of Theodore, and yet none of them took another into her confidence.[27]

In the end the crimes that shocked England in this case were not the financial victimizations of the women so much, said White, "as an offense committed against several of them in which Mrs. Jackson's part was one from which the most depraved of her sex with any lingering trace of womanliness would turn with loathing." Daisy Adams had come under the control of the Jacksons when her mother met them at a religious meeting in London and gave Daisy into their charge. Three other minor girls also testified against the prisoners. Detectives said they might well have brought forward "two-score more victims of the unclean pair." None of the victims (including Vera) ever got any of their money or property back and, indeed, the Jacksons pled poverty at the trial. Although the court offered to provide counsel for the Jacksons at the trial Mrs. Jackson acted as lawyer for both. Said White, "Fat and short enough, with her 300 pounds avoirdupois and her 5 feet of stature, to have served as a museum freak; arranged in a grotesque white robe, low at the neck, which she declared to be the correct costume of a Swami ... she contested a forlorn hope" of escaping conviction.[28]

Details of the crimes were considered too horrific to be printed in the papers. White observed, "The unprintable details of the crimes committed by husband and wife in the house in Eaton Square, as testified to in the central criminal court, were so loathsome as to cause judge, counsel, jurors, and spectators to doubt if either the man or the woman had a scintilla of human feeling left, and to put both entirely outside the pale of human sympathy." On December 20, 1901, Ann O'Delia Diss Debar was sentenced to seven years of penal servitude. Theodore was sentenced to 15 years. In passing sentence Justice Pigham said it was difficult to conceive of more revolting and abominable conduct than that which had been attributed to the pair. Upon her release from England's Pentonville prison in 1907 (she was released early for good behavior) she went directly to a fashionable hotel in London where she lived with no mind to the cost (in spite of her pleading poverty at her trail) for a short time until her identity was learned, whereupon she was thrown out. Her next stop was the Detroit/Windsor area.[29]

Late in March 1907, in Detroit, the faithful followers of Mother Elinor, self-styled Queen of the House of Israel and head of the Flying Rollers group, pondered the story she was in reality the notorious international ex-convict Diss Debar. It was also reported that Mother Elinor carried away about $10,000 in jewels and cash, which did not belong to her, when she vanished from Detroit 10 days earlier. All the allegations were denied by David Livingstone Mackay, private secretary to Mother Elinor, as "red-hot lies straight from hell." Mostly the followers simply did not believe the story. Edward Preston, one of the trustees of the New Ever Flying Roll House said it was hard to think of Mother Elinor as anything "but a good woman who has been mighty helpful to us all." When she first arrived in the area, in Windsor a few months earlier, she passed herself off as Mrs. Emily Mason and let it be known that great wealth was at her command. Mason proposed to build a great religious colony in the Windsor/Detroit area, she told anybody who would listen. Mother Elinor never returned to Detroit and further communication with England left the Flying Rollers with little choice but to accept that Mother was indeed Diss Debar and that they had all joined her growing list of swindled victims.[30]

One year later she was living on West 25th Street in New York as Mrs. James Thompson with Mackay as her factotum. In the fall of 1908 she rented a house in Metuchen, New Jersey, where she lived with Mackay and a young woman who was passed off as her daughter. She gave séances and held poker parties that were attended by the young men of the town. The next stop for the group was in the somewhat exclusive Long Island residence colony of Douglas Manor, where they appeared in January 1909. Reportedly they again held "disreputable" parties and poker games. One of the women was described as a good-looking blonde while the other one was short and stout with a red wig.[31]

During the summer of 1909 a woman named Mrs. Lillian Hobart French rented a house in New York at 32 East 33rd Street, fixed it up and put a sign on it that said herein was the Mahatma Institute of New York — a school for the study of Oriental (especially) and Occidental religions and philosophy. Her patron, she said, was wealthy copper magnate F. Augustus Heinze, who had supposedly financed the venture or at least a part of it. French hired a few people for staff, one of whom was "an elderly woman savant of the occult, who said she was Mme. A-diva Veed-ya and a friend of this savant, who was known to the youthful Mrs. French (who was president of the institute) merely as David [Mackay]." According to the institute's literature A-diva was hired to give "financial, social, domestic, and spiritual advice." Apparently the pair met French one day coming out of a New Thought meeting at Carnegie Hall. Somehow reporters found out about the real identities of the pair and told French A-diva was really Diss Debar. French confronted the pair later that day and when they did not deny the obvious she was said to have told them to "beat it." Reportedly they packed up their stuff and left in "ten minutes."[32]

French claimed she did not know the relationship between the pair except that they addressed each other as "mother" and "son." Explaining the first meeting French related she had asked the speaker some questions and after the talk people were standing around discussing it. David approached her and said he was impressed by the intelligent questions she had asked and could he introduce his mother to her. Several meetings between the two women followed, including dining engagements at the Waldorf, culminating in Diss Debar's suggestion that she be included in the teaching staff of the Institute. It was agreed, said French, that A-diva was to lecture Wednesday afternoons at 3 P.M. on Esoterics and was to receive $50 a month for her services. It was said to be Mackay's idea that the line about advice on all sorts of matters was included in the literature and that she, French, did not know anything about it until it was too late to stop it. At this time she denied that Heinze supported the Mahatma Institute in any form. Such improbabilities led to speculation that French was really the young woman — she fit the general description — that had hooked up with Diss Debar a couple of years earlier but who had never been identified.[33]

All that publicity led to the police putting Debar through close questioning, the "third degree," on August 28, 1909. But at the conclusion of "the sweating process" it was determined no law had been broken, no charges were to be laid and for the present at least, there would be no interference with the Mahatma Institute. Diss Debar gave a bizarre interview to a reporter following her questioning by the police in which she predicted the end of the world in 1917, declared she could destroy New York City through musical vibrations, but would not do so, spouted Biblical gibberish, and insisted she was then 95 years old, when she was most likely 65 to 70, and maintained that she could live in the flesh forever.[34]

Diss Debar was notorious enough that in September 1909 she was signed to appear as a headliner on a vaudeville bill at Hammerstein's Theatre in New York. She was paid $1,000 or so a week on a one-week contract with an option for more weeks. Her act was to appear in a replica of her reception room at the 32 East 33rd Street house and to talk to the audience about her experiences; she was not conjuring up spirits. When her 13-minute "freak" act was reviewed (as all acts were designated wherein the performer did not entertain in the usual way with conventional talents — from criminal personalities to athletes and so on), *Variety* observed she was an excellent speaker, who appeared in her white robes but played fast and loose with the truth. For example, she said she had been arrested in England for nothing more than holding meetings. During a period when some of the members of the audience hissed her remarks, Diss Debar adlibbed that only two living things hissed, geese and snakes. Of course, that only drew more hisses. Concluded the review, "She said nothing of interest, excepting to claim that she is immortal.... Vaudeville doesn't want to hear the Madame confess herself a convict and tell what she was pinched for. Ann's troubles are her own."[35]

At the end of her career Frank White tried to sum up the mysteries of her appeal and successes. He wrote, "Imprisoned and exposed again and again, and in spite of a personality so striking as to make it impossible to conceal her identity once she might be suspected, she has levied upon the credulity of new dupes since she was a mere child.... Commonplace of feature, ungainly of figure, and illiterate as she is, and almost masculine in appearance and manner, she yet finds mankind an easy prey."[36]

Love and marriage was another area women were not slow to exploit in the endless search for the lucrative scam.

3

Love and Marriage

Sarah Hitchcock

Authorities in Meadville, Pennsylvania noted the August 1889 arrest of Seymour Hitchcock and his wife Sarah (née Hugell) there by Post Office Inspector Nash, charged with using the mails for purposes of fraud. Their scam was alleged to have been to place an advertisement in Western newspapers to the effect that a widow of 35 desired a Western correspondent with a view to matrimony. Dupes who answered those ads were drawn into a long correspondence, helped along by the picture of a "handsome young woman" (not Sarah) that was sent in due course. The object of the correspondence, of course, was to work up to an engagement of marriage, the obtaining of a ring and/or other presents, and last of all, a remittance of money to allow the woman to travel west to join her newly found beloved. When remittances were received the dupe got a receipt signed "Sarah H. Hitchcock, per Seymour Hitchcock." Reportedly that put a quick end to any further correspondence. Besides Meadville, the pair were said to have operated out of many other eastern cities, including Erie, Ashtabula, Olean and Oneonta, New York. Between March and July they received through the Oneonta post office money orders to the amount of $100 and 19 registered letters. Seymour was said to have admitted his guilt but said his wife assisted him under protest. Both were in jail.[1]

Special interest in that case came from Delhi, New York, where the offenders were well known and where they began their swindling career. As well, people in Delhi looked upon the individual culpability of the pair quite differently from the above account. Seymour was the son of

Matthew Hitchcock, "a well-to-do and highly respectable farmer" from the Delhi area. "He grew up to be an idle but inoffensive young man, and is now, it is believed, the victim of an unscrupulous adventuress, rather than of his own evil propensities," remarked a reporter. Several years earlier, while Seymour was still living at home with his parents, he saw an ad in a matrimonial newspaper, setting forth that a young woman wanted a husband, and invited correspondence. He wrote to the advertiser who proved to be Sarah Hugell, who was the daughter of "respectable" parents who lived near Smethport, Pennsylvania. When she was 16 she ran off with a "good-looking fellow" who later ill-treated her and then deserted her. Following that, Sarah lived for a year or two, went the story, the "gay life on the strength of liberal drafts upon the bank account of a wealthy oil operator." When that resource dried up Sarah turned to seeking a husband through the columns of the matrimonial newspapers. According to this account "She is not notably handsome, but she is bright and artful, and of winning ways." Figuring that Seymour was a good enough catch she set out to land him, and did. But, "After a time old Mr. Hitchcock got tired of maintaining an idle son and a gay and extravagant daughter-in-law, and cut off the supplies."[2]

Faced with a lack of funds Sarah took her husband to Oneonta and from that point sent ads to Chicago and San Francisco papers stating that a respectable young widow desired to hear from a Western gentleman of means with a view to marriage. She got letters "by the score" from all parts of the West and sent back ardent replies, enclosing "the likeness of a beautiful young woman." In this account it was reported that Sarah took in $400 in postal money orders at Oneonta, along with 19 registered letters containing remittances in cash of unknown amounts, together with packages of jewelry. "When arrested, with characteristic cunning and audacity, Mrs. Hitchcock attempted to shift the entire load of guilt upon her husband," concluded the newsman. "She induced him to make a confession to the effect that he was the chief criminal and she an unwilling accomplice. The chances are that the adventuress will go scot free, while the weak and infatuated husband will go to the penitentiary."[3]

Dora Ponder

Mrs. Dora Ponder, and her husband Levi, moved to Los Angeles on April 20, 1899, from Santa Ana, California. Just four days later she was arrested there on a charge of using the mails to defraud. W. F. Smith of Pasadena swore out the complaint, against a woman he knew as Dora Morton.[4]

Ten days later a United States grand jury returned an indictment against Dora. Smith, employed as a waiter at the Royal Bakery restaurant, had entered into a correspondence with Dora that in due course led to a proposal of marriage. Then on March 15 Smith got a letter from her in which she asked him to send her money (to Santa Ana) to pay the freight on half a carload of household goods, which had been shipped from Kansas City and was then being held for her at Orange, California. A suspicious Smith investigated and it was determined the woman had no goods at Orange, nor had any been shipped to her from Kansas City. Smith claimed to have given her money earlier, however, upon the belief that she would marry him, although throughout their correspondence Dora was living with her husband. Dora had led Smith to believe that while she had been married she had secured a divorce from Ponder and it was because of that divorce that the goods were shipped to her from Kansas City by her ex-husband, who still resided in that city. On May 3, 1899, Dora Ponder pled guilty to a charge of using the mails to defraud. She was sentenced to 10 days in jail and to pay a fine of $1.[5]

Catherine Durand

Judge Fitzgerald's courtroom in Los Angeles was jammed with spectators in March 1900 in one of the oddest matrimonial cases on record. A woman appeared there calling herself Mrs. Bauer, who told the court she married a man by the name of Claude Albert Durand in New York City in 1876 and that he afterward deserted her, living together for more than a year before the desertion. Some two or three weeks after her marriage, she alleged, Durand, a waiter by trade, came to her and told her his true name was Thiebaud Bauer (Bauer, 53 years old in 1900, was an ex–world champion wrestler from a couple of decades earlier and very well known in his day, although Catherine said she was not familiar with that fact at the time Durand made his admission, nor had Durand elaborated at all). After 1881 she lost all touch with the man. Then, around 1894 or 1895, she made a trip to Alsace, Germany. There she accidentally became acquainted with an old woman who had pictures of her son hanging in her bedroom; the son was Thiebaud Bauer. Catherine declared she recognized him as her deserted husband, and finding out who he really was, set out at once for Los Angeles (where Bauer lived) to prove her case.[6]

She asked the court for recognition that Bauer was indeed her husband and for $300 a month in support payments. Bauer's real estate holdings in New York City yielded him an income of $1,000 a month. He denied in court that he ever saw the woman in his life until she started to pester him some five or six months earlier. Many witnesses clearly refuted Catherine's claims. One was Julius Dentel, who owned a restaurant in New York from 1874 until 1885. She worked for him there starting in 1876. As well, he employed her husband C. Alfred Durand as a waiter for about 10 months. Dentel did not know Bauer and had never seen him until the trial but said definitely that Bauer and Durand were two different people. Other witnesses made similar statements. Some showed Bauer was in a different part of the world when Catherine said they were together someplace else. Other witnesses testified when Durand met Bauer in the streets of Los Angeles a few months before the trial she admitted to Bauer she had made a mistake. Another witness was Dr. George W. Burleigh. He testified that the pair had come to his office to have him examined. She gave Burleigh a list of marks supposedly on her spouse's body (for the purpose of identifying him) but when the physician conducted the examination he found none of them.[7]

In view of the weight of the evidence — Catherine had no witnesses or evidence save her own word — Judge Fitzgerald, of course, found her to not be the wife of Bauer. He ordered her to henceforth call herself either Mrs. Durand or Mrs. Jelsch (from the trial it was revealed she had first married Jelsch and then Durand but no documents existed to indicate she had divorced Jelsch). No charge of perjury was preferred against her because the prevailing feeling was she may have been "dementedly mistaken" and thus a conviction would be unlikely. Fitzgerald remarked the evidence was so "crushingly overwhelming" in favor of Bauer "that it is difficult for me to understand how a case of this character could ever have been permitted to enter a court of justice." If she had started her quest in good faith, said Fitzgerald, once she arrived in Los Angeles "she was thoroughly satisfied in her own mind (in fact, she so stated) that Bauer was not her husband" but then she got the idea "she might be able to get something out of it. From that time on her case has all the earmarks, the unmistakable earmarks of a blackmailing suit." Despite those comments, the judge exonerated her lawyers as innocent. Taking 4½ days in all, the trial involved an expense of over $5,000 to Bauer even though there was not "a particle of evidence" in the case that Bauer ever knew or laid eyes on the woman until a few months before the trial.[8]

Etna Dungan

Extending over six years, from about 1895 until 1901, Etna Dungan of Gold Hill in southern Oregon had been in correspondence with a large number of men, all anxious to secure a wife and, under promise to marry every one of them, she is said to have secured various sums of money ranging from $5 to $300. Through the suspicions of one of her correspondents (an Idaho man wrote the Gold Hill postmaster asking for information about her) the attention of postal authorities was called to her, resulting in her indictment by the Federal grand jury and her subsequent arrest. Dungan was alleged to have answered the ads of men looking for wives and after a certain amount of correspondence and the exchange of photos she would say she was willing to marry the letter writer and would suggest that money be sent her to help defray the expenses in coming to her future husband's home. Testimony at the grand jury hearing revealed that Andrew Nutson of New Whatcom, Washington, received such a letter from Dungan and sent her $50 while A. Sagendorph of Aberdeen, Washington, under similar circumstances, remitted $25 to her. A cash bail of $500 was provided for Dungan by her father, who was described as a "wealthy man."[9]

Ida Grace Macumber

Even an "insane" woman was able to run a matrimonial bunko game. As of 1905 Ida Grace Macumber had been confined to a federal insane asylum in Lincoln, Nebraska for a number of years. She was described in one account as "a handsome widow" whose mind was affected by the death of her husband, which led to her commitment to the asylum. Curiously, it was reported, she developed a mania for remarrying. Seeing the advertisement of a Denver matrimonial bureau, Macumber enrolled herself as a member, categorizing herself as an attractive widow of marriageable age whose first husband left her with "boundless" wealth. Within two months she had reportedly received over 1,500 letters from as many different men. She had asked for photos and had a collection of some 1,100. Answering many of these letters and apparently promising marriage, she soon began to receive packages containing rings, jewels, articles of clothing, and so forth, from her suitors. The volume of mail arriving for Macumber alerted authorities at the facility but under Federal law, as construed by the courts, the State (in this case asylum authorities) had no legal right to interfere with the mail of insane patients. Hence, asylum officials placed the matter in the hands of a post office inspector who, after an investigation, issued a fraud order against the woman.[10]

Due to the complications of the case it took almost a year from discovery of the scam until the U.S. Postmaster General issued an order against Macumber prohibiting her from using the mails. After the order was issued, it meant that all letters addressed to her in the future relating to matrimony would be marked with the word "Fraudulent" and returned to the senders. In that year or so when she worked the fraud, Macumber was able to victimize an unknown number of men, on the strength of her promises to marry them, out of an unknown amount of cash and goods.[11]

Elizabeth Young

The grand jury of the circuit court adjourned in Rockville, Maryland, in March 1910 after, among other things, returning two indictments against Mrs. Elizabeth Young, the "aged woman" who, it was charged obtained several hundred dollars from Roger P. Murphy and Henry B. Gardiner, well known farmers of Clarksburg district, by false pretenses.[12]

Supposedly a "wealthy Baltimore widow," the 60-year-old Young seemed an unlikely person to run a matrimonial bunko game but she was said to have been successful. Elizabeth was charged with having separated many farmers of Montgomery County, not just the two named in the indictments, from small sums of money. However, the majority of her victims were too embarrassed to come forward and publicly press charges. Young, who apparently did not care for whiskers on the faces of her numerous admirers, once ordered one of them, an 82-year-old "prosperous" farmer, to shave off his beard; he did so in the hope of winning her hand. Once the beard was removed, said the man, Young called him "the ugliest man I have ever seen; as ugly as sin," and declined his marriage proposal. Further testimony showed Young not only procured small sums of money on the story that she would shortly come into a large fortune "but that she was the woman in the case in several feuds among farmers in the vicinity of Clarksburg, who had been friends and neighbors for years," so hot did the contest for her hand become. According to the account of the trial on the two counts of obtaining money by false pretenses, after several hours spent in taking testimony, "the court announced it had heard enough, and told the prosecution that a final argument was not necessary." One of the subheads of the article asserted, "Mrs. Elizabeth Young, sixty years old, fat and shabby, faces in Rockville court an array of farmers who charge her with being a mercenary coquette."[13]

Fay Loewenstein

Fay Loewenstein's Los Angeles scam was more in the nature of a commercial sting but when one of her dupes fell for her she was able to extract even more money by using the matrimonial ruse. At her preliminary court hearing in February 1909 the main witness was George Harmer, a Santa Monica, California artist who answered Fay's pitch to become a partner in her phony 1,600 acre cattle ranch. On the stand Harmer admitted falling in love with Fay, proposing to marry her, and setting a wedding date for December 25, 1908 (it was later postponed). He bought her a $157 diamond ring and she also got an unspecified amount of cash out of him. Harmer candidly admitted he had been an easy mark for Fay and was ready to fly away with her as her husband to her non-existent ranch, supposedly located in San Luis Obispo, California. After the wedding date had been fixed Fay announced regrettably that it would have to be postponed because her mythical stepmother (with whom she did not get along and with whom she had various legal disputes) persisted in staying at the equally mythical ranch.[14]

After the hearing a 70-year-old man named Paul Durand approached a reporter to say he immediately recognized Fay as a woman he knew a year earlier as Blanche Black and who lived on South Flower Street between Tenth and Eleventh. Back then Paul had read an ad in one of the Sunday papers asking for a partner with $500 to invest and an expected return of $100 to $200 a week. Durand explained he answered the ad, visited the woman, and got the same story that Harmer originally received, that of a cattle ranch up country in San Luis Obispo. On his first visit, believing the investment scam, Durand left a $25 deposit and invested $50 more on a second visit. However, then he got suspicious and refused to invest any more money.[15]

A. Wolter and H. T. Martin

On December 15, 1909, Mrs. A. Wolter and Mrs. H. T. Martin were arrested in San Francisco and those arrests were said to have "uncovered one of the biggest matrimonial agencies' frauds ever revealed in this city." The complaining witness was Bernard Deppe, "an aged man" who said that after marrying Mrs. Martin, Mrs. Wolter took his money from him to purchase a lodging-house for his new wife. Deppe was given a small room in the house, but Mrs. Martin did not adopt his name, nor live with him, so he complained to the police. Detective Bunner, who conducted the investigation, was offered a wife by Wolter, who assured him that she would herself perform the ceremony without publicity. Bunner then placed her under arrest and next located Martin at the lodging-house she was running. Upon being arrested there Martin confessed that she had been one of the principals at several of the marriages performed by Wolter and that on each occasion the money of the man involved had been used for the purchase of a lodging-house.[16]

May Clark

Federal charges of using the mails to defraud were laid in October 1912 in Los Angeles against Mrs. May Clark. She formerly resided in Denver, Kansas City and Topeka and was described as well known in all four of those cities for using the old marriage swindle. The complainant for the Los Angeles charges was J. T. Kelly of Stilwell, Oklahoma, well-to-do rancher, widower, and the father of six boys for whom he was anxious to secure a mother. Kelly alleged he was swindled out of his money through the pages of one of the better known American matrimonial newspapers, published in Denver. After he paid the enrollment fee, explained Kelly, he was sent a series of descriptions of various women looking to marry. He was struck especially by the information he received for #435, "Age — 35; Nativity — American; Religion — Presbyterian; Disposition — Kind and loving; Weight —120 pounds; Height — 5 ft. 4 in.; General characteristics — Fond of home life, can do all kinds of housework or can assist in business. Eyes blue, brown hair, fair complexion." May Clark was the woman described and Kelly entered into correspondence with her at her Los Angeles address. Contained in one of those "letters of a loving character," added Kelly, was a picture of a "remarkably beautiful girl of about 25," which he was persuaded was a picture of Mrs. Clark. Eventually Kelly proposed marriage to her and was accepted. He said she told him she would be delighted to make a home for his six boys "and that their names — Claude, William, Abner, Charles, Richard and Eddie — had always been favorites with her." Kelly said he did not care to marry her in Los Angeles and was unwilling that his Stilwell associates should know that he had secured a bride in that matter. Therefore they were to meet in Springfield, Missouri where they were to be married. Then Clark wrote to him that she had suddenly become ill and been taken to the hospital. Might he be able, she wondered in a second letter to him, to send her some money both for medical expenses and to cover travel costs to Missouri. He could and did immediately and without question. Suddenly her letters to him stopped and when his letters to her produced no replies, he contacted the authorities.[17]

Olga Hurst and Anita Johnson

Two men and two women, Olga Hurst, Anita Johnson, George Turner, and Emil Hurst, were said to have operated in many American cities, defrauding older men of their life savings by a matrimonial scam. All four were arrested in May 1913 in San Francisco following a complaint against them from Charles Laine, a lawyer in Cheyenne, Wyoming, who, in a letter, accused them of carrying on wholesale fraudulent operations. In his letter to the San Francisco police, Laine declared the two men introduced the two women to wealthy men of advanced years with the women doing their best to marry the targets. After the marriages, Laine charged, the women decamped with the money and other valuables of their elderly husbands. Laine cited the specific case of Henry Smith, 76, of Cheyenne who, he said, married Olga Hurst some time ago after Olga first won him over by a series of letters from San Francisco. After the marriage, continued the attorney, Olga disappeared, taking with her cash and securities amounting to between $3,000 and $5,000 in value.[18]

One of the most popular scams used by women was to present sob stories and rely on them to generate so much sympathy in the listener that money was forthcoming. Babies were often a popular prop women used in conjunction with a good, sad story, and cynics sometimes summed up such ruses as, "rent the baby; grind the organ." Mostly these women and their fraudulent stories represented not so much a criminal mentality but a measure of their desperation in trying to survive in the midst of a ruthless patriarchal capitalist economic system.

4

Sob Stories

Margaret Hartley

Late in August 1865, a "respectable-appearing" old woman was found by the authorities wandering the streets of New Jersey in an apparently agitated state of mind. However, on the following morning she seemed to have recovered and was quite rational. At that time she gave her name as Margaret Hartley, a resident of Springfield, Illinois, and said that she had been robbed of $200 in cash, a check for $400 and her baggage claim tickets, after having been drugged. A few days later, after her story had been checked a reporter said, "It now appears that the old woman, who is of good address and intelligence, is an imposter, and a successful actor in that line of business."[1]

Some 10 days before she was found in New Jersey she played the "drugged and robbed game" in Boston, explained the newsman, and considerable sympathy — and donations — was generated by the story. A man named Priestly took a great interest in her case and spent about $60 on her for clothing and then personally accompanied her on the train as far as New York, in her supposed journey to Springfield. When they arrived in New York Priestly consulted with friends as to the best way to get Hartley on to Springfield, spent more money on her by paying her fare, procuring a double berth for the entire trip for her, and got her food for the journey. He assumed she made her way home. That is, until Mr. Tift (one of Priestly's New York friends) happened to read the account of the old woman found in New Jersey. Tift went to the hospital in Jersey City where Hartley remained, and confronted her. Hartley attempted to explain the matter by saying she had stayed in New York for the purpose of recovering her baggage. Then, said the account, she was "required to take a sudden departure" from New York. She was described by a reporter in the following fashion, "Mrs. Hartley is between sixty and sixty-four years of age, slim built, five feet seven or eight inches in height, long features, face very much wrinkled, very lady-like in her deportment and apparently well educated."[2]

Jane Doe

Panhandlers of this era worked the same as they do today in the sense of stationing themselves at a particular spot and working passers-by. Something they did in this period they no longer do was to go door to door (and in commercial areas they went store to store), spinning out their stories and hoping for the best. In fact, going door to door was just as popular, or perhaps more so, than working a spot, one reason being that panhandlers could be, and were, arrested for vagrancy in this period. Going door to door likely made it easier to avoid the police. Many of these panhandling women became notorious in certain areas for their fraudulent sob stories.

Over the last few months of 1867 a German woman with a little child had been in the habit of calling at the residences of leading citizens of New York City, asking for money so she could afford to bury one of her children who had just died from the effects of burns received some months earlier in a house fire. Usually her story was that the son had died the previous day at Bellevue Hospital, being the fourth child of hers to die from burns received in that fire. Authorities proposed, she continued, to inter the body in Potter's Field (where the state buried the indigent), which she hoped to prevent by raising enough money so she could bury the child by the side of her husband and other children in Greenwich. After a reporter determined her story to be "wholly false" he added, "The woman plays her part to perfection with tears and sobs, besides skillfully using the names of well-known physicians and clergymen, she generally succeeds in obtaining a liberal sum from her victims." Her story was exposed after two clergymen were so impressed by her tale they volunteered to perform the burial service and only discovered the truth on reaching the hospital. Concluded the reporter, "Any one seeing this imposter will do a service by giving her into the custody of the Police."[3]

General

A lengthy article critical of the large number of beggars to be seen on the streets of New York was published in April 1870. Mostly it was about male beggars but it did have a section on women. Estimated by this article was that there were about 15,000 men and women "who make it their daily object to wander through the streets of the metropolis in quest of food and money at the houses of the rich and poor." According to the reporter one of the most familiar objects in the mendicant line, "and one that is thoroughly disgusting and inhuman, is the stout, thinly-clad Irish woman who tramps from saloon to saloon, day and night, all the year round, with a sickly and emaciated babe bundled in her arms." Once she entered such a place the woman was constantly "pinching the helpless little creature in her arms until it screams with pain." Then going from person to person she almost coerced money from reluctant donors, thanks to the screaming infant, in order, she explained "to buy coal wid and feed the childer." However, the reporter insisted, none of the money collected was ever spent on either coal or children, but rather was spent by the woman and the mother who rented out the child (after the latter had received her share of the collector's take) in the "low gin-mills." Summing up his view of these women he had just described the reporter fumed, "There are about one hundred women of this class in the City who eke out a miserable existence by this style of begging and it would be a good thing for the public if a law were enacted to forbid their cruel and inhuman practice."[4]

Caroline Wilson

On a Monday night near the end of October 1878, "a handsome woman of good address" drove up in a coach to the door of the Reverend Mr. Langford in Elizabeth, New Jersey. She explained to the clergyman that she had been involved in the Civil War and had exhausted her finances in providing for Union soldiers and thus, she was appealing to him for financial assistance for herself. The woman showed letters of recommendation bearing what purported to be the signatures of prominent men in different parts of the country. Langford was suspicious of the woman, for unreported reasons, and, believing she was a fraud he had her arrested. When arraigned before Justice Osborne she said her name was Caroline S. Wilson, that she was 51, that she was born in Springfield, Massachusetts, and that her husband had died of pneumonia during the war.[5]

Arrested along with Wilson was the driver of the carriage that delivered Wilson to Langford's door. His story showed she went out on her begging excursions in good style and that she had been for some months at least "a professional solicitor of aid." Carriage driver Edward B. Kett said he first met Wilson in July 1878 when he drove her from a railroad station to an address in Trenton, New Jersey where she was staying. Wilson told him she would need his services frequently and he agreed to carry her for 50 cents an hour. Kett had been in her employ ever since. Then he listed by name 17 different towns and villages in New Jersey and Pennsylvania (among others) to which he had driven her. Kett added that she paid him from $3 to $6 per day and that she always boarded in first-class hotels, paying $21 a week for room and board, and $3 for fire. According to the driver's account, "She wanted to board in hotels, as she wanted waiting on; since she engaged me I have at her request refitted the inside of my cab, putting in a fine Brussels carpet and other things to make it warmer and more comfortable." Found in her luggage by the police were papers that were said to show Wilson had been traveling around in that style soliciting aid since 1871. Among her letters, which were thought to be forgeries, was one bearing the signature of William Cullen Bryant. Kett was discharged by the police; Wilson was held. On their excursions Kett probably made better time than many modern-day commuters, averaging eight to 10 miles an hour.[6]

Mary White

During the summer of 1881 "a well-dressed and rather fine-looking woman" made the rounds calling at houses in Paterson, New Jersey, telling a sorrowful tale to the effect that her husband had died some time earlier and left her destitute. As a result she had been compelled to sell all her furniture and other property until all she had left to her name of any value was her wedding ring, which she was now forced to try to sell to get the wherewithal to support herself. The wedding ring appeared to have been worn, was marked "18k" on the inside, and carried the initials "M.C." At that point in her tale, "She wept as she told how this was the last souvenir she possessed of her departed husband and how it grieved her to part with it." Worth about $15, she sobbed, she was willing to sell the ring for just $4, so anxious was she to get some money. Apparently more than a few listeners purchased the ring, leaving the bereaved one to travel on to another house where she related the same story and displayed the same ring. Exposure came when one of the buyers casually showed his bargain purchase to a neighbor who, as it happened, produced an identical ring, right down to the same initials. Fearing they had been had the pair took the rings to a jeweler where they were found to be made of brass and worth about 10 cents each. When she was arrested and charged with obtaining money by false pretenses, the ring seller gave her name as Mary White.[7]

Elizabeth Whitford

Elizabeth Whitford, about 40, "with a strongly marked red nose, heavily built, apparently American, claiming to be the widow of a physician, dressed in a red shawl and dark merino dress" went door to door among the "charitable" in New York in 1883 collecting money to clothe a deceased child that she said the Superintendent of Outdoor Poor was supposed to have agreed to bury, explained an account. It added, "She has an ever ready flow of tears at her command." An agent of the Charity Organization Society (an umbrella group of charity associations) investigated the case and declared Whitford to be "an arrant imposter." The address given to listeners by Whitford turned out to be that of a brewery and no person with her name lived anywhere else on the block. Generally, Whitford directed her appeals for money to ministers.[8]

Elizabeth Daly

A well-dressed woman of 46 was brought into the Tombs Police Court in New York in August 1884. The arresting officer told the court he had seen her go into a building at 203 Broadway where he observed her to beg 10 cents. She then "accosted" several other people on Broadway and at a store she successfully begged 25 cents from a clerk. At that point she was arrested. She told the court her name was Elizabeth Daly, that she lived in Jersey City, New Jersey, and that she had a large family to support. Several police detectives who happened to be in court for other matters told the judge Daly was known as the "Queen Beggar" and had been plying her trade for 14 years. She was sent to prison at Blackwell's Island for six months.[9]

Mrs. Meyers

A 55-year-old woman who confessed to having swindled 600 men out of small sums between February and September in 1888 was locked up by the police near the end of the latter month. About one week earlier William Thompson, a coffee broker, and Charles Haynes, a stockbroker, had called separately at the police station to report they had been swindled, the former out of $20, the latter of $15 "by an old woman." She told both men the same story: that her only son had just died in the Home for Incurables, and unless she obtained some money he would be buried in Potter's Field. She showed them a card with the name of the Reverend Asa Reed Dilts on it and said that he had told her they were very charitable men. Thompson and Haynes were members of a church in Plainfield, New Jersey, of which Dilts was the pastor. Each man gave her money and when they next saw Dilts they discovered they had been swindled as the pastor did not know the woman at all. When police arrested her she gave her name as Susan Smith but Captain McLaughlin recognized her as a "notorious swindler known to the police as Mrs. Meyers. She had already served several terms in prison.[10]

General

An editorial in the *Washington Post* in March 1892 complained the arriving fair weather had again brought onto the streets that class of mendicants that charitable institutions found it hardest with which to deal, "namely, the woman who crouches on the curbstone droning a mournful tune from an organette and nursing a sickly looking baby to attract sympathy and alms from passers-by." Explained the editor, "These women are fixtures. They haunt the same streets from year to year, always with a baby exactly the same age. The child is usually drugged to keep it quiet. It is rented by the month from none too careful parents.... The women get enough by their curbstone begging to make them refuse all offers of help from charitable sources, and it is next to impossible to get them off the street." Admitting the police had the power to order them to "move on," he felt they did not do so because they felt sympathy for them. Also, said the editor, agents for prevention of cruelty to children societies could usually make a case against these women on behalf of the babies but for some reason never did, with the result that several such women were "familiar sights to the pedestrians on the business streets" of Washington.[11]

Louise Schenke

The elderly woman who was detained at the Washington, D.C., police station at the start of 1887 for having imposed on the generosity of Samuel Ross proved to be Mrs. Louise Schenke, 54, of Rossville, Baltimore County, Maryland. She had a husband, was the mother of five children and, it was reported, "they have a nice little home and are well supplied with the necessaries of life." Although she had never been convicted on any charge, the police of Baltimore saw fit a number of years earlier to take her photo for future reference. Whenever lately she had been charged with falsely representing her condition for the purpose of securing money, her age had worked to get her discharged. According to her story her maiden name was Louise Myer and during the Civil War she was connected with the secret service of the War Department. From that experience she maintained she learned all that was bad there and it led her to be less scrupulous, and when she retired from the service she attempted to make money in the easiest way possible.[12]

Schenke explained that one day years in the past she told a pitiful tale and obtained a sum of money from a female friend. When the friend learned she had been scammed she had Schenke arrested, but for one reason or another no conviction was registered. Emboldened by the fact she had escaped conviction, Schenke resorted to a similar fraud whenever she found herself short of cash. In the case of Samuel Ross, she had represented to him that her daughter was in trouble and $20 was needed to help her out. After giving her that amount, Ross learned she was a fraud and went to the police who, after a time, arrested her on a charge of obtaining money under false pretenses. Judge Miller, however, discharged the woman, for reasons not reported.[13]

General

The *New York Times* ran a long article about male and female beggars again, this time in 1898. Reportedly a great watchfulness was then kept over beggars because the special agent of the Charity Organization Society (said agent was devoted to investigating possible fraudulent solicitations both on the part of individuals and organizations) had two police officers in plainclothes from each police court in New York assigned to help him in the work of suppression of begging. Supposedly it worked to keep the number of beggars down. According to this account female beggars never attempted the physical subterfuges attempted by male beggars (such as pretending to be blind, adopting a fake limp, painting an ugly scar on the body, and so on). "Perhaps she does not need to. The general regard paid her sex may bring her a sufficient income without a waste of brain power. When women do attempt something in the nature of subterfuge they are apt to let the unusual use of brain power run away with them," concluded an observer. An example given was of a woman who played an organ on the streets and announced she was in need of assistance also by the use of a framed placard that stated she had seven small children, the youngest less than six years old. But the unconvincing part was the fact the placard was dated and then was over eight years old. Another woman beggar displayed the following placard to passersby: "To the Public: I recommend you this poor woman Mrs. Grannelli, she is a widow, and mother of six children. The Hon. Mayor gave her permission to play this hand organ in the city of New York, as a means of supporting her family. I know her personally to be a very poor and very good woman. Very respectfully, R. H. Hayes, M. D., 333 E. 65th St." But a reporter had determined there was not a word of truth in the placard. Grannelli was not a widow and not the mother of six children. There was no Dr. R. H. Hayes, nor any Hayes at the listed address. Finally, the mayor of New York did not sanction anybody to play musical instruments in the streets.[14]

By this account female beggars could be classed into different categories. One category was to place them with "the tramps," the class of beggars most commonly known and most often seen. "They are old, degraded and dirty, and they are to be seen sitting in the parks and on the streets, asking the passer-by to 'Please help an old woman.'" Their age was said to work in their favor in helping them raise enough money for their night's lodging and something to eat and "what is more important to them, something to drink." Usually they lived in the worst class of lodging houses in the city, facilities kept by other old women who rented basements usually in rear houses where they had one, perhaps two, rooms for which they paid a rent of $3 or $4 a month. In that flat were then accommodated some 12 to 15 "women tramps" who slept on the floor and paid a rent of 10 cents a night.[15]

Another class of New York beggar woman described by the account were those who went door to door at certain area houses and were kept supplied, at least with food, by "warm-hearted servant girls." And "Whether they are worthy or unworthy, this class of beggars is difficult to catch, for the servant girl will declare that her visitors have only come asking for work or refuse to answer inquiries altogether." The special agent of the Charity Organization Society reportedly caught one of this class at his own door. Provisions had been disappearing from his household more rapidly than the stomachs of family members seemed to indicate, so one day he hung around outside his own house. In due course he stopped a beggar woman leaving his door and found she had collected "all kinds of foodstuffs" from his house. "Women support entire families in this way," remarked a journalist. "They have their regular customers to whom they go, some on one day and some on another. A woman frequently finds that begging is so easy that when the need is past she keeps up the practice."[16]

Yet another class were the women who asked for car fare. Many were to be found in the city and some made it their special business. One was a neat, nice, well-dressed little woman with gray hair. Most who worked the car fare dodge were said to be well advanced in years and "They have respectable homes and make a comfortable living by begging." The special agent had also had a run-in with one from this class and, despite attempts to suppress her, she was still working the car fare dodge. Younger than most, at 32 or 33, she always carried an umbrella and was respectably dressed. Approaching passers-by she told the same story of having lost her purse and being in great need of a nickel so she could get home. When she made her appeal to the special agent he gave her the requested five cents (the full fare at the time) but the woman did not then head out to board the train to her Harlem destination, but continued to approach passers-by for more nickels. All that was done in the presence of the special agent who became infuriated at such cheek. He went to her, called her a "professional beggar," and demanded his five cents back. She gave it to him.[17]

Elizabeth Brady

Around Christmas 1898 Mrs. Elizabeth Brady disappeared from her old stand for parts unknown. For years she was said to have earned a living on East 23rd Street and on East 14th Street between Second and Third Avenues by grinding out tunes on the hand organ "and putting up hard-luck stories, gems of plaintive ingenuity. To gullible passers-by she was a bundle of rags and a picture of physical misery. A Quaker bonnet partly concealed her features and the bent figure and plaintive wails did the rest," commented an observer. She had rented a room in the neighborhood for $1.10 a week and, while she had lived there for years, her age (estimated at 45 to 60) and origins were unknown. One conclusion drawn by a reporter was that underneath the less than promising physical exterior "was a sturdy constitution, an alert mind worthy of a better occupation, and a general capacity for touching sympathetic persons."[18]

Hester Smith

One of the spinners of sob stories most reported on was Hester Smith, who operated in Washington D. C, with the first account of her activities appearing in print in 1899 and the last in 1923. Mrs. John B. Wight, wife of a District (of Columbia) Commissioner aided materially in the capture in March 1899 of Hester Smith, a black, who had been soliciting money on the representation that her home in Montgomery County had burned down and her two children, together with all her household goods, were consumed in the flames. Wight helped her financially but later discovered that many of her friends had also been approached and an investigation proved that Smith's story was false. Some time later Wight happened to spot Smith on the street, whereupon she called a cop and had the woman arrested. A couple of days later she was arraigned under the vagrancy act and not for obtaining money under false pretenses as she was charged at the time of her arrest.[19]

Eight years later Hester, 26, was arrested again by Washington police, charged with obtaining money by false pretenses. For the previous week or so the police had been receiving complaints against a black woman. That woman would appear at a house and solicit a dollar or two, explaining that she lived in the country and would deliver in payment for the "loan" five dozen eggs. Her husband was an invalid, she explained to her listeners, and she was compelled to earn a livelihood as best she could. Several people who advanced her money and who did not receive the promised eggs reported the matter to the police.[20]

Twelve more years passed before Smith made the news again when the police yet again arrested her, in June 1919. She confessed to various scams, some 11 cases of false pretenses and one of petty larceny, promising the police she had still more to confess. Detectives on the force were unsure as to whether or not to believe her as she seemed to them to confess too often and too readily. She also promised the police to lead them to other people doing the same things but, noted a reporter, "She has a bad habit of steering the detectives to vacant lots and unoccupied houses." As Smith gave her background information to the police she punctuated her account with terms such as "in the cooler," and "United States hotels" (that is, federal jails). With respect to her current arrest it was alleged Smith went door to door and misrepresented herself to people as a laundress who was calling on speculation for washing work. When people decided to employ her to do their wash, and went off to collect the laundry for her, Smith stole everything that was within reach and not nailed down, and fled. During this most recent period of incarceration, during her questioning and her confinement in a precinct cell an amazed reporter commented about her deportment, "She had consumed enough cigarettes to demoralize a whole village. Without 'coffin nails' she cannot find the proper artistic atmosphere for her confessions, and so they have been furnished her by the police regretfully, but in profusion [it was very unusual for a woman to smoke in 1919 America]."[21]

Smith appeared in court in February 1922 with the police testifying she had visited 11 homes in different sections of the city (she faced 11 counts of fraud but had visited many more houses) and told the women who answered the doors that she would supply a domestic for less money than they were currently paying for their maids. Hester explained the girl who was to come to work lived in the country and needed railroad fare, which Hester solicited on the girl's behalf. Once they advanced the money that was the last they saw of Hester. Also, she confided to the housewives that she had a place in the country, and would furnish eggs for 35 cents a dozen. Here again, railroad fare was borrowed. Eleven victims appeared in court to testify they had been scammed by Smith for sums of money ranging from 25 cents to $8. Pleading guilty to all 11 counts, the prisoner commented, "I'm guilty all right. All I did was to get a few dollars out of some people who tried to get something for nothing at some other person's expense." Assistant United States Attorney Ralph Given told the court that because Smith had borrowed enough railroad fare in total to take a trip to California, a stiff sentence should be imposed. A sentence of 30 days was given for each of the 11 counts.[22]

Just one year later Smith was in court again. This time it was alleged she had gone door to door with a woeful tale of twins born to her the day she represented her husband had died. In her house-to-house canvass in Washington she told people who answered their doors she was the mother of 13 children and had been left destitute by the death of her husband. Before the police arrested her she had collected sums of money from $1 to $5 from an estimated 100 people. In police court Judge John P. McMahon sentenced her to 360 days in jail on four charges of false pretenses.[23]

Bridget Redmond

Bridget Redmond, who described herself as the "guardian angel" of the Guardian Angel nursery, was sentenced to one year in the penitentiary in June 1900 for petty larceny, in the Court of Special Sessions. The complainant against her was Simon Nachtigall, a cotton merchant. He said that on May 21 he contributed 25 cents for the aid of the nursery, at the solicitation of Redmond, and that later on he found out that the nursery did not exist and that Redmond appropriated all the money she had collected ostensibly for the nursery for her own use. Redmond declared she was supporting several children at the nursery to those she approached for money (it was supposedly a home-based nursery run by herself alone, a common enough situation at the time), but when the police reached her residence they found no children, nor any sign of any having been there.[24]

Jennie Page

Forty-year-old Mrs. Jennie Page was arrested in Washington, D.C., in April 1901 on a charge of vagrancy and sent to the House of Detention for the night. Her arrest came about after a complaint was made by Norman Luchs, who reported a woman had been asking for money from storekeepers. About one week earlier, he said, the woman came to his store and, acting in an excited manner, told him she had lost her pocketbook and as she lived a long way off she had no means of getting home unless she could raise some change. Luchs gave her 25 cents. One week later she called at his store again. This time she told him she was a stranger in Washington and while out shopping had become separated from her sister, and needed money to get to a friend's house. As he recognized Page, Luchs refused to help this time. When she left his store he followed her and learned she had visited various stores that day and told various stories of misfortune. Calling on the police, Luchs had her arrested. When she was picked up she gave a home address but when the police checked it out it was found she had boarded there 15 years earlier, but had not lived there since. Also ascertained by the authorities was that a woman answering her description had visited stores all over the city and solicited money on various pretexts.[25]

Ada Much

Mrs. Ada Much, of Washington, D.C., widow of George W. Much, was held for the Grand Jury by Judge Scott in March 1899 on the charge of obtaining $1.50 by false pretenses from Mrs. Andrew Wilson, also of Washington. Wilson told the court that Much had asked her recently for a $1.50 donation towards a sum, it was represented, charitable people were contributing to effect the removal of the remains of a poor man, "Mr. Robinson," to Alexandria, Virginia for burial. Much was said to have given her name as Davis during the solicitation. Wilson was touched by the story and went to the address given by Much, to see if she could give any further aid to the Robinson family, if necessary. Andrew Wilson was the Treasurer of the Vermont Avenue Church and Much represented that the late Robinson was a member of the same church. When Mrs. Wilson arrived at the address and found no Robinson family the fraud was exposed. When arrested Much denied the charges and said if she had called on the Wilson home she did not remember doing so. Also, she claimed to be the mother of eight children.[26]

Much, alias Mary Agnes Murch, Murray, Davis, Anderson, and so on, was arrested again in August 1901 and locked up in the House of Detention charged with "larceny by trick." The complainant this time was Mrs. Carl Hoffman, although the woman was expected to face a total of seven separate fraud charges (different victims and different stories). Reportedly Much had been arrested three times on similar charges but in every case the persons complaining asked the judge at the Police Court to not be severe with her. As a result she was dismissed from court twice and in November 1900 she had a sentence imposed but suspended and was released on her personal bond to insure her future good behavior. A history of Much's operations in Washington for the previous two years, obtained by a reporter from the official records of the Police Department and the Associated Charities, revealed that she used at least eight different names over that time period, and that she used at least three different stories to elicit sympathy from potential victims.[27]

She called on many well-known charity workers and the Associated Charities and several of its agents were numbered among her list of victims. Ada was then about 45 years old and did have eight children, although two were adult sons who had left home. One was in the U.S. Navy while the other was employed in the Navy Yard. The first record of Ada appeared on the books of the Associated Charities for 1895 when a report was compiled on the activities of a woman who solicited money to enable her to remove a load of kindling wood from the Navy Yard. Much told people she could get the wood for free but she did not have the money to transport it from the Yard to her home. Several people gave her sums ranging from 50 cents to $1 for hauling the wood home but a subsequent investigation showed the money was not used for that purpose. When the Associated Charities found the woman had a large family of children, efforts were made to help her in a "legitimate" way by the charity workers, and it was thought that Much had been relieved of the necessity of begging, when she was again reported to be working the same scheme to obtain money, "which her neighbors said she used to purchase liquor." As soon as Much came under suspicion in one section of Washington she would move to another and use the same process to obtain money. According to a newsman, "She appealed to several ministers as a woman in distress, and her general appearance went a great way toward proving her statements."[28]

After using the kindling wood scam for some time, with varying success, Ada branched out into a new field and began to collect money on the plea she needed it to bury her husband. In this story (a slight variation on the Mr. Robinson, a stranger, theme) she told people she desired to send her husband's body to Alexandria, so it could be buried in the old family burial ground. The cost of shipping the body there, she said, was $5 and she usually managed to get a small sum from the person approached. One of those approached was a "prominent" Presbyterian minister who gave a small sum. Then he engaged Ada in more conversation with the end result being she requested the minister to preach the sermon at her husband's funeral. He consented, and was given an address, date and time by Much. However, when he showed up on time only to find no such address existed he concluded he'd been had and reported her to the Associated Charities. An investigation was undertaken by that group and it was discovered the woman was Ada, although she had used a different name. Apparently Much had never used her real name in any of her scams. Police and charity workers had a difficult time in suppressing the woman's activities because, for one thing, she invariably gave false names and addresses, which slowed down investigations as officials tried to determine real identities.[29]

With respect to her most recent arrest, on Hoffman's complaint, it appeared the woman had returned to an earlier scheme. According to Hoffman, a woman giving her name as Mrs. Schrader called on her to ask for money so she could pay for hauling a free load of kindling wood home from the Navy Yard. Hoffman gave her some money but became suspicious a short time later when a relative visited her and happened to mention she also received a visit from Schrader. When Hoffman reported the matter to the police they, of course, immediately recognized the method as that of Ada Much and arrested her. During that canvass of Hoffman's neighborhood that day Much had called on other people under the name of Mrs. Slater. Police admitted they did not know what to do with the woman. The six younger children in the Much family were turned over to the Board of Children's Guardians for "safekeeping," while Much was under detention. One of the woman's adult sons told police the night of her arrest that efforts were being made to have his mother committed to the insane asylum.[30]

When Ada was arraigned in court the next day only Hoffman appeared against her although, said an account, "The police attempted to secure the presence in court of a number of persons whom she is said to have victimized, but, despite their efforts, could not persuade them to prosecute. Numbered among her dupes, the police assert, are many prominent clergymen and charity workers, who shrunk from the publicity police court proceedings would entail." Judge O'Donnell was disposed to be lenient with her, though he heartily endorsed the plans of the police to bring her schemes to an end. Thus, he sentenced Much to six months in jail but suspended sentence upon her promise to leave the city of Washington at once. She was told by the judge that if she was found in the District of Columbia after the time limit to be set by him expired she would be arrested and required to serve the six months imposed by O'Donnell and also the sentence (duration not stated) imposed by Judge Kimball at an earlier court session. Much promised to leave town and her eldest son, in court with his mother, assured the judge that he would do what he could to send his mother away to an institution.[31]

Jennie Gold

On a December afternoon in 1901 at around five P. M., socialite Mrs. Mary D. Carey (daughter of the late Samuel T. Carey) was returning home after a social engagement. As she walked along Madison Avenue she was accosted, she said, by a young woman who asked her for money, saying she had not eaten all day. Carey, after questioning the girl, decided not to give her anything and was about to walk away whereupon the girl spat on her. Then Carey hurried away, but was followed by the girl, "who became offensive." As a result, Carey called a police officer and had her arrested. At the station she gave her name as Annie Kramer. Later in the evening her father showed up at the station house, but only to declare her to be "incorrigible."[32]

On the following day Carey appeared at the Jefferson Market Police Court to press a charge of begging against the young woman, whose name turned out to be Jennie Gold. In this longer and fuller account, no mention was made of the spitting, which apparently did not happen. As a high flyer in social circles Carey told the court that prior to being accosted, "I had been taking luncheon at the home of Mr. Pierpont Morgan." After being solicited by Gold who said, according to Cary, "Won't you help me? I have not eaten in two days, and I am starving," Carey responded by saying, "I told her that she was well dressed and unlike a beggar, and that she ought to be ashamed to ask for alms." Explaining further, Carey added, "There was no sign of want about the girl, and I decided that she was one of a number of beggars that infest the neighborhood and try to pester passers-by into giving them alms for the sake of getting rid of their importunities."[33]

When Gold continued to beg for money Carey declared, "'I shall give you nothing,' I declared finally, but found upon walking away that the young woman was following me, and evidently intended doing so till I paid to get rid of her. 'Please help me,' she said, dripping into another whine, 'You are rich and I am poor and starving.'" Carey walked on without paying any more attention to Gold, whereupon the latter became so enraged that she made insulting gestures and remarks. At that point Carey decided to have Gold arrested. Carey argued she wanted to press the complaint, not because she felt vindictive, "but because the girl is a disgrace to the decent poor and does harm to those that are really deserving and in need. By her own father's statement she is a professional beggar and quite incorrigible." A reporter indirectly indicated where he stood when he wrote about the prisoner Gold, "She was dressed in an exclusive tailor-made walking skirt and jacket, with a handsome deep green waist."[34]

Gold told the court she was temporarily unemployed, was a hardworking person, and that her family was starving. Policeman Flynn identified the girl as a beggar that he knew well. In passing sentence Magistrate Cornell stated, "Your own father called last night at the station house and complained that you were an incorrigible beggar, and that he wished you locked up. I'll let you off with a ten-dollar fine this time, but next time you are brought here I will send you to the workhouse." Whereupon Gold broke down and sobbed she did not have the money. However, soon thereafter, it was reported, a well-dressed man who gave his name only as Curtis appeared and paid Gold's fine.[35]

Mrs. Pratt

The Associated Charities reported in 1903 that for six years, since 1897, it had been looking up successive false addresses given by a woman who went door to door in Washington, D.C., soliciting money. According to the group, "The agents of the Associated Charities consider it desirable that thoughtless alms at the door be withheld and such charitable treatment substituted as will enable, and even force, the woman to help herself and prevent the steady deterioration of character caused by her begging." A bewildering array of aliases had been used by the woman, one of which was Mrs. Pratt. Different stories were told by Pratt as she canvassed houses, with a main one being that she had an old mother dependent on her. Another recurring one was that she herself had been dependent on a daughter who had just died of consumption or cancer.[36]

In a typical approach she usually began by asking for work, such as sewing, but always ended with a request for money to buy food and/or medicine for her aged mother or for herself. When work was given her Pratt asked to have part of the pay given to her in advance as she was under a pressing need for money. Of course, she never did the work, or returned the material she had been given. Pratt generally introduced herself by saying she had been sent by a specified person known to the one upon whom she was then calling, and she claimed to be a member of the church attended by the latter. But investigation always showed her to be unknown to those she cited as a reference. One of her methods of securing those references was suggested by the experience of a woman in Chevy Chase, Maryland, who received inquiries concerning the woman from a large number of her personal friends soon after Pratt made a pitch at her home. Apparently Pratt had extracted from this lady's card receiver (it was a common practice when members of the middle and upper classes went visiting to leave a calling card containing their name and address — much the same size and format as the modern business card — at the residence they visited; they did this whether the household they were calling on was at home or absent) a number of her friends' calling cards and had told the ladies whose names were thus secured that she had been recommended to them by their friend. Other aliases Pratt used included Chase, McKenzie, Scott, and Stevens. Addresses she gave always turned out to be vacant lots or empty houses. In conclusion the Associated Charities declared its "agent thinks that this excellent appearing woman should be treated with such wise kindness as will make these practices both unprofitable and unnecessary."[37]

Elizabeth Hennery

When Elizabeth Hennery appeared in court after being arrested in February 1903 when Policeman Hartigan noticed her going door to door soliciting money, it was the officers of the Charity Organization Society, through Assistant Superintendent Godfrey, who appeared as complainant. According to that group, she was one of "the most troublesome and persistent beggars they know, having been on their records for no less than twelve years." Godfrey exhibited a "huge mass of correspondence" on her — complaints. It was said to consist of hundreds and hundreds of letters, most of them on fashionable stationery "for the little old woman scorned to prey upon those of humble fortune." Every missive, declared Godfrey, "was a letter of inquiry or complaint from householders she had attempted to inveigle." Not all the offended ones, he added, complained of her begging alone, "for there were in the heap many stories of household articles, ornaments, and other things, generally of small value, that had been missed after her departure."[38]

Other aliases the woman used included Hendricks, Hennessy, and Lucy Henderson, and "The little old woman, who wept all through the hearing, is about sixty-five years old, four feet six inches tall, and weighs not more than eighty pounds. She is clad in deep mourning, and is tidy in appearance." Godfrey added that she came from a family of "expert beggars, who live at 300 Henry Street, consisting of two other sisters, one a hunchback, and a brother, all well known to the society." The prisoner sobbed in court that she had no other means of making a living and had to live somehow, that she had no idea that what she did was wrong and that she was too old to work. As he passed sentence on her in New York's Yorkville Police Court, Magistrate Deuel said he was sorry for her but nevertheless committed her to six months in the prison at Blackwell's Island. Thus, summed up a reporter, the "maraudings" of "The Little Old Woman in Black" would cease, at least for that amount of time.[39]

Helen Estel

The Widow Wallace, or Estel (sometimes Estelle) as she sometimes called herself, was said to be making "easy money" in the summer of 1904 among the fashionable homes of the Westlake district of Los Angeles by canvassing for aid, although the *Los Angeles Times* declared the woman was exposed in the pages of that newspaper a few months earlier. She simply changed her location of operation, revised her method of soliciting and resumed business as usual. The Mrs. Wallace doing house to house canvassing in the Westlake area was described by the newspaper as "a pitiful-looking, thin little woman, wearing rusty black, and proclaiming herself a widow with no resources." As well, she told people she had an application on file at the Hollenbeck Home (apparently a care home for the aged) and that she had been given assurance that she would be admitted at the next vacancy. And all she lacked to complete the required deposit was the small sum of $3.50. Reportedly, that story usually worked and in numerous cases the importuned householder made the donation an even $5, or sometimes more. Then the widow, after profuse thanks, hesitatingly asked the householder whether she didn't have some old clothing that she could have as she only had a meager wardrobe. Any clothes she managed to collect quickly found their way to a second-hand store. According to the matron of the Hollenbeck Home, Estel had never been there, nor did she have any application on file. Staff at the residence had received several calls from people within the past few days and told of donations to the woman to aid her in getting admission to the home.[40]

Several months earlier Estel was working a similar scam among the business offices of Los Angeles, claiming that she lacked only a few dollars of having enough to pay to get her baggage out of impound — she said the luggage was held at the Natick Hotel until a board bill was paid. "She made a good living at this until exposed by the newspaper, when she changed her place of residence and proceeded to the suburban districts with her new tale, concocted for the purpose of bringing forth money from the liberal-hearted," explained the newspaper. Estel had been a boarder at the Natick. She remained there until she ran up a large bill, and sought other quarters when she was urged to settle her Natick bill. Among the effects left in her room at the Natick were long lists of names of people who appeared to have been "worked' in various other cities. Some of the names, for example, were those of well-known New Orleans business firms. Her bill at the Natick was run up to $200 before she was finally evicted. Although one of her scams was to say she was collecting money to reclaim her luggage, she never returned to the hotel to collect her trunks. When opened those trunks were revealed to contain nothing of value. Estel was about 66 years old.[41]

Estel first came to Los Angeles in May 1904 when she moved into the Natick. When she was evicted she appealed for aid to the Associated Charities, telling them she had recently lived at the Hotel Hudson in Gainesville, Georgia for five years and, overall, spent 14 years in that city and that she owned property worth about $1,000 in Atlanta, Georgia. Other details she revealed about herself to the group were all designed to show that she was an unfortunate Southern woman who had come to Southern California on account of her health. She was recommended to several Los Angeles families originally from the South by Associated Charities, with the idea the legendary hospitality of Southern people would display itself to Helen's benefit. It did for she was said to have lived well until she was discovered to be "only a common, every-day grafter." Reverend E. P. Ryland, pastor of the Trinity Methodist Episcopal Church in Los Angeles, wrote to friends in Atlanta to check out her Georgia stories. All were completely false. Exposure was completed when the *Los Angeles Times* published an account of the woman's frauds. And that stopped business for a time.[42]

Changing locations, Estel then went door to door relating "with much pathos" that upon coming to California she visited her sister in Los Angeles only to find her sister very ill and impoverished and that she was trying to raise enough money to take her poor sister back home to Philadelphia. The Associated Charities received numerous calls from people in various parts of Los Angeles making inquiries regarding a certain old lady who was soliciting aid for her sick sister. She was described "as a little woman, with slightly bowed shoulders, hair gray, rather sharply-cut features, dressed in black and with all the smaller details of dress indicating refinement." During her most recent rounds of canvassing she was surreptitiously followed by a reporter who remarked that among the places visited by her after she had finished soliciting for the day, "were several cigar stands, and inquiry revealed the fact that she smoked cigarettes. She did not purchase the five or ten cent packages, but obtained a well-made and rather expensive cigarette that reflected credit upon her judgment."[43]

Felice Lawrence

Women beggars were said to have become so numerous in the Williamsburg section of Brooklyn that the police had started a crusade against them. "Many of these women have infants, which, the police say, they hire for the purpose of creating sympathy, while they grind an organ which they rent from a concern in Manhattan," explained a news account. According to the Society for the Prevention of Cruelty to Children these women, in order to make the infants cry, "pinch them with great severity." A couple of days earlier a woman had complained to the Brooklyn police that a woman with an infant and an organ working a particular street corner was "cruelly pinching the little one" to excite sympathy. A police officer was dispatched and took the woman and infant into custody. She said she was Mrs. Felice Lawrence of Hoboken, New Jersey. When she was arraigned the next day before magistrate Higginbotham an agent of the Children's Society was present to press a complaint against Lawrence. "It is high time your Honor that the practice many women beggars have of pinching little children who do not belong to them for the purpose of creating sympathy while playing an organ should be stopped," the agent said to the judge. "It has been called to our attention that some of these infants are black and blue as the result of the cruel treatment to which they are subjected." Lawrence stated she had not ill-treated the child, that it was her infant, and that she was poor and compelled to beg. Higginbotham discharged the woman after warning her to keep away from Williamsburg.[44]

Kate Dunn

New York City had a Mendicancy Bureau in 1904 with seven detectives in it, all under the command of Chief Mendicancy officer James Forbes. Reportedly, that was the reason that there were then comparatively few beggars in New York. In just one day in December 1901, 19 beggars were arrested and by 1904 they had practically been driven out of the city, or so went the boast. Over 1,000 arrests of beggars were then made each year, "which keeps the city free from the nuisances and swindlers." A generic name given the women beggars was "Blackhood" because they usually wore a black bonnet or hood. One example of the type was Kate Dunn, who had exercised her profession for some time outside the Church of St. Vincent de Paul on 23rd Street. Most of the women in that category were past middle age, wore shawls in addition to the black bonnet and were comparatively respectable in appearance. Few people were said to refuse their importunes because "they are women and old." However, officer Forbes remarked, "But there is not one deserving one among 'em. Decent people don't go on the street. Some of these women are misers and have good bank accounts. Others, and nine-tenths of them, are begging for whisky."[45]

Elizabeth Hogan

Seventy-year-old Mrs. Elizabeth Hogan was arraigned in the West Side Court in New York in April 1905 on a charge of vagrancy and was paroled in the custody of the Probation Officer, Miss McQuade. Policeman Pierce told the judge he had found Hogan going store to store in the vicinity of Amsterdam Avenue and 96th Street, asking for financial assistance, and showing a bandaged hand. Pierce explained that when the woman was taken to the station house and the bandage removed it was found there was nothing wrong with Hogan's hand. Special Agent John Godfrey of the Charity Organization Society said the woman owned two houses on West 49th Street worth at least $27,000 and had a bank account with a balance of over $7,000. Hogan lived with her niece, Mrs. Dwyer, who told the court her aunt had a good home and plenty of money but that her eccentricities took the form of going out into the streets and looking for sympathy.[46]

Jane Doe

Two Italian women wearing the garb of Roman Catholic nuns were arrested and locked up by New York police in July 1905, charged with obtaining money under false pretenses. When asked who they were the women gave the following particulars to the police: Sister Marie Adele, 28, and Sister Marie Agnes, 52. Initially agents of the Charity Organization Society, who had been searching for them for weeks, detained them for the police. Many complaints had been made to priests in the city, who were informed that two women clad in religious attire were collecting money around town and could give no satisfactory explanation as to who authorized them to do the collecting. Archbishop Farley was much annoyed over the matter and urged the police to make greater efforts to effect their capture. When agents of the Charity Organization Society finally spotted the women they trailed them to a tenement house on East 29th Street. After the police were called in and started to make the formal arrest (the women were still dressed as nuns), a crowd gathered and began to mutter angrily. Several other policemen had to be called in to deal with a growing and increasingly restive crowd. A mob of Italians followed behind the officers who were trying to take the nuns in and it stopped only when an Italian officer explained to the crowd, in Italian, what had happened. Reportedly, the two women had collected many hundreds of dollars which they told donors were to be used in establishing a chain of hospitals.[47]

Mrs. Gordon

Several Masons who resided in Orange, California were deceived in 1907 into giving money to a woman who called at homes and identified herself as Mrs. Gordon. She told a hard-luck story, complete with tears, and presented a note purportedly to have been written by Mrs. John Morris of Tustin, California (the wife of a high-ranking Mason). That note stated that Gordon was known to the writer as a hard-working and deserving widow, the daughter of a thirty-second degree Mason and that she was in great need of $27 in order to care for her sick little girl. After acquiring about $46 the woman was said to have left town.[48]

Rifka Siskind

In Special Sessions Court in New York in September 1911, officers of the Gerry Society appeared against Mrs. Rifka Siskind, who was charged with "impairing the morals of a minor" as she used two children with her as she preyed upon the sympathies of people on the east side. On September 6, agents of the society found Siskind sitting in the midst of a pile of broken and shabby furniture on the sidewalk with "a wretched child huddled in her lap" and another by her side. A plate located in a conspicuous place invited the contributions of passers-by. An investigation showed the whole scene was a phony eviction scam that had been staged carefully and one that Siskind had played many times. When she was arrested the plate held about $18. Officials explained the woman had once been really evicted and, after accidentally finding it could pay well, took to the fraudulent eviction business. According to the Gerry Society, "With her children and an assistant to help her she had been making $150 to $300 a month" and has "a comfortable home on the upper east side."[49]

Mary Stafford

Many who used the sob story in an effort to generate money skipped the bother of going door to door, or the problems of working a street corner. From the relative comfort of their own homes they mailed off hard-luck letters, usually to a targeted audience. The doings of society people were regularly reported by the press, and usually the media reported names and addresses. Sometimes these con artists operated even more efficiently by placing ads in newspapers or by using newspapers in other ways to generate publicity for them, and ultimately money. Around June 1, 1888, Mrs. Joslyn, superintendent of the Women's Exchange, part of the Benevolent Society of Los Angeles, received a "pathetic" letter from a Mrs. Mary E. Stafford of Tustin, California, asking if she could not obtain employment for her in Los Angeles. That letter dwelt at great length on her destitution, saying she had been very sick, and had two little boys who were dependent on her. Stafford added she had once been engaged in literary work, and was anxious to eventually get to San Francisco where she felt she could resume such work.[50]

Joslyn was a sympathetic woman and at once started to search Los Angeles for a job for Stafford. In her letter she claimed she was ready to do any kind of work but remarked that her children were a drawback in landing and holding a job. Even that was attended to as Joslyn got a commitment from the managers of the Orphans' Home to take them in, if that proved to be the only way to get Stafford a job. Also, Joslyn got $50 subscribed to a fund for the family, and a ticket to San Francisco. In the meantime she decided she should write to contacts in Tustin and find out something about Stafford, before doing any further work on her behalf. Answers to those inquiries, however, turned out to be disappointing. People who responded to the inquiries felt Stafford was perhaps needy but also reported her as unwilling to work and rumors were that she had been sexually involved with a married doctor in Tustin. On the basis of those responses the officials of the Women's Exchange declined to have anything more to do with her. Nevertheless, she came to Los Angeles around July 1 and called at the Women's Exchange where she was told she had been exposed and then received the cold shoulder.[51]

Notwithstanding the above treatment, Stafford stayed around Los Angeles for a few days and went about the city soliciting aid, using Joslyn's name as a reference, after which she dropped out of sight. Several days later a newspaper account told of a woman, accompanied by two children, who had her pocket picked of $42 at the Southern Pacific train depot in Pasadena, and that had she had been left destitute. She gave her name as Mrs. Stanwood of Santa Ana and told a very sad tale. That account came to the attention of the women at the Benevolent Society, who were reminded of Stafford. An investigation revealed that Stafford had gone to Pasadena. Authorities returned Stanwood to Los Angeles and held her at a station house until Joslyn and a Mrs. Bath (also of the Benevolent Society) arrived, whereupon both identified her as Stafford. However, after being given a "sound lecture" the police discharged her. According to a reporter, "Mrs. Stafford is a woman about 27 years of age, of rather good appearance, and a very smooth talker, and it is more than likely that she will try to work other towns in this vicinity on the 'literary racket,' and the ladies of the Benevolent Society wish to put all charitably-disposed people on their guard against her."[52]

Lillian Hall

In the United States District Court in Hartford, Connecticut in 1891, Mrs. Lillian Hall of Ellington, Connecticut, pled guilty to fraud, to devising and operating a scheme whereby she received gratuitously various articles from charitably-inclined people. In September 1890 Hall advertised in newspapers that gifts of any kind for a girl who had one leg amputated and the other one stiff, as the result of a fall, would reach their destination if sent to Clementine St. George Ray (herself) at the listed address. Reportedly, she received hundreds of replies to her ads. There was no such person as the luckless girl described and in court Hall was fined $300 and costs.[53]

Jane Doe

Late in 1894 the Charity Organization Society in New York issued a warning to the public against six con artists then working the city. Two were men, in two cases the gender was not specified, and the other two were women letter writers. In all cases the details were skimpy. One was described as "The young woman with the initials L. F. G., who writes begging letters from New Jersey" and the other as "The woman who wants clothing for her infants and often includes a dispensary ticket or a bogus bill for rent" in her letters. While no names were given, the Society noted all six were "flagrant" frauds but the perpetrators used so many aliases "that it is idle to give names." Concluding its warning the Society called the attention of the charitable public to the fact that the success of such fraudulent appeals presented to numerous men and women struggling under very tough circumstances to earn a living "an almost overwhelming temptation to attempt similar dishonest schemes. Hence to give money to persons of whom nothing is known is to run the risks of unintentionally leading or confirming a person in a course of fraud.[54]

Mrs. Andrew Clark

A fraud case up before the U.S. Post Office Department resulted in the issuance in August 1897 of a fraud order against Mrs. Andrew Clark and her son Samuel Clark, both of Norwich, Connecticut. For a number of years the pair had been in the habit of writing begging letters to prominent people. Having selected someone they believed would respond they would write them a touching letter to the effect that a member of their family was sick and destitute. By limiting their demands to a small amount they were said to have secured many responses and by changing the name of the party said to be ill they sometimes managed to catch the same donor twice. Husband and father Andrew Clark was described as a hard-working man perfectly willing and able to support his wife and son appropriately and while he had repeatedly asked them to give up writing begging letters they had persistently declined to do so. Finally the postmaster at Norwich heard of their operations and notified his superiors. After due consideration Postmaster General Gary notified the Clarks that if they gave up their scheme they would not be prosecuted. On July 15, 1897 they were so notified and apparently desisted for several days but on July 24 Samuel deposited in the mail several letters, one of them addressed to H. A. Chittenden Jr., of New Rochelle. In that letter the writer claimed that he was helpless as a result of poverty and disease and pleaded for assistance. When the U.S. Post Office was notified of the mailing of that letter it issued the fraud order. That meant from then onward neither Mrs. Clark nor her son could receive any mail whatever, even letters from their friends and relatives, and they could not send any mail whatever, until the fraud order was revoked.[55]

Anna Mayers

Another woman the Charity Organization Society in New York kept an eye on was Anna Mayers (also known as Annie Myers, Mary Boman, Mary Ida Smith, and Ann Williams, among other aliases). She was described as fond of simple aliases and direct methods. When the Charity Organization Society was established in 1884, it inherited Anna as a sort of legacy and she had occupied a conspicuous place on their rolls ever since. Enough letters of complaint against her had been received by the Society, it said, to "fill a barrel." Although she once did her soliciting and begging in person it was said that by this time she worked her frauds by letter because her face was so well known. Usually in her begging letters she enclosed a bogus rent bill that looked very genuine and told in general a "piteous" story. Sometimes she told in her letter of a sick child, or sometimes of a sick husband, but nearly every letter ended in an appeal for money to help her pay the rent. Frequently she described herself as a deserted wife, but in other letters she related how she had to take care of an invalid husband who had an affliction of the brain. Many of her appeals were made to women and some of those went to see Anna in her lodgings to try and aid her. On one occasion she had represented to her victim that her child was dead and she could not afford to bury it. Her visitor looked around for the dead infant and, when she could not find it, asked where it was. Anna sobbed in reply, "I had to put it on the roof to keep." So overcome by that answer and display was the visitor that she reportedly contributed generously to Anna.[56]

Harriet Taylor

Frank Barkley, a New York Gerry Society agent, took into custody in March 1900 the three children of the woman known as Mrs. Harriet Taylor, who was said to have made her living by begging. In fact, the police and the Gerry Society officials argued that in "skill and fertility of imagination" Taylor had only one equal in recent years, and that was the notorious Ann Myers (Mayers), who eventually disappeared from her familiar haunts in New York. Their methods were said to be much the same, with both partial to prey on the sympathies of ministers, their congregations, and wealthy people in general. Taylor had been known to the Gerry Society since 1890. Barkley explained that charity organizations had made numerous complaints against her but she had always taken the precaution to move whenever things got too hot for her in a particular locale.[57]

Back in 1890 she was known as Mrs. Kate Mulholland and the Gerry Society believed that was her real name. Since then she had been known as Kate Sheridan, Harriet Milholland, Kate Anderson, Harriet Merrill, Kate Merrill, Kate Conklin, and most recently as Harriet Taylor. Her begging was done by letters and a year earlier, as Mrs. Mulholland living on West 45th Street, she received as many as 20 letters a day in answer to her appeals. She always ensured she rented a ground floor flat so she could watch for the letter carrier and rush out when she saw him arrive and get all her mail (she regularly used a number of aliases at the same time). Sometimes she detailed one of her children to deal with the arriving mail and make sure all was collected. People to whom she had written would also sometimes come in person and leave money, food, or clothing. Another scheme she worked was to send her children to some Protestant Episcopal Sunday school. Sad stories and fervent appeals by the children usually brought aid, and when one church was worked dry, one or two of the children would be withdrawn from the Sunday school and sent to another, to start the racket all over.[58]

Mrs. Zobrist

The Associated Charities of Los Angeles exposed Mrs. Zobrist and her husband in 1904 as frauds. Their game was milking certain Los Angeles newspapers which persisted in starting up collections for alleged needy families. The Zobrist method was said to involve phoning up the newspaper, identifying themselves as a different family, and calling editorial attention to the "distressing condition of a family named Zobrist" (themselves). Many such calls were made to each paper, in disguised voices, to try and pretend many people were worried by the plight of the Zobrist family. Apparently it worked a number of times, with collections being taken, and supplies delivered "by the wagonload" to the Zobrist house at 1920 North State Street. Finally, Mr. Zobrist joked to a neighbor that if people did not stop sending in groceries, he would have to begin burning the stuff. When the Associated Charities investigated the whole affair they learned the couple was given the tip on working gullible newspapers by a next door neighbor who said he used to do the same thing himself. In their cover story the Zobrists named their landlord C. A. Isbell as their ogre, a man who wanted to evict them. However, in reality Isbell let them stay in the house for some time without paying rent, furnished them a cow and chickens, and advanced them $2 or $3 a week to live on. Finally the couple were exposed when their voices were recognized at the office of a newspaper they were in the process of trying to scam.[59]

Mrs. Bush

During that same year, 1904, in Los Angeles, a dramatic incident occurred when a Mrs. Bush threw herself in front of a Main Street streetcar, a supposedly impoverished woman trying to commit suicide — she threw her three children with her. Actually she knelt down with the kids in the street well before the car reached the spot, giving the car plenty of time and distance to stop. As an added safety measure she had a confederate standing by off to one side a bit — to rush forward and save her in the unlikely event that became necessary. The gambit was effective in the way Bush intended as it produced plenty of sad, sad stories in the papers that, in turn, produced donations from the public. Later Bush admitted to Miss Carver of the Associated Charities she had no intention of killing herself or her children but to create public sentiment and perhaps even force money from the street railway company. She explained to Carver her landlord had come up with the scheme and he was the one on the scene as the back-up confederate. According to a reporter, "Mrs. Bush's ten-second melodrama has netted her several hundred dollars and a house is to be erected for her — shameless grafter that she is. She must have, incidentally, derived considerable amusement from the tearful stories that have been printed about her in the yellow journals.... The fact is, the dictionary has been squeezed flat and dry for pathetic words."[60]

For the journalist reporting the Bush story the most deplorable result from the escapade was, "A number of female grafters have quickly seized the opportunity to rob charitable people of their coin on the strength of the Bush stories." Reportedly, no less than eight women were separately going through the city representing themselves to be collecting money for Bush. The Associated Charities was then on the trail of two of them. One was a girl of 18 to 20 ostensibly collecting money and clothes for Bush, claiming she represented the Associated Charities. A second girl, about the same age, was working the South Figueroa Street district. She claimed to represent the *Examiner* newspaper and was also collecting money and clothes for Bush. Embellishing the story in the *Examiner*, this woman, as she went door to door increased the size of Bush's brood from three children to eight with another on the way. That newspaper had apparently started a collection drive of its own. Concluded the reporter, "The Associated Charities, like the Merchants' and Manufacturers' Association has made repeated protest against subscription funds like this by the Examiner, for this very reason — grafters."[61]

And then there were the women who passed bad paper — checks, notes, and other financial instruments. Some of them were forgeries, and all were worthless. Some of the schemes were elaborate and netted the confidence woman a relatively large amount of money; others got only tiny sums at best. Some of the women were never captured, or even identified accurately; some undertook frauds so ill-conceived and ill-advised as to almost guarantee they would be caught.

5

Passing Bad Paper

Jane Doe

In the course of doing business in the spring of 1872 with the firm of Caswell, Hazard and Company in New York, C. Kimberly of Branford, Connecticut mailed them a check for $15.43. It never arrived. Kimberly made inquiries and it was discovered a signature had been forged to the check and it had been cashed. The check had been uttered to a New Haven merchant named George Lamb who related he had taken it from a woman who said she was Kimberly's wife. Lamb then went in search of the woman and he learned, after a conversation with a man from Branford, that a woman lived there who answered the description of the check passer. When Lamb went to Branford he recognized the woman, who was a clerk in the post office there, as the one. At the time she denied everything when Lamb confronted her. A couple of days later he returned to Branford, accompanied by Postmaster Sperry. During an interview with Sperry the woman reportedly confessed she was guilty not only of the crime in question, but also of several earlier pilferings from the mail. She returned the $15.43. While she was not immediately arrested or discharged from her job, Sperry sent the details of the case to Washington, D.C., authorities for further action. A news account stated, "The young lady is connected with a respectable family, is of very prepossessing appearance and but eighteen years of age. She has been about the Post-office four or five years, and has not only been free from suspicion, but admired for her amiability and excellence of character."[1]

Caroline Pells

Thinking big, Caroline Pells entered the Nassau Bank in New York in April 1875 and tried unsuccessfully to get a forged check for $19,400 cashed. When tendering the check she explained to the bank clerk it was payment for a farm lately belonging to her deceased husband, which she had sold. Suspicions at the bank were raised, the police were called and the woman later arrested. Arraigned in the Tombs Police Court she said only, "My name is Caroline Blank, I am twenty years of age, am a native of Vienna, am a dress-maker, reside in Hoboken, and am not guilty of the charge preferred against me." She was committed to the Tombs jail in default of a $6,000 bail she could not raise. At that arraignment Justice Smith and his Chief Clerk Mr. Rockwell both expressed the opinion she had been arrested before, as her face seemed familiar to them. In court she needed a German interpreter, which struck those in the court as an obvious fraud since the woman had conversed fluently and easily in English with the bank clerk when she had tendered the check. Police received varying accounts from the woman as to how she came into possession of the check.[2]

Caroline Pells stood trial for forgery in July 1875 but the jury was unable to agree on a verdict. By then her real name had been established, along with the fact she was of German origin and that she had used the aliases of Hoffman and Blank. A second trial was held in September. On the day in question, April 17, a young woman dressed in mourning and calling herself Mrs. Caroline Pells presented the check to the Nassau Bank, drawn by Warder, Mitchell & Company to the order of Mrs. Caroline Pells and endorsed by Warder and by Pells. She told the Paying Teller she was a widow and had received the check in payment for a farm in Springfield, Ohio and sold by her to Mr. Warder. Satisfied the check was a forgery the bank sent her away and told her to return later. Pells suspected nothing but in the meantime the police were notified. They followed her and arrested her at the St. Nicholas Hotel. At police headquarters she said she had arrived in America from Europe a few days earlier on the ocean liner Schiller. During the passage she became acquainted with passenger Aloise Hammer with whom she started to live, in Hoboken, after the ship docked. On the morning in question Hammer had given her the check to take to the bank while he awaited her completion of the transaction at the St. Nicholas Hotel. She was utterly ignorant of the nature of the check, according to Pells.[3]

She told the above story in court during her first trial "weeping piteously while detailing her experiences through the medium of the court interpreter." As well, her lawyer presented her as the dupe of some forger. Apparently the strategy worked. At her second trial Assistant District Attorney Relima "cautioned the jury against being influenced by the youth and beauty of the prisoner, whose shamming had already succeeded in humbugging one jury." Also emphasized was that she pretended a lack of understanding of English to strengthen her claim of ignorance. After a short time spent in deliberation the jury found her guilty with a recommendation for mercy. On hearing the verdict Pells broke down and wept although, supposedly, she would not have understood it since it was delivered in English. Recorder Hackett, in the Court of General Sessions, said he agreed with the verdict and were it not for the recommendation for mercy he would have imposed the maximum sentence. Hackett sentenced her to two years and six months in the Penitentiary. Subsequently it was learned, said a reporter, that she was an "accomplished adventuress" and the mistress of a notorious Philadelphia forger by the name of Gottlieb Hoffman. The pair had earlier traveled to Europe to visit the Vienna Exposition, where it happened that Warder, Mitchell & Company was among the exhibitors. In payment for some services performed for them in Vienna, Hoffman, on his return to Philadelphia, received a check drawn on the Nassau Bank in New York. In that way the pair learned the Warder firm kept an account there and obtained the appropriate signature, which they later forged.[4]

Ellen Tupper

People in Iowa were reported to have been greatly surprised by the 1876 discovery that several forgeries had been committed by Mrs. Ellen S. Tupper, a woman who had been a lecturer on bees and their care at the State Agricultural College and was also the editor of several journals devoted to bee culture. As it turned out she had been practicing "a bold scheme of swindling and forgery" for two to three years. Tupper uttered forged checks and passed drafts signed by her when she had no money to cover them. About two years earlier she had even forged the signatures of local dignitaries Governor Carpenter and the Honorable John A. Kasson. Additionally, "Several other well-known business men also were victimized, but allowed the matter to be settled without exposure yet with some sacrifice." In December 1875 she forged several notes in different names, payable to her, and then sold them to a bank, netting over $1,000 in total. When those forgeries were detected and traced to Tupper she acknowledged the crime and promised full restitution. The bank accepted the offer, received restitution, and no prosecution was made. However, she made restitution then, as she had done before, by passing still more bad paper. Finally, early in 1876 she was arrested on the complaint of a bank that had purchased notes from her, all forged, with two of them being for a total of $675, and three others totaling $1,191. According to a reporter the whole business was a "sorrowful" tale considering Tupper's connection in business and social circles. About two years earlier it became known by her friends that she became "much embarrassed" in money matters. She had two daughters at school that she was anxious to educate and a husband said to have been an invalid for many years. "About that time she broke down in body and mind from overwork and passed through a protracted illness, and so soon as she resumed labor she appears to have resorted to this means [uttering forgeries] to relieve her financial pressure, as often as necessity required, redeeming her fraudulent paper with money got by either forged paper, or replacing it with fraudulent drafts."5

Josephine Trau

On a spring day in 1881 Mrs. Josephine Trau presented a forged check for $1,800, purported to be signed by Gill, Baird & Company to the Commercial Bank of Brooklyn, and received the money. Pushing her luck she turned up at the same bank on the following day and presented another forged check on the same firm for $1,150. This time a forgery was suspected, the police were called in and Trau arrested. Tried on a charge of forgery in the third degree, along with her partner Adolph Bessie, in the Kings County Court of Sessions, the three-day trial was said to have attracted a good deal of attention. Trau, in court, claimed she had received the checks from a man named Steele in payment for a Long Island farm, on which she lived with her family. However, no such man as Steele was ever found. When the jury declared the woman guilty a reporter observed, "Mrs. Trau went into hysterics when she heard the verdict, and her little daughter fell to the floor in a faint." Trau was sentenced to one year in the King's Country Penitentiary.6

Florence Ducat

When Florence Ducat was convicted of forgery in 1881 in Columbus, Ohio and sentenced to five years in prison it was reportedly just the second conviction in Ohio of a female for forgery. Ducat had forged the name of John Mercer, a farmer, to a check for $900, payable to a fictitious female. Then she presented the check to the bank, which obligingly cashed it. Upon reaching the door of the bank on her way out, Ducat returned to the counter to say she did not want to take all that money away with her and would leave some of it at the bank. Thus, she opened an account, deposited $400 and took away the other $500. Some time passed before Mercer was notified of the cashing of the check and the forgery discovered. Police went to work but another woman was arrested and charged with the crime. But she had an alibi and was eventually discharged. Suspicion fell on Ducat finally when it was discovered she had made a large cash purchase of furniture that she had delivered to friends in the country. Said a reporter, "She was arrested on suspicion, became frightened and confessed her guilt. Her conviction followed, of course. Had she not confessed, she could not have been convicted."[7]

Margaret Weiss

One day in September 1881 a woman who gave her name as Weiss entered the store of T. Leeds Waters, a piano dealer on 14th Street in New York. She said she was interested in a second-hand piano; Waters showed her a few and she picked out one priced at $105. In payment she offered a note drawn by an alleged builder Herman Gerke, explaining her husband Adolph had sold some property to Gerke and received the note in question in part payment. Strangely enough, the note was for the exact same amount as the price of the piano. Waters asked her to leave the note with him until he could check on Gerke's ability to pay. Weiss argued and told him where Gerke could be found, at a site where he was building some houses. Sure enough, Waters went there, met a man who said he was Gerke and was told the note was genuine and that he was the owner of the houses being built. Still somewhat leery, Waters told Margaret when she returned he would not accept the note in payment for the piano but he would hold it and let her have the instrument on a written obligation to return it if the note was not paid. If the note were paid he would give her a bill of sale. Weiss readily agreed and the piano was delivered to her address. Of course, the note bounced but by then both Weiss and the piano had disappeared.[8]

People who lived in other parts of the house wherein Weiss resided said she had moved away without saying where she was going. They also said she had received several pianos and one organ at different times during her stay in the house, but with the excuse that the action was too hard or that something else was wrong about the instrument had sent each away in turn after keeping it for no more than a few days. She led her neighbors to believe the instruments were returned to the people or firms from whom she obtained them. Waters hired a private detective to find her and to find the other firms from which she had obtained instruments. He found Weiss had gotten one piano from Sohmer & Company for $160 where, having offered a note from Gerke for $165 in payment, she demanded $5 in cash. Mr. Sohmer refused to give her the $5 but said she could call and get it as soon as the note was paid. Jacob Brothers was victimized for two pianos while the organ owner's identity was not ascertained. Weiss had been traced to Brooklyn and to different places in Jersey City, New Jersey. Her whereabouts were said to then be known to the police who were keeping a watch on her and, said an account, "There is considerable excitement in the piano trade over the discovery of the plot, and the leading manufacturers and dealers have all subscribed to a fund for prosecuting the swindlers."[9]

Late in January 1882 Margaret Weiss was arrested in Jersey City and arraigned for examination in the Essex Market Police Court. On the day Margaret was arrested Herman Gerke was sent to State prison after a conviction for swindling, not related to the piano scam.[10]

Louise Watson

Giving her name as Louise Watson, "a plain-looking young woman of good address" appeared in Jefferson Market Police Court in New York in September 1883 on a charge of having obtained money under false pretenses from Joseph Martin. It was further reported, "The prisoner is respectably connected and her father, Mr. Stephen Wilkins, holds a responsible position in the banking house of White, Morris & Co., No. 6 Wall-street." Until a month or two earlier Watson lived with her parents, until a quarrel with her mother led to her moving out. Her aunt Mrs.

Ella Hall had once been in "comfortable circumstances" but after her husband died a few months earlier she was induced by friends (one of whom was Martin) to set up her own dressmaking business, necessary due to her reduced financial situation. Martin was one of the people who loaned her money to get the business started.[11]

Then about three weeks before Watson's court appearance Martin received a note (by messenger boy), purportedly from Hall, asking for the loan of $35. He sent the money back with the messenger boy. That was followed by other notes asking for small loans until the sum totaled about $150. Finally Martin, worried that Hall was getting into financial difficulties, investigated further. He learned Hall had made no requests for loans and had received no money from Martin. Police were called in and they discovered all the notes had been sent from a specific messenger location and from the messengers who worked there obtained a description of the woman and enough of her habits to find she was in the habit of meeting John Daly (a bricklayer who had taken one of the answers to a note for the woman) at a particular street intersection on Friday evenings. It was there they arrested Louise Watson.[12]

Researching Watson's background it was found that in 1879 she was married to F. H. Underhill, a New York City store clerk, with the couple living with her parents for nearly three years. On July 17, 1882 they were divorced. In the following month she married James A. Walker but he deserted her in June 1883. At the time Louise married Walker she did not know he had a wife in Pennsylvania. Around May 1883 she made the acquaintance of James Daly in the street and the pair quickly became intimate. According to one report, "Louise says that Daly suggested the plan of obtaining money from Mr. Martin and compelled her, under threats, to write the letters. All the money she received, which she says amounted to $115, she gave Daly, and the clothes he now wears were paid for from this money."[13]

Jennie Saxton

When 20-year-old Jennie Saxton arrived in Burlington, Vermont on November 16, 1886 for her sister's wedding, she found herself arrested on a charge of forgery. Then the "charming-looking" woman was taken to the Police Court and arraigned on the charge of forging two checks on the Burlington Savings Bank in the name of John L. Mason of Richmond, Vermont, one for $500 and the other for $800. Her home was in

Richmond but for the past year she had lived with her brother in Willsborough, New York. While she admitted writing the two orders she claimed she had been authorized to do so by Mason, and the town of Burlington professed itself to be shocked over a looming scandal. At arraignment, said a reporter, "The prisoner, who is a fine-looking brunette, was handsomely dressed in seal wraps, fashionable hat with long plumes, and a rich dress with beaded front." Allegedly Saxton went to the bank on September 4, 1886, presented the order for $500 and had it cashed. Just as she left the bank the paying teller, on closer inspection was said to have realized the check was a forgery but did nothing, content to wait, as he was certain she would do it again. It happened on November 16 when the order for $800 was tendered by a messenger as Saxton feigned indisposition at home. That time the police were notified and made the arrest. Her explanation that Mason authorized the withdrawals and would make the matter right caused an adjournment in the proceedings until Mason could be summoned before the court. In the meantime her brother-in-law, Mr. Delaney, told the court Mason had been furnishing her with money for some time, sending to her on one occasion at her home in Richmond $150 concealed in an apple. Mason was an older man with a married daughter, and himself was married for the second time. It left observers feeling certain that Saxton had some relationship with Mason but what it was "could only be conjectured" and "the gossips have not been so busy here for years."[14]

A few days later the hearing resumed wherein Mason, 66, declared his interest in Saxton was merely in the form of a paternal feeling. That caused a reporter to observe, "The evidence thus far indicates that his affection was greater even than brotherly love." In a courtroom described as "thronged before the hour set for opening" Mason testified he never signed the checks tendered by Saxton and never authorized her or anyone else to do so. He admitted he had known the accused since she was two or three years old and that he had met her often in Richmond and in Burlington and that he frequently rode on the railroad with her. Agreeing he was very fond of apples and that he gave them to others, he said he never gave Jennie an apple containing $150 but, "He often gave her fruit, though." Also admitted by Mason was that he and Saxton had exchanged many letters and he had one letter with him in court, but it was not put in evidence. Several years earlier he had a farm some distance from his home; Saxton went there daily to milk the cow and he regularly drove her back and forth from her home to do that chore. After the hearing adjourned for the day it was learned that the letter given by Mason to counsel for the accused, addressed by her to Mason, stated that she was in trouble and a young man was to blame. He was poor and if Mason would lend her money she would pay him a high rate of interest.[15]

Mary Davidson

Mrs. Mary P. Sturgess had held a prominent position in religious works for some 14 months in Albany, New York, at the time of her arrest in November 1886. Reportedly, that event caused considerable excitement in church circles. Arriving in that city from Boston, Mary became active in "Christian labors," earned a livelihood by selling insurance and, said an account, "made many friends by her agreeable manners and conversational powers. She is a stout, prepossessing woman of middle age, with gray hair." However, it was revealed she was Mrs. Mary A. Davidson, of Lynn, Massachusetts, who had allegedly committed a crime there and, as a result, had been sought by the police for 18 months. She was born Mary Alice Abbott in Bucksport, Maine, where her father was a man of prominence. For a time the family resided in Washington, D.C., where Mary made her debut into society and "in the heyday of her youth and beauty, shone as a belle in Boston and Washington."[16]

While still young, she married a Mr. Davidson, a wealthy resident of Lynn. Some years later, according to her story, Davidson lost his wealth through "unfortunate speculation" and they were thrown on their own resources. Mrs. Davidson went to Boston for a while and taught music. It was alleged that she then procured an insurance agency from Oliver Ditson & Company of Boston, and opened up a promising business in Lynn. Things went wrong, however, and it was alleged that after mortgaging the company stock she sold it for several thousand dollars and disappeared — only to resurface in Albany under an alias. It was said Mary was "dazed" by her arrest "and said it was due to the work of enemies. She acted as if her mind was affected."[17]

Sophie Jerome

Arrested in Philadelphia in October 1888, Mrs. Sophie Jerome was described as "a handsome woman of middle age, the widow of a wealthy manufacturer, who has squandered a large fortune during the last eight years." She was locked up for passing worthless checks. When arrested "she was richly dressed and was on her way to call on a fashionable dressmaker to whom she has paid thousands of dollars" over the years for her wardrobe. Jerome visited the Philadelphia National Bank just after it opened on October 12 and discussed with its president the possibility that she might open an account there and deposit $10,000. After discussing interest rates and terms, Jerome left the bank saying she would consult with her counsel and would return in an hour to open the account, if so advised. As she exited the president's office she was observed to pick up several blank deposit slips and blank checks, but no other attention was paid to that matter. Some two to three hours later a young man walked into the bank and presented a $25 check signed by Sophie Jerome drawn on that bank. After glancing at the check, the Paying Teller knew it was worthless as he knew no such person as Jerome had an account at his bank. The man was detained and the police sent for. He turned out to be James Carr, employed in the C. Buckle & Company livery stable. A woman had appeared there, rented a carriage for the day and tendered the check in payment. Because she did not wait for her change the stable keeper became leery and sent Carr to the bank immediately to cash the check. Police waited at the stable all day for Jerome to return but she did not and the vigil was eventually given up for the night. Jerome was captured the next day.[18]

Kate Dooley

Kate Dooley, "a handsome young woman" in the employ of dressmaker Mme. E. Cooley Ross of New York, purchased $3 worth of buttons at the Stern Brothers store and tendered in payment a check for $25 purportedly signed by Mme. Ross. The check was accepted with Dooley getting the buttons and $22 in cash. However, the check was a forgery but by the time the police were called in the woman had disappeared from her residence. A couple of weeks later, in April 1889, she was arrested at the home of a friend. Arraigned before Justice Duffy at the Jefferson Market Police Court she was reported to have "wept continuously." Dooley was held for an examination on a complaint of forgery.[19]

Mary Beck and Dolly Vernon

Check passers Mrs. Mary Beck and Dolly Vernon were in court in May 1889 before Justice Patterson for examination on the complaints made by retailer Lord & Taylor and furniture dealer R. J. Horner. The latter had taken checks from the pair to the total of $800 to furnish two apartments; both at 1723 Madison Avenue, New York. The pair was charged with passing a series of forged checks, all bearing the name of Seth B. French. In court French was shown 10 such checks, all of which he declared to be forgeries. Speculation was that Beck got the idea of signing his name to checks from the fact that nearly three years earlier French had rented a flat in a house and paid his rent monthly by checks, giving them to Mrs. Beck who acted as a collector for her mother, Mrs. Barnett, from whom the flat was rented. Both women were committed for trial. Meanwhile, Horner had obtained a writ for the return of his furniture and carpets. On the basis of that writ City Marshall McDermott went to the flats at the Madison Avenue house and stripped them completely.[20]

Julia Lippincott

A series of forgeries by a woman, amounting to an estimated $35,000 then, had just come to light in February 1890 in Mount Holly, New Jersey, involving "a member of one of the best known Quaker families in the State, who has long been considered an ornament to society and a man of strictest integrity." Those people were Edwin Lippincott, the proprietor of Hadden Hall, a large hotel in Atlantic City, and his wife Julia, who had for a number of years been associated with him in the management of the hotel. Reportedly, Edwin had by then used up the bulk of his fortune in paying off a lot of the forged paper in order to save his wife from exposure and disgrace, but such could no longer be averted as lawsuits had been commenced on a dozen or more of the forged instruments. Charged with having uttered the forged paper, Julia was described in a news account as "a bright, pleasant faced woman with an unusual capacity for business. She was considered to possess more than ordinary shrewdness. She is now nearly 50 years of age." During a portion of the winter the couple lived in Medford, New Jersey, with the rest of the year spent in residence at Hadden Hall.[21]

In her childhood Julia was adopted by a Mrs. Scattergood, a wealthy resident of New York State who also adopted another girl — Minnie A. Haines of Medford, widow of Casper Haines. So close were the two girls that they became known in the neighborhood as the "adopted sisters." Upon the death of Scattergood each received a legacy of $30,000. Minnie lived in Medford year round and possessed "considerable property." Apparently Julia launched her forgery career in 1883 when she placed several mortgages on Minnie's Medford property for $1,800, $1,000, and $1,200. All were forgeries as Minnie declared she never put any mortgages on any of her property. Another lot of bogus mortgages, again all on Minnie's property, totaling some $19,000 on property that was worth only $6,000, were placed a few years later. All were phony said Minnie. Some of the documents were placed with business firms and some with private individuals. Each piece of property was mortgaged repeatedly. Many of the bogus mortgages did not surface for some time, leading to speculation that perhaps Julia paid the interest on some of them for a time, probably out of the proceeds of other bogus mortgages floated later. Firms scammed included the Atlantic City Building and Loan Association and the United Security Insurance and Trust Company (Philadelphia). For the $14,415.68 mortgage obtained at the latter institution a personal visit to the firm had been required, although Minnie had never gone there. Other forged notes used the name of Edwin Lippincott and were put on Haddon Hall, including mortgages from the Union National Bank of Mount Holly, the National State Bank of Camden, and Philadelphia Trust. When the discovery was finally made Edwin endeavored to buy up all the bogus paper. When he had paid out over $4,000 his wife assured him that was all, and he said he felt secure. But then evidence of additional forgeries continued to pour in and eventually he stopped paying them off, fearing he would be broke before they stopped turning up.[22]

The biggest mystery remaining was what Julia had done with all the money. It was rumored she bought heavily into the stock market but "generally got on the wrong side of the market, which probably accounts for the disappearance of a good deal of the money." Edwin told a reporter, "She has ruined me. I won't have a dollar left. If I had enough money I would voluntarily assume the payment of all these bogus notes, but that is out of the question. I cannot do it. It is a terrible blow to me. I have no idea what she has done with the money unless she has lost it in stocks. It must be all gone, for I know that she is out of funds and has been borrowing." The first he knew that anything was wrong was in 1889 when he was approached by the teller of the Atlantic City National Bank with a lot of notes that bore his name but which were forgeries, "It was a complete surprise to me. At that time I went to my wife and demanded an explanation. Then she admitted her guilt, and said she had forged my name to the notes. These I paid off in order to avoid trouble and save her from disgrace, little thinking there were thousands and thousands of dollars more of just such paper afloat at that time." Minnie said she trusted Julia with all her business and it was Julia who held the sole key to the safety deposit box that contained all the papers, and so forth, belonging to them from the Scattergood estate.[23]

A few days later, still in February 1890, Julia disappeared, with the police looking to arrest her for forgery. During her absence more forgeries of notes, mortgages and checks came to light. According to the Philadelphia *Times* newspaper, the fugitive was an inveterate stock speculator and the fraudulently obtained money (over $100,000 by its estimate) was used for stock speculation. When the safety deposit box was opened in the presence of Minnie's lawyer, it was discovered that many papers were missing and nothing of value remained. All they found were a lot of receipts from stockbrokers for margin calls and those receipts dated back as far as 1881. Said the lawyer, a Mr. Brightly, "She has evidently lost a great deal of money. She no doubt lost the estate left her and Mrs. Haines in stock gambling, and to pay margins on the bonds and stocks still carried for her she forged her husband's name."[24]

According to Brightly, only a few days prior to her discovery she went to Philadelphia on a shopping excursion and while in one prominent store she uttered a $500 forged check drawn to the order of Edwin and signed by Mrs. Haines. It was estimated here that Julia forged some $60,000 worth of paper in Minnie's name and over $40,000 in Edwin's name. Additionally, it was thought she had obtained another $20,000 through forging the names of other people; for example, Lewis Groff, a councilman for Atlantic City, received a notice from the Camden National Bank that a note (forged) of his for $352 was due; the name of James A. Somers of Atlantic City had been forged to the extent of $2,000; and that of George Myers to the amount of $10,000.[25]

Julia remained a fugitive until June or July 1890 when she was arrested at the house of a relative in Baltimore. Returned to Camden, New Jersey, she remained in custody there until almost the end of the year. During the period she was incarcerated her husband died. Late in 1890 she was tried five separate times in the Camden court and acquitted on every charge brought against her. On December 13, Julia was released from the Camden jail by the order of Wilson Jenkins, Prosecutor of the Pleas of Camden County, who had tried without success to convict the woman. Several indictments remained outstanding against Julia but the prosecutor, despairing of obtaining a conviction, decided not to prosecute in the remaining cases. It was understood that in the day or two after her release a warrant for her arrest had been issued in Atlantic City, where she faced one charge of forgery.[26]

Annie Murphy

A gang of swindlers was thought to be operating throughout the U.S. late in 1892 by procuring a draft from a bank and then having a lot of them printed up exactly like the original. The leader of the gang was said to be Mrs. Annie M. Murphy. On October 27 the First National and the German American National Bank of St. Cloud, Minnesota each cashed a draft to oblige Murphy; one was for $700, the other was for $800. Purportedly, they were drawn on the National Bank of Commerce of Tacoma, Washington, and on the Chase National Bank of New York. In due course they were determined to be frauds and the banks were then offering a $300 reward for Murphy's detection. Those financial institutions sent out the following description of Annie: "Five feet eight inches high, weighs about 190 pounds, very dark hair, cut short and curled, dark grey eyes, heavy lips, about twenty-four years of age, good looking, of pleasing address, dashing manners, and may at times assume male attire."[27]

Shortly thereafter she was spotted in Montreal with the police said to be hot on her trail. Then about one month later it was reported that she had been arrested and was in jail at Huntsville, Alabama on a forgery charge. She was said to have been the wife of a Tacoma, Washington merchant from whom she had recently separated "to begin a systematic draft forging business." Within a month she had uttered $2,895 in forged drafts drawn on the two financial institutions. Cryptically, it was again observed, "Mrs. Murphy appeared in male attire."[28]

Edna White

Arrested in Marietta, Georgia in July 1894 was a woman who gave her name as Mrs. Edna White. Authorities believed her to be a professional swindler and that she might even be the famous Mrs. Kate Bradford who disappeared from New York a few months earlier. White had operated extensively in the Atlanta area for a few days. Her method was to give a check (generally for $15 or $20) for a small purchase of goods, receiving the goods (usually worth only $1 or so) and the change in cash from the check. She worked the Atlanta area in May of that same year and swindled several firms before returning to business again in July. Edna was arrested by chance when a man, whose firm she swindled in May, recognized her on a train.[29]

Jane Doe

In the summer of 1895 a woman forger worked Washington, D.C., merchants for goods and cash in exchange for bogus checks. One victim was storekeeper T. G. Hoover. One day a woman attired in "a striped gossamer and a high bonnet" entered Hoover's meat store and inquired for Hoover's son, who died some time earlier. Told of the boy's death by Hoover, the woman expressed great sympathy, claiming to have known him quite well and to have done a good deal of trading with him. Then she selected a quantity of meat and tendered a check drawn on the Washington Loan and Trust Company signed by A. J. Moore. The check amount was for several times the purchase price and she asked Hoover to let her have the balance in cash. Based on their earlier conversation, he readily agreed. Later he took the check to the bank, found it bogus, and reported it to the police. On the same day several other bogus checks with the same signature were tendered to Washington storekeepers, and later reported to the police.[30]

Maud Craig Burke Davis

When Mrs. Maud Craig Burke Davis, along with her husband, was arrested in San Francisco in June 1895 on a charge of forgery, the announcement caused a great sensation in Rochester, New York, where she was well known. They were accused of having passed bogus checks drawn on a mythical New York bank at various stores in San Francisco. Thirty-year-old Maud was first married to Dr. J. J. A. Burke, an ex-president of the Rochester Board of Health, in 1887. Two years later they separated. Maud's father was Henry H. Craig, a wealthy Rochester lumber merchant said to be worth at least a half a million dollars with the family belonging to the "upper ten in Rochester society." Mrs. Burke married Davis in April 1895 when the latter was advertising manager for a Rochester clothing house, having arrived fairly recently from New York City. Prior to the marriage the couple were acquainted for only a short time. According to a reporter, "Davis, whose real name is said to be Zalinsky, came to this city about a year ago and represented himself to be a New York journalist. A young man of this city, who it is said, introduced Davis to the lady who became his wife, says that Davis was the oiliest and smoothest scoundrel he ever met. It is believed here that Mrs. Davis is innocent of wrongdoing. It is thought that Davis gave her the checks and told her to pay for the goods and get the difference in cash." Others were said to believe the man's real name was Harry Silverberg and that he was married twice with his first wife having been a woman of means at the time of their marriage.[31]

Anna Bellah

Mrs. Anna D. Bellah, when she was arrested on January 16, 1895, in Kansas City, Missouri, was described in one news account as "probably the cleverest woman swindler that ever obtained money on fraudulent checks in the United States." She was held by police in Kansas City awaiting word from police authorities at Excelsior Springs, Missouri, and elsewhere. Registered in a Kansas City hotel as Mrs. Dennison of Baltimore, she was recognized by chance in a hotel corridor and her arrest soon followed, along with her admission of her real identity. During the summer of 1894 in Excelsior Springs, she became acquainted with Lemuel Lincoln, a distant relative of Robert T. Lincoln, son of the murdered President. Bellah told him she was preparing to write a history of President Lincoln and his descendants. Lemuel readily gave her the desired information and she finally got him to cash a worthless $125 check from her. With the biographical information obtained from Lemuel, Anna went to Plattsburg, Missouri and worked the same deal on Mrs. McMichael, a sister of Lemuel. Bellah then disappeared and although the police searched "scores" of towns, she managed to elude them successfully until the chance discovery in Kansas City. Estimated to be 40 years old, at the time of her arrest she was described as "fashionably dressed."

Kansas City Police Chief Speers had on file a record of the woman, furnished several months earlier by authorities in Boston where Anna and her husband Joseph T. Bellah were defendants in several suits that had been instituted by people they had allegedly defrauded. Reportedly the Bellahs conducted their fraudulent operations over at least five states.[32]

Sadie Hubbard

W. F. Thomas, an employee of a real estate office in Los Angeles, was arraigned in court in April 1895 on a felony charge preferred by M. N. Avery, cashier of the German-American Savings Bank. Thomas, while admitting a connection with a questionable financial transaction, claimed he had been victimized by a designing woman. The crime for which Thomas was arraigned was obtaining or helping to obtain money by false pretenses. On February 23 that year Thomas came to the bank with a woman whom he introduced to the cashier as Mrs. Sarah E. Stebbins. That woman presented a draft issued by the Citizens' National Bank of Baltimore on the Third National Bank of New York for $200, payable, as she alleged, to herself. She endorsed the draft Sarah E. Stebbins. Thomas added his endorsement and gave his personal guarantee; then the $200 was paid over to the woman.[33]

Meanwhile, the real Sarah E. Stebbins, the wife of a prominent Baltimore machinery contractor, was in Los Angeles wondering why her husband had not written to her and sent her the $200 he had promised her. After a time she wrote to him and he replied that he had sent the letter and the money. That led to an investigation and in due course it developed that the letter containing the draft had been taken from the Los Angeles post office by some one other than the real Stebbins. As soon as the fraud was discovered, Thomas was arrested as he had endorsed the check and given a personal guarantee. According to Thomas he became acquainted with the woman in a business way. She came to his office to list some real estate he was to sell for her, and later when he thought he knew her well she asked him to identify her at the bank to get a draft cashed. He did so, he claimed, believing her to be the real Mrs. Stebbins.[34]

However, the police alleged when Thomas first came to know the woman she called herself Mrs. Sadie Hubbard, that he became infatuated with her and their relations were intimate and that Thomas knew she was not Mrs. Stebbins when he identified her as such. Also alleged by the police was that Thomas accompanied Hubbard to San Francisco where they were going to establish an employment agency with their limited capital. But the scheme fell through and Thomas returned to Los Angeles where he was arrested. Thomas laid all the blame on the woman and after his arrest swore out a complaint against her for having forged the name of Stebbins. Hubbard remained at large with the police having intercepted a number of letters the woman had written, both from San Francisco and from Los Angeles.[35]

On April 11, 1895, Mrs. Sadie Hubbard walked into a Los Angeles police station and surrendered herself, explaining she had just arrived back in the city and wanted to have the charge cleared up. Her attorney presented the bizarre story that her real name was Sarah Stebbins (no initial E.) but she had been in the habit of using the initial E (for unexplained reasons) in her name, which accounted for her receiving the letter and draft not intended for her. According to her story, as related by lawyer Peck, she came west some two years earlier for her health, stopping at Denver, then Portland, Oregon and from there on to San Francisco and then to Los Angeles. Her husband was a speculator who from time to time had been sending her money. In February she inquired for her mail at the post office as usual and was handed a letter addressed to Mrs. Sarah E. Stebbins (the letter with the draft) and a note saying, "I understand you are having a pleasant time in Southern California. I hope your health will continue to improve. I enclose draft for $200. (signed) Your husband." Not having the slightest doubt that it was from her own husband she hunted up Thomas, with whom she had done business, and got him to assist her in cashing the draft. At Thomas's suggestion, she accompanied him to San Francisco to open an employment agency but the idea fell through. In the meantime she heard from her husband and discovered, for the first time, that he had not sent the draft and that it must have been intended for another Mrs. Stebbins. On learning of her mistake, Peck explained as he continued to relate her story, she hastened to Los Angeles at once to rectify it, but when she arrived there her friends advised her to keep quiet because trying to explain the matter would only get her in trouble. She did not deny that she went by the name of Hubbard during most of her stay in Los Angeles and that her daughter's name was also Hubbard, nor did she offer any explanation of the name change.[36]

Later in April Justice Morrison, on a motion from Deputy District Attorney James, dismissed the felony charges against Thomas and Hubbard. As the elated defendants left the courtroom they were arrested by the police on a warrant from the United States Court charging them with a violation of the postal laws. Specifically, the charge against Hubbard was for taking from the post office the letter and draft intended for Sarah E. Stebbins.[37]

Mary A. Miller

Late in the summer of 1897 a couple turned up in Niagara Falls, New York, using the names Mary A. Miller and P. J. Baynes, of Richmond, Virginia. Once in Niagara Falls the pair set in motion a scheme that was described as "in the main, simple, and seldom unsuccessful." They had secured a number of blank checks from a local financial institution, the Bank of Niagara, and they also had a rubber stamp, similar to those used in banks, which stated, "Certified to by Bank of Niagara; George J. Howard, Cashier." Howard's name was forged and it was said to be a good copy of the original. One problem with the forged document was that the word "cashier" had been misspelled. The checks were all made payable to Mary A. Miller and were signed by various firms and individuals. Amounts of the checks were always less than $100. Once they had a number of checks ready to tender the pair went on the road and passed them in cities such as Toledo, Detroit, St. Louis, and Chicago, with commodity houses being a favorite location in which to utter the bad paper. Letters from Miller were sent to brokers in various cities as they traveled asking if they wanted her business as she wished to invest in May wheat futures, for example. Usually the brokers took her business and at that point Miller tendered one of her checks, usually for $70 to $90, getting the balance in cash. Reportedly, Miller thus cleared from $10 to $25 on each check. They were detected once in St. Louis and almost arrested but just barely managed to elude the police. Miller was described as "a small, very slender and delicate looking woman about forty years of age. She has blonde hair and is of a very nervous temperament, and while here [Niagara Falls] was frequently under a physician's treatment."[38]

May Kellard

Based on a complaint made in June 1897, by New York florist Mrs. Mary D. Spencer, May Kellard was arrested on a charge of forgery.

Spencer alleged that Kellard obtained from her $750 as the discount price for a $1,000 note with the name of Mrs. Virginia Wood forged on the note as maker. Mrs. Wood was the wife of William D. Wood, once a wealthy resident of Harlem but who was adjudged insane some time earlier and was then a patient at the Middletown Insane Asylum. While the commission that ruled on his sanity was sitting, testimony developed, according to a reporter, "that showed that all of Wood's fortune has been dissipated and much of it upon Miss Kellard."[39]

Kellard's trial was held in November that year. William H. Chandler, the fifth juror selected and seated to try Kellard, was suddenly challenged by Assistant District Attorney D. Frank Lloyd, after all 12 jurors had been selected. Chandler was replaced. After court adjourned for the day, Lloyd explained to the press why he had unexpectedly issued the challenge, "I challenged Juror No. 5 for smiling and flirting with the defendant. I saw him exchanging smiling glances with May Kellard, and several other persons saw him at different times do the same thing."[40]

During that trial it was reported that Kellard had "cajoled" some $250,000 from Mr. Woods "in the old man's dotage, through her fascinations." In her testimony Mrs. Woods said she paid $20,000 to redeem forged notes rather than run the risk of having her husband sent to jail. Spencer told the court that altogether she had discounted nearly $10,000 worth of notes tendered to her by Kellard, all bearing the forged signature of Mrs. Woods. Despite such testimony the jury was not able to agree on a verdict — a decision the judge apparently let stand even though the jury had deliberated, reportedly, for not quite five hours.[41]

Three months later, in February 1898, May went on trial in the General Sessions Court in New York before Judge Newburger for stealing a harp valued at $650. It was alleged she agreed to buy the harp but before she paid for it she had sold it. Each prospective juror was closely questioned concerning his views on hypnotism and was asked whether he thought he would succumb to the glances of a hypnotic eye. Such questions were put by Assistant District Attorney Lloyd, who apparently believed such a phenomenon must have had an effect at May's earlier trial. A reporter, without making a direct connection, still made the point when he wrote, "The reason hypnotism is thus playing a part in the case is that Miss Kellard is supposed to have a hypnotic eye, at least so rumor says, and Mr. Lloyd evidently places some faith in the supposition."[42]

Bessie Bangs

Twenty-two year old servant girl Bessie Bangs of Washington, D.C., was arrested in March 1898, charged by Mrs. Bessie Bowman with forgery and by Herbert Allen with obtaining goods by false pretenses. For some time the Bangs family had been receivers of charity, for whom Bowman, who was Superintendent of the Western Division of the Associated Charities, had issued supplies. Also for a number of years, Bowman had been aiding the family financially from her own pocket. On March 26 Bessie presented an order for groceries, bearing Bowman's signature, to Allen, a clerk in the grocery store owned by James E. Thompson. Later that day Bessie returned to the store to complain that the order had not been properly filled, but in the meantime Bowman had entered the store, been shown the order, which she repudiated as a forgery, and the police were called.[43]

Harriet T. Clogg

Another of the wealthy passers of bad paper was Harriet T. Clogg of Baltimore (also known as Mrs. William A. Busnau). New York City police arrested her in March 1900 as she disembarked from an ocean liner after a European vacation. Reportedly, she confessed to arresting Detective McClusky that she had been engaged in swindling in Baltimore by means of bad checks. Harriet was locked up the night of her arrest, with her two-month-old baby, awaiting extradition to Baltimore. One specific charge was that on December 15, 1899 she represented that she had an account in the Astor National Bank (of New York) and thus obtained $400 from the Bank of Commerce in Baltimore, her hometown. McClusky said she also told him she got a diamond ring worth $500 from Frederick Gruebel jewelers of Baltimore with a worthless check from the same bank and that she got a sealskin muff and jacket from Albert Sigmund furriers of Baltimore, paying for it with a worthless $300 check drawn on the Astor National Bank.[44]

Clogg also declared she was not really the wife of Dr. William A. Busnau. According to her story, Busnau came to Baltimore about four years earlier with a hockey team from Canada, and after a whirlwind courtship she married him. Afterward they took a trip to London, Ontario where she found out Busnau had a wife in Canada from whom he had never gotten a divorce. Within hours of the announcement of the arrest of Clogg, merchants Gruebel and Sigmund both declared they would not prosecute the woman. Perhaps the reason could be found in the words of a reporter, who remarked, "The woman is well known here [Baltimore], and had a good social position. Her father was a prominent merchant, and left her $15,000 at his death, which money she is said to have taken with her to Europe."[45]

M. A. Morgan

As 1900 drew to a close, Brooklyn police detectives hunted for a "clever young woman swindler who succeeded by a bold method" in scamming one of the big Fulton Street department stores of furs worth around $400. The woman visited the store and asked to see some sealskin sacques. Reportedly, "She was handsomely dressed and impressed the salespeople as being a person of means." After selecting a sealskin sacque worth $360 and a matching muff worth $35, she ordered the furs sent to herself, Miss M. A. Morgan, at her hotel, the Pierrepont House. A special messenger was dispatched with the furs and was directed to Morgan's room on the first floor, where she took the furs and gave him a check in payment. However, the messenger explained he could only accept cash. "Oh, that will be all right," she told him, "just step down to the hotel office and they will cash the check for you." Naively, he went downstairs with the check leaving the furs with the woman. Of course, the hotel people would not cash the check and by the time he hurried back to the room she was long gone. It was learned later that Morgan, as soon as the messenger had left her, had fled quickly down a back stairway and out through the side entrance of the hotel. Morgan then stopped a passing hansom cab and was driven away. Police arrived at the hotel later in the day but learned nothing. The woman had registered a day before as Miss M. A. Morgan of Washington, D.C., but was a stranger to all the hotel staff.[46]

Mary Langdon

For 18 years, as of 1904, Mrs. Mary Langdon of St. Louis had raised money by passing forged paper; for 18 years her aged mother had kept her out of prison by making good the losses of her daughter's victims. But the mother was just about broke by 1904 and as a result Mary had been arrested and brought to trial as a forger. She was the daughter of an old, wealthy, and respected family, the wife of a man who had held government positions of responsibility, and the niece of the Episcopal bishop of North Carolina. In court Langdon faced the 12 men in the jury and confessed she had been a forger for 18 years and in that time that she had victimized people in all parts of the country. She was born Mary Hoffman in 1861 in Quincy, Illinois to well-to-do parents. At the age of 23 she married Addison Langdon (who was five years older than her mother), who was in the newspaper business in Quincy. Prior to her marriage her father had died and her mother had married a Mr. Blakeslee (she was widowed from him at the time of the trial). Langdon was placed in jail on her 20th wedding anniversary. When she was on the stand in court Mrs. Blakeslee testified she had spent $18,000 in covering the forged paper passed by her daughter over those 18 years, always for small amounts ranging from $50 to $500. Over time the mother sold off all her property, then sold off all her jewelry, and so on, until she had nothing left. Two days after her arrest Addison Langdon went to California for his health, but sent "cheering" letters to his wife from there. That arrest marked Langdon's first interaction with the police over forgeries. Despite the evidence and apparent confession in court the jury could not agree on a verdict. A second trial was promised.[47]

Catherine Bolch

Mrs. Catherine Bolch was arraigned in the Jefferson Market Police Court in New York in December 1906, charged with forging the name of William A. Jones to a check for $10, drawn on the Chemical National Bank. Special detectives of department stores that had lost money by accepting checks from Bolch had Bridget J. Ryan, the landlady of the New York boarding house where Bolch lived, and Mrs. H. J. Reiseng, a lunch-room owner, whose names had been forged to checks for $25 each and passed in department stores, in court. Also, Mrs. Elizabeth Lewis was in court and identified the prisoner as the woman who, three years earlier, lived with her in South Brooklyn and carried away $300 worth of her furniture and clothing. Lewis said that Bolch had completely "cleaned her out," taking even her sewing machine and selling it to a second-hand store while Lewis was out at work. Bolch was arrested at the time, explained Lewis, but escaped trial by jumping a $1,000 bail bond. Police said in court that Bolch was wanted in Atlantic City, Providence, Philadelphia, and Washington.[48]

On December 14 Recorder Goff sentenced Bolch to five years and one month in the prison for women at Auburn for a forgery committed soon after her arrival in New York from Washington. Before he passed sentence Goff asked the prisoner if she had ever been convicted. When she said no Goff asked, "How about the Brooklyn transaction?" to which she replied, "I was not convicted. I jumped my bond." Goff asked her about several other incidents of a similar nature before he told her she should not expect any clemency from him, and then he passed sentence.[49]

A. T. Rowland

A woman most widely known as Mrs. A. T. Rowland, but who also operated under a large number of other aliases, was being sought at the start of 1907 by the police and various private Pinkerton detectives throughout the country. In the words of a news account, "She is regarded as the cleverest hotel beat in America. She suddenly disappeared from this city [New York] after she had left unpaid bills at more than half a dozen hostelries, to say nothing of stacks of worthless checks." Reportedly Rowland had been born of a noble family of Norway, had once been the wife of a prominent Philadelphian, and was also wanted in London, England, where she was said to have operated on even a greater scale than in America. Her past was revealed through the arrest of Florence Scott (accused of stealing $75 in cash and some bonds from Mrs. Mary Giles). Scott and Rowland stopped at the Wellington Hotel but left suddenly without paying their hotel bill. They said they were going to the country for 10 days and left Giles (employed as their maid) behind and on the hook for the hotel bill. During their absence Giles discovered her loss and swore out a warrant for the arrest of the pair. Scott was picked up; Rowland escaped. Detectives learned Rowland's father was a Count Yarde; she came to the U.S. when she was 20 and her "sensational" actions after her marriage caused her husband to sue for a divorce, "and since that time the police have heard from her often under her many aliases."[50]

Antoinette Barris

Sixteen-year-old Antoinette Barris was arrested in Newark, New Jersey, late in 1907 on a charge of forging the name of Miss Rose C. Lynch, who was teaching her dressmaking, to a check for $40. Barris confessed and was paroled awaiting the action of the Grand Jury. Subsequent investigation connected her with many so-called Black Hand letters sent to residents of Newark during the last few months demanding money. All of those communications stated that unless money was paid "death by revolver" would follow. One who received such a letter was a young girl, Maria Pariso. When she received the first letter she was greatly frightened and tried to borrow $5 from a storekeeper, but without success. Pariso's parents, upset by her nervous state, finally found out and called in police. A sting was then set up whereby Maria paid the $5 at a pre-arranged meeting spot to a messenger (ignorant of the scheme) who took the payment to Barris. The police simply followed the schoolgirl messenger Maria Redice to the Barris residence.[51]

Mrs. N. Oster

After following her trail for several days, police detectives Ingram and Cowan finally arrested Mrs. N. Oster on December 24, 1910 after she alighted in downtown Los Angeles from a suburban streetcar. She was locked up in the City Jail on a charge of passing bad checks. According to the police, she tendered a worthless check only a few hours before her arrest. When arrested, Oster had in her possession 13 more checks, written and numbered alike but varying in amount from $15 to $20. Complaints had been made to the police since early in September that a woman about 35 years old had been passing bad checks in the city, but the description of her varied so much that a picture of her was said to be hard to form. Then on December 24th she purchased $3 worth of goods at the Moore Pharmacy at 2080 Pico Street. Oster paid for her purchase with a $15 check, and took away $12 in cash. In a very short time it was discovered to be worthless and police were notified that she had been seen boarding a Pico Heights streetcar bound for the city. Ingram boarded the same car, spotted the woman, and he and his partner Cowan arrested her when she got off at a downtown stop. At the police station she told a "pitiful" story of having three small children and being much in need of medical care. Because of her handwriting a number of checks dating back to September 17 were attributed to her. In nearly every place she made a small purchase and took the remainder of the tendered check in cash.[52]

Mrs. Francis A. Christy

Los Angeles hotel executives were notified in September 1911 to be on the lookout for a pair of check forgers thought to be headed their way after, in the previous two weeks, having passed bad paper at the Hotel Grant and at the Hotel del Coronado, both in San Diego. When they tried to pass another bad check at San Diego's Lankershim Hotel, they were refused due to lack of identification. The forgers were a man and a woman who traveled together as Mr. and Mrs. Francis A. Christy and who used only certified checks drawn on the Union Savings Bank of Pittsburgh made payable to the husband, signed by the wife, and finally certified to by the signature of O. P. Gregory of the Pittsburgh bank. According to Gregory his signature was a forgery. Mrs. Christy was described as partial to dressing in blue serge, large hats, and tan shoes. A reward for their capture was offered by L. F. Nicodemus of the Plains Hotel, Cheyenne, Wyoming, from where they managed to get away with "considerable" of the hotel's cash.[53]

Mamie Mack

Mamie Mack was a black servant in the employ of Mrs. Frances Mayers of New York City. On November 10, 1910 she drew $25 from a savings bank in which her mistress had an account, signing Mayer's name on the withdrawal slip. Mack was arraigned before Judge Mulqueen, pled guilty, and was paroled in the custody of Grace Campbell, a probation officer. Campbell soon found Mack a job but the latter abandoned the job not long after taking it, leaving a note behind to say she hated work. Mulqueen issued a bench warrant for her arrest. Eventually she was located in a New York building and placed under arrest. However, she made an excuse to leave the policeman for a moment and got away by means of a fire escape. A few days later she was again located but she ran away from her police pursuers and was said to have tried to jump out of a fifth story window before a police officer grabbed her just in time.

Once in the street the woman broke free again and made a run for it only to be hauled down after a chase of two blocks. In General Sessions Court on June 9, 1911, Judge Mulqueen sentenced Mack to 11 months and 29 days in the penitentiary.[54]

Adelle Winifred Wade

An old-fashioned Ponzi scheme was uncovered (before Ponzi had arrived on the scene to lend his name to a particular type of fraud) at the start of 1911 in Washington, D.C., with the arrest of Mrs. Josephine Harris along with Mrs. Adelle Winifred Wade, both charged with forgery. Harris pled guilty, turned state's evidence, and explained, "I first met Mrs. Wade when I was selling soap and soap powders on commission. She told me of a plan to make more money and with less effort, and unfolded to me the money lending and borrowing plan, which unfortunately has placed me where I am today. I don't mean to say that I am entirely blameless in the matter, but I have been foolish." When Harris first went to work for Wade she spent much of her time going from place to place paying people interest on the money they had loaned Wade. The scam was to pay exorbitantly high rates of interest that was covered, for a time, by the principal sums loaned to the woman from an ever-increasing number of investors drawn to her by the high interest rates. Apparently Wade was not too skillful in running her scheme — one investor who loaned her $30 was paid $24 interest per month, another who loaned Wade $150 had collected over $500 in interest at the time of the scheme's collapse — and Wade and Harris turned also to using forged notes to raise cash.[55]

On the stand during her trial Wade admitted she had obtained thousands of dollars from Washington citizens by making promises to pay extremely high rates of interest. She was convicted by a jury in Criminal Court on one charge of forgery and on one charge of uttering a forged note. Counsel for Wade gave notice of intention to file a motion for a new trial, and sentence was suspended.[56]

Rosa Zindel

Rosa Zindel, president of the Zindel Manufacturing Company (maker of tortoise shell goods), was carried "hysterical and crying" into the Tombs Prison in New York in August 1912, following her arrest on a bench warrant issued by Chief Magistrate McAdoo. She was locked up and charged with the forging of a $5,795 note purporting to be from a firm of Philadelphia merchants, E. & R. Quinn & Company, which she allegedly discounted at the Century Bank. Two days earlier the note fell due, at which time it was found to be a forgery. When two policemen arrived at Rosa's apartment to arrest her, said an account, "She began shrieking and tried to climb out the windows, according to police. She said she was sick and could not leave her apartment." Her doctor was sent for and the four started for the Tombs by car. On her way down the stairs "she became hysterical and twice fainted." Two weeks earlier a lawyer representing several creditors of the Zindel Company began bankruptcy proceedings against the firm along with a separate bankruptcy proceeding against Rosa personally. She was notified to appear before U.S. Commissioner Gilchrist in those proceedings a couple of days before her arrest but she failed to appear, submitting instead a certificate from her doctor that she was too ill to attend.[57]

A month later, in September, Rosa appeared before Gilchrist to be examined as to the whereabouts of some of her property. William Henkel, receiver for the then officially bankrupt Zindel Company, wanted to know what became of her assets, especially some expensive jewelry. After answering evasively, observed a reporter, Rosa had "a hysterical attack" and shouted out, "I have been trailed about the city by detectives in taxicabs and as I have spent the last three weeks in the Tombs I don't care what becomes of me. Hounds and curs have driven me from business and now if they will only give me poison they can have my life." When she had recovered somewhat she referred the examiner to the company's books but then declared they had been tampered with by the men who had ruined her.[58]

After she pled guilty to a charge of forgery in the second degree, Rosa appeared in court on October 10, 1912, for sentencing; her lawyer made a plea for clemency on the ground of ill health. However, Jesse Epstein, counsel for the Century Bank — it had cashed the forged note — claimed the woman had spirited away about $150,000 worth of property in anticipation of bankruptcy. Epstein further declared that one of the causes of bankruptcy was the forging of notes and a proof of that was the discovery among her belongings at her place of business a card index that showed she had carried on a regular system of forgery for years. Judge Blanchard said he would not consider the plea for clemency until the $150,000 had been accounted for and appointed a commission to investigate where Rosa's assets had gone, with sentencing held in abeyance awaiting that report.[59]

Emma Richardson Burkett

A claim for $69,000 against the estate of Theodore Roosevelt was filed in 1920 by Mrs. Emma Richardson Burkett. Following that filing a bizarre story emerged. According to Burkett she resided in Danville, Illinois, where her husband was a portrait enlarger, when the loan was allegedly made on June 21, 1912. Supposedly she had inherited $70,000 around that time and she had asked a Judge Peyton (deceased by 1920) for advice on what to do with the money. Peyton told her the best thing she could do was to lend the money to the Bull Moose political party. With that party's convention underway Peyton informed Burkett he had arranged for a loan to take place and for her to go to the convention city of Chicago. When she got there she made a loan of $69,000 with the note signed by Charles Shunson (one of Roosevelt's Rough Riders) and by Theodore Roosevelt. When asked if she was sure it was really Roosevelt and not an impostor Burkett was adamant it was really Teddy and she was positive as she had met him several times in the past. Shunson paid her the interest on the loan, seven percent, up until 1917 but then stopped. As the note expired on June 21, 1920, she waited until then to make her claim. Besides the promissory note Burkett had other documents including affidavits signed in February 1921 by alleged witnesses to the interest payments made in 1913, 1914, and 1915.[60]

An investigation revealed that before she became housekeeper for an aged retired farmer in Hillsdale, Indiana, where she lived in 1921, she represented herself in Danville as a short story writer while she conducted a sham matrimonial agency, which caused her to spend two months in jail for using the mails to defraud. She advertised her services as "housekeeper, object matrimony." In answering replies she said she was without clothes or money to make the trip to prospective husbands, and when they sent the money that was the last they heard of her. Burkett was arrested in Danville on November 29, 1913, and charged with using the mails to defraud. Since she had supposedly inherited $70,000 in 1912, investigators found it curious that Emma was compelled to remain in the county jail from the end of November until her case was called in March 1914, unable to raise the $1,500 bail. She was found guilty and sentenced to serve a 60-day sentence that started on March 9, 1914 and ended with her discharge on May 7.[61]

Many people came forward to declare the signature on the Roosevelt note a forgery, and not a very good one at that. Burkett's note held a signature with the prefix "Col." Yet none of Roosevelt's family or friends knew Teddy to sign his name in such a fashion on either personal or business documents. No such person as Shunson could be found, nor had such a name ever appeared on the rolls of the Rough Riders. Assistant District Attorney Dooling observed that in his investigation, besides the mail fraud instance, "We also learned that some time before that she was arrested on a charge of attempting to defraud the executors of the estate of another prominent man through the filing of a claim similar to that which she presented to the executors of the Roosevelt estate.[62]

In due course she was arrested for forgery. At her trial later in 1921 witnesses again refuted all of her documents. One piece of evidence introduced at the trial was a letter Emma wrote on July 19, 1921, while she was a prisoner in the Tombs. She wrote to a friend living near Hillsdale explaining she wanted him and two other men to sign affidavits to the effect they saw her turn over the $69,000 to Shunson, and so on. Emma promised a payment of $10,000 to the friend, if that was arranged.[63]

On October 13, 1921, Burkett was found guilty, whereupon the prisoner swooned and fell to the floor. In his charge to the jury Judge Talley commented on the fact the husband and stepson had not appeared at the trial to testify on her behalf. That was a situation remedied at the sentencing portion of her trial when George Burkett made an unsuccessful plea for the release of his wife to his custody. Emma was believed to then be around 40 years old. Judge Talley sentenced her to the penitentiary on October 24, which meant a minimum period of three years. George was said to be Emma's fifth husband and in his pitch to Talley he remarked, "I have always looked upon her as a sort of cracked pot. I thought the Roosevelt note she talked about was just another one of her peculiarities and never paid much attention to it."[64]

Mary Cameron

After having passed bad checks at half a dozen or more New York City hotels, Mary Cameron was arrested in that city in August 1914.

According to a journalist, "The process used in extracting money from the hotel cashiers was simple, requiring only fairly good looks, a breezy manner, and some nerve." A woman would arrive at a hotel, say that she had left her trunks at an address on the upper west side, and ask that they be sent for. In the meantime she confessed to an awkward predicament — a lack of cash — caused by mistakenly having packed her purse in her trunk. Could the hotel cashier be so good, she wondered, as to cash her check. The cashier at the Biltmore did, to the extent of $25, as they did also at the Algonquin and Belleclaire, for amounts between $20 and $50. Reportedly, other hotels did likewise. On June 13 the woman appeared at the Manhattan Hotel where she registered as Mrs. V. Maxwell and gave the same story. When the porter arrived at the address (supposedly the home of a friend where she said she had been staying) to pick up her baggage he found only a vacant lot. By then, though, the cashier at the Manhattan had cashed a $40 check for the woman, who then promptly disappeared. Soon thereafter a woman calling herself Mary Cameron tried the same scheme at the Hotel University. But the clerk became suspicious when he noted she fit the description of the bad check passer (by then her description had been circulated to all New York hotels) and declined to cash her check, whereupon she left. Hotel detectives trailed her, though, and later that day she was arrested at the Palace Theatre. When she was arraigned before Magistrate Deuel she gave her name as Mary Cameron and said she was 38 years old. Police detective Ernest Moore said the woman was an actress who had once performed with vaudeville's well-known comedy team of Weber and Fields.[65]

Annie Sharpley

For several months in the spring and summer of 1903 postal authorities had received complaints of a systematic raising of the value of postal money orders by a woman operating under the names of Annie Sharpley, Charlotte Cross, A. Thompson, and many other aliases. All of those money orders had been issued by one of the smaller post offices between New York and Philadelphia, usually for 25 cents and, with the aid of acids, had the sums raised to amounts ranging from $65 to $100. Many futile efforts were made to catch the woman with the matter finally turned over to two government Post Office Inspectors, Jacobs and Meyer. For several weeks they worked at catching her but without success. Then they got word she had passed a money order raised to $100 at the Belmont Hotel in Bath Beach. Jacobs and Meyer missed her there by only 10 minutes but, acting on information they had, the pair waited for her at the general delivery window at a New York City post office and arrested Annie E. Sharpley in August when she showed up to collect mail she had forwarded from Philadelphia. On her person they found half a dozen raised money orders, all issued for 25 cents, but raised to $65, $75, or $100. She admitted she was Sharpley and that she had been raising postal money orders since March. Inspectors agreed she did excellent forgeries and was good at imitating handwriting (to match that already on the note). By the time of her arrest many victims had already come forward. For example, the Knickerbocker Hotel of New York, the Palace Hotel of Newark and the Bronx Hotel had each cashed a $100 money order for her.[66]

Sharpley's home was in Philadelphia where she had resided for many years, although English by birth, and where she formerly conducted a small express business that she had sold in March. She was described as "a short, stout red-faced little woman, apparently about forty-five years of age." Up until March, as far as was known, Sharpley had lived a "very respectable life" and was well thought of in the area where she and her husband, who had died several years earlier, resided. After selling her express business, according to the private Pinkerton detectives, she started on a career of crime and made her debut in that field in Chester, Pennsylvania, where she passed a number of forged and raised checks drawn on the Chester National Bank and the National Security Bank of Philadelphia. These were for amounts ranging from a few dollars to $185, purported to be signed by bank depositors and which she cashed with local tradesmen. Next she surfaced in smaller villages in Pennsylvania where she first began to pass raised postal money orders. When police asked her why she had embarked on a career in crime, and so on, Sharpley always declined to answer. She was extradited to Philadelphia, tried and convicted on a charge of forgery and sent to the Federal penitentiary in Philadelphia.[67]

Nothing more was heard of Sharpley until the fall of 1916 when she filed a petition in bankruptcy in Chicago, listing $80,000 in debts and no assets and her affairs became public. She admitted she was the same Sharpley who had done time in Philadelphia. During her stay in Chicago she was said to have borrowed $80,000 from wealthy Chicagoans without security, "by her mere power of persuasion." An extensive poultry farm from which she sold eggs to many wealthy Chicago families had been sacrificed to her longing to have produced a play she had written, *Lights*

Ahead. The entire value of the farm, she said in her bankruptcy petition, had been spent in inducing noted theatrical figure David Belasco to produce the play. However, she later admitted her adventure in the theater world had cost her only $800 and that she had never dealt with the New York producer, but with an imposter who had defrauded her. Sharpley confessed the money she had obtained from forgeries and borrowings in Chicago had all gone for the support of an Englishman, whom she had loved in her girlhood, and who had since lived on the money she made. Conveniently, that man had recently died, she solemnly declared. Her creditors included Mrs. T. B. Blackstone (to the extent of $47,000) and pawnbroker Herman Cohen ($20,000). Cohen finally took over the poultry farm as security for $4,000 of his loan after which Sharpley promptly borrowed a further $350 from him to pay the first month's rent on the farm (apparently she stayed on as a tenant). Despite all they heard about Sharpley, for the first time, her persuasiveness could be seen in the fact that Cohen and Blackstone both were prepared to continue to stand by her. Blackstone said she believed thoroughly in Sharpley's honesty and was prepared to lend her even more money, if necessary.[68]

Minnie D. McLean

Alleged to have posed as a relative to many wealthy Los Angeles residents in order to cash forged checks, Minnie D. McLean, 50, was brought to Los Angeles in March 1919 from San Francisco after her arrest in that city. Reportedly she cashed forged checks totaling $700 on local merchants, using the names of A. J. Blanchard, Mrs. May Wiley, and many other prominent persons. According to the police she was known to them under several aliases and to have been arrested under the name De Graf in 1913, and since then to have lived under her various names at the most fashionable hotels in Los Angeles and in Westlake and Wilshire district apartment houses. Her arrest came, said the police, after a countrywide search.[69]

Florence Langdon

A police search for a mysterious woman in black who passed worthless checks in downtown department stores in Los Angeles kept them busy for over a year trying to find her until it all came to an end on October 31, 1919, when they arrested Florence Langdon at, of all places, their own City Jail. It happened when Langdon showed up at the jail to visit Elizabeth Warren, 19, also being held for passing bad checks, but in incidents unrelated to Langdon. Until three months earlier checks amounting to several hundred dollars in total were cashed by a woman who always wore a black dress and a black hat but she always escaped before police arrived. A few days earlier Warren had been arrested and confessed to the police that she knew the mysterious woman in black but did not knew her name or address. Then, a couple of days later, the police chanced to notice a woman who showed up to visit Warren — wearing a black dress, black silk stockings, and a black silk hat, she matched the description — and held her for questioning. Eventually she identified herself as Langdon and when confronted with a number of returned bad checks she confessed to passing several hundred dollars worth of bad checks over a period of months; she said she had not been operating in Los Angeles in the most recent three months, hence explaining the lull. Langdon added that by chance she saw an account of Warren's arrest in the newspaper and came to see her to offer her assistance.[70]

6

Passing Bad Paper — Mabel Parker

When Mrs. Mabel Parker was arraigned in court in New York on August 16, 1903, charged with forging the names of several Broadway merchants, a reporter asked her to comment on her case. She declared, "It is hardly necessary to say anything, and I cannot talk much under the circumstances. As you see, I am securely under arrest, and I wish I wasn't.... I hope to be able to clear myself, but my dear friend, [police officer] Mr. Peabody, tells me a number of persons will appear against me." Her husband had also been arrested for the same offenses, but separately from her. To that point the only cases of forgery cited against her involved R. H. Macy & Company, Alice Kauser, a theatrical play broker, Benedict Brothers company, the Shoe and Leather Bank, and Rogers, Peet & Company, with the amounts involved ranging from $150 to $1,200. When the judge remanded her for a day she left the courtroom with Detective Peabody, who was charged with returning her to her cell. According to a reporter, Mabel "asked the detective to walk over to Fifth Avenue and down past its churches and through Washington Square to the station." That is, she wanted the officer to take her by way of what she considered to be the scenic route to the jail. Peabody complied with her request.[1]

On the next day a "serene and smiling" Mabel Parker was held for examination in the Jefferson Market Police Court. Magistrate Flammer took the same action with regard to her husband James Parker (each also used the last name Singerley). To that point Mabel had spent two nights in a cell at the Mercer Street police station and, commented a journalist, "Veteran policemen said they had never seen a woman prisoner maintain such an air of nonchalance for so long a time. Her manner so far indicates that she will take all the blame she can on herself in the hope of helping her husband, to whom she seems devotedly attached, admitted criminal though he is, according to the police. Morphine, too, is supposed to have something to do with her unusual bearing."[2]

Parker went on to regale the police and reporters with stories that were more fanciful than real. All she had said before about her background was that she came from Minneapolis where she had married four years previously, after which she and her husband came to New York City. This time she told of having been a novitiate in the Ursuline Convent at Bedford Park in New York and of leaping from a window 30 feet to the ground to elope with James four years earlier, he having driven the thought of being a nun from her mind. Upon being contacted at the convent, the Mother Superior explained the girl's only experience with that institution had been as a regular pupil in the boarding school. Mabel came there early in December 1898, being enrolled by her foster mother Mrs. T. J. Preece of Minneapolis who was then in New York. Parker left the school of her own free will on January 15, 1899. Subtracting out the school Christmas vacation it meant her time there amounted to less than one month as a pupil. Another tale spun by Mabel was that she claimed she had written extensively for magazines under the name of Mabel Singerley but when a reporter conducted a "careful canvas" of the leading periodicals of that class, he failed to find a single editor who had ever heard of her. During her time at the Mercer Street Station, for some reason, Mabel decided to display her forgery skills to Detective Peabody. She asked him to write a name, any name, on a piece of paper. He obliged by writing down "William J. Clark." Then she had him turn around and less than a minute later showed him the paper which now contained the Clark name written down three times. So skillful was she as a forger that Peabody could not tell which was the one he had written. Not surprisingly, at a later stage Peabody showed that paper in court.[3]

During her trial in December 1903 Mabel told the court she had been adopted by Mr. and Mrs. Thomas Preece of Minneapolis, who sent her East to attend school. She went from Minneapolis to the school at the Ursuline Convent where she remained until January 1899. A few months later she became acquainted with James Parker, whom she married in June 1899. In the following August James was arrested and sentenced to a term in the Elmira Reformatory. No verdict was reached at Mabel's trial, as the jury could not agree on one.[4]

A second trial was held in January 1904 with the Parkers facing six forgery indictments. Wallace B. McSweeney was a key witness in court testifying against Mabel. McSweeney was brought down to court from the Elmira Reformatory especially for the purpose of testifying as a witness for the prosecution. He had been arrested in September 1903 and sentenced to a term in the reformatory after having pled guilty to a forgery charge. According to him he was a member of the Parker gang, which included a fourth person by the name of Dutch Gordon. Unemployed when he met James, he visited him at his apartment where he was introduced to Mabel. She asked him what he was doing and he said not much, just walking the streets. Mabel suggested he get into the check game with them but he said he did not think so as he worried about ending up in jail. In response she told him he might as well be in prison as walking the streets and there was nothing like taking a chance to get some money in a hurry.[5]

McSweeney explained he had over time stolen a few letters from mailboxes and Mabel suggested he become the fisherman for the gang. His job was to get hold of checks sent through the mail. "I fished letters from letter boxes at her suggestion. I fished them with a piece of wire and soon became an expert at it. Now and then I found a check in a letter and turned it over to the Parkers, who looked after the checks that were fixed up for passing," he told the court. When the check was for a small amount it was just used to get a copy of the signature for making out a new check for a larger amount. Letterheads were printed with the names of business concerns to match the stolen checks and then a signature was copied from the stolen check and attached to a letter on the fake letterhead. Then that letter was sent as a request to a bank for a checkbook, and if the checkbook came back with the messenger a regular check with a forged signature was then taken by Mabel (or James) to a jewelry store or other retail outlet. When she made a purchase she tendered a forged check in payment but then remarked she would leave the purchase and the check so the retailer could take it to the bank and have it certified. When Mabel returned the next day the check had been certified by the bank (it took longer to discover the forgery due to the method employed by the Parkers) and Mabel was able to walk away with the jewelry and sometimes cash in change. Wallace also testified that he had personally seen Mabel forge names on checks.[6]

Approximately a dozen businessmen appeared in court, all to testify they had received forged checks from the Parkers. Another witness was Bella Van Rensselaer, employed by the couple as their servant, who admitted under close questioning that she had seen Mabel and James tear up many checks. Florence Creighton was their landlady (she knew them as Mr. and Mrs. Singerley) and she told the court, "I was curious to know how they earned their living and asked Mrs. Parker why she wrote so many checks. Every time I entered her room to clean it I found her writing checks. She had many checkbooks there, so I became suspicious of her and her husband. When I asked her about it she said she had several bank accounts." On the day after her husband was arrested, Creighton recalled that Mabel "tore up a number of blank checks which were in the room. There were also a number of checks which had names attached to them. I saw one check with the name of Alice B. Kauser on it." While Creighton testified Mabel occupied herself by making a pencil sketch of the witness.[7]

Mabel's trial drew much attention and, observed a reporter, "When the courtroom doors were thrown open a crowd of fashionably dressed women who were waiting in the corridor made a mad rush, pushing and elbowing each other in an effort to get front seats." Detective Sergeant Clarke was called as a witness and he related what happened in the days after the arrest of James, but before that of Mabel. When Mabel visited James at the jail after his arrest, Clarke and Detective Peabody were assigned to follow her and to infiltrate her gang. It was agreed by the two officers that Peabody would pose as a burglar and ex-convict who had occupied a cell next to James. After the pair trailed Mabel home Peabody knocked at the door with that story. According to Peabody she outlined the workings of the gang, and so on, in what amounted to a full confession, after he expressed an interest in joining the gang. She had even forged some names for him to show him how easy it was to do. James took the stand to declare that Mabel did not know anything about the forgery racket and was not involved in any way. Mabel took the stand and denied all charges and allegations against her. According to her, she had told Peabody she forged the checks only after she felt sure he was a plant — a policeman — and she did so only to try and help her husband. Prosecutor Train asked her if she gave the name of Mabel Wright when she had been arrested earlier for larceny in Buffalo. Parker admitted she was once known as Mabel Wright.[8]

During the course of her trial she said she was 21 years old, born in Jefferson City, Missouri and had been married for about five years. She denied she had ever been convicted in the past but admitted to having been frequently arrested in various parts of the country. After having been out for six hours the jury returned a verdict of guilty against Mabel for forgery in the second degree. Judge Foster immediately sentenced her to the State Reformatory for Women at Bedford, in Westchester County from where she would be released after 13 months, if she behaved herself. If she failed to display good behavior her incarceration would continue for another year, or even longer. Mabel's husband James was sentenced to 10 years' imprisonment in Sing Sing Prison at hard labor. When he sentenced her Judge Foster remarked, "You are a dangerous woman to be at large. I could send you to State prison, but as you say you have never been convicted before I'll sentence you to the Female Reformatory at Bedford, where you may have a chance to forget your cleverness with the pen." A journalist observed how she would spend her time at that facility, "While there she will be employed in making baskets, working half a day and attending school during the remainder of the day. In the summer time she may amuse herself on the lawn playing croquet and basket ball with the other young women prisoners."[9]

Then there were the con artists who used business interests in some way as a cloak for their fraudulent schemes: women employed in the world's oldest profession who extracted something beyond the agreed-upon fee, women operating phony schools, women going door to door soliciting homework for their small business, and women advertising in the media for partners with cash or for victims who wished to make their fortunes by working at home.

Commercial Interests

Sophia Price

Hiram Walker, a visitor to New York, stopped at Lovejoy's Hotel on a November evening in 1860. There he met a streetwalker by the name of Sophia Price. Walker reportedly allowed Price "to take liberties with him" but in the course of their "conversation" she managed to steal his wallet containing $14 in cash and a note for $60. As soon as Walker discovered his loss he caused the woman's arrest. Judge Welsh held her to answer a charge of larceny.[1]

Mary Ann Hanfent

Acting on the complaint of Mrs. Laura Howard in May 1865, New York City police arrested Mary Ann Hanfent, who was alleged to have fraudulently obtained and disposed of two silk dresses and other wearing apparel, to the total value of $210. Operating by going door to door, Hanfent took the dresses under the pretext of repairing and cleaning them, after which they would be promptly returned to the owner. When her clothes were about a month late in being returned Howard made her own investigation of the situation and learned the clothing had been hocked at Barnard's pawnshop. It further appeared that Hanfent had obtained clothing from at least three other women, using the same ruse, and hocked those at Lanagan's pawnshop.[2]

Mrs. Valentine

At the start of 1883 the Charity Organization Society in New York warned the public against a woman who usually gave her name as Mrs. Valentine and who had defrauded several "prominent" ladies in a door to door scam. Arriving at someone's door Valentine portrayed herself as being skillful with the needle and offered to collect any unfinished embroidery and fancy work the householder may have had, take it home to her place, complete the work, and return it. Of course, none of the work she managed to collect was ever returned. In fact, Valentine exhibited those pieces elsewhere as samples of her own work and took orders to generate similar pieces, with advance wages solicited, or some part of them, and, again, no work was ever done. She was described as about five feet two inches in height, with a fair complexion, dark hair, around 40 years old, "and with artless and plausible manners." Valentine gave different home addresses out and what they had in common was that they were always vacant lots. According to a news account, "she had been quite successful in imposing upon a number of wealthy and charitable ladies."[3]

Jane Eliza Foote

With the word "Missioner" printed on her calling cards, along with her snow white hair and a "devout manner of speech," Jane Eliza Foote was said, as of 1887, to have managed to live a comfortable life over the previous few years. She spent a lot of her time among the poor in the uptown districts of New York City and was a regular visitor at the county institutions, in particular the almshouse and the hospital, with the result her face became known to those in charge at such places. Also, at such places, Foote encountered charitable individuals out on errands of mercy. To them she pitched her own modest ambition, which was to take into her home the destitute, the sick, and the helpless. Whenever anyone called on her at her residence they were said to be always impressed when they saw that while she could afford only a tenement flat of three or four rooms, she seemed always to maintain one or two "helpless" people therein. All of this meant, said a reporter, "Her desires soon became known to quite a circle of charitable people and they sent her clothing, provisions, and money. In that way she made a living."[4]

Foote might have gone along in the same fashion indefinitely except for her temper. When she scolded or beat one of those helpless people she had taken into her home and under her care as a charge she did it loudly enough for other families living in flats in the house to hear her. Neighbors talked among themselves and became angry when Foote went out for a day, and sometimes longer, leaving her helpless wards without food or fire. Finally, at the beginning of 1887 the neighbors complained to the authorities and when Foote returned to her tenement flat at 2312 Second Avenue she found her rooms empty of people. A note left on the door by the authorities informed her that Hattie Brice, 10 (one of her charges), would be taken to Police Court the next morning by a representative from the Society for the Prevention of Cruelty to Children, on an application to have the child taken from her because of ill treatment. Her other charge, Martha Thompson, an elderly woman subject to epileptic fits whom Foote picked up at the Charity Hospital, had also been removed and the same note informed the missioner that Thompson would also be found in court the following morning.[5]

When the authorities collected the two wards they found the pair locked in a room, cold and starving while Foote had been out all day making collections for her missioner work. Reportedly, "Both woman and child told pitiful stories of neglect and abuse." The charges had to do all the work of the house and got only abuse for it. Rarely could they obtain anything but crusts to eat, although Foote always managed to place "appetizing dishes" before herself. Neighbors appeared in court and detailed what they had seen and heard. Brice's mother came down from Yonkers, where she was a housekeeper, and explained that she had allowed Foote to take her child, in the hope of getting her the nice home that the missioner had promised. Mrs. Brice was a widow with several children.[6]

After two hearings Justice Patterson ordered Hattie to be placed in the care of the Society for the Prevention of Cruelty to Children, with the mother's consent, until a suitable foster home could be found for her. Thompson was sent back to Charity Hospital. Upon returning to Foote's apartment to get the clothing belonging to Brice and Thompson the authorities found a quantity of other clothing and provisions, donations that had been sent to her for her work with the poor. After investigating her past the Society concluded, "It appeared that she was not new at this business. She took children as a matter of business, and then half starved and beat them. Before taking her present rooms she lived in the same section on Fourth-avenue, where she annoyed the neighbors so much by her abuse of her helpless charges that the landlord put her out. The Society for the Prevention of Cruelty to Children will see that she lets children alone hereafter."[7]

Alice Webster

In Baltimore the case against Alice Webster (alias the Reverend Dr. George Goodwin of New York) was declared in U.S. Court there in April 1894 to be one that would not be prosecuted. She was charged with using the U.S. mails for fraudulent purposes. Allegedly, she advertised bicycles for sale in newspapers and magazines at remarkably low prices, soliciting buyers. Would-be purchasers were informed by the ads that Dr. Goodwin was a pastor of a well known church in New York and that having met with an accident he could not use the bicycle and that it would be sold for $30. Correspondents were requested to remit $5 as a deposit and for express charges. Letters for Goodwin were addressed to an uptown private letter box in New York and when the woman was arrested at that mail drop a few weeks earlier, a number of letters had just been delivered to her. Government officials claimed that hundreds of letters addressed to Goodwin had been delivered to her and "many persons in all parts of the country had been mulcted." Needless to say, nobody received a bicycle from Webster. However, District Attorney Ensor decided there was not enough evidence to convict her and the case was abandoned.[8]

Ruth Howard

Mrs. Ruth Howard, 28, and Herman Cohen, 30, were arrested and locked up by the police in New York in March 1899, charged with grand larceny. They were alleged to be members of a gang of swindlers that operated the previous month under the name of W. B. Deming & Company in the Hudson Building at 32 Broadway. Howard and Cohen obtained credit from the other firms by representing themselves as an established but fake firm, with Howard reportedly having made a full confession to Captain McClusky. Cohen, she said, was the gang leader and she acted as an agent in acquiring goods. Cards were printed up giving her name as May Chambers and Cohen gave her a list of merchants from whom she was expected to get goods. She visited Boaz & Lichtenstein and obtained from them $500 worth of silk shirts, on credit, as the representative of the W. B. Deming firm. From the Acme Knee Pants Company she secured $300 worth of goods. A. Friel, furrier, gave up $500 worth of furs, the same amount as obtained from another furrier, John Russig. Many other merchants fell victim to the swindle with all the goods, Howard related, delivered to the offices of W. B. Deming and then sold by the gang. Howard added that she had reformed and had joined the Daughters of Independence as well as being in attendance at the Young Women's Christian Association.[9]

When her background was investigated it was learned that Ruth Howard began to appear in the offices of the American Ring Company (a dealer in novelties) in Chicago in the latter part of 1897, accompanying R. M. Agee, employed by that firm as an agent, whom she had recently married. Then one day late in that year Mrs. Agee appeared in the American Ring office on her own and told the manager a story of desertion and theft by her husband. According to the story she told the manager she married Agee thinking he was a "prayer-meeting" sort of a man only to quickly learn he was of the "confidence" class when he deserted her and took away everything she had. In November of 1897 Ruth stopped in at the American Ring office to tell them she had assumed her maiden name, Ruth Frost, and was running a shoe agency, the Ruth Frost Shoe Company. Still later she returned to American Ring to say she was employed buying bankrupt shoe stock for George P. Gore. And that was the last of Howard's visits to the American Ring Company.[10]

Later she married George B. Martin, but he turned out to be a swindler as well. One reporter commented that her alliance with Martin appeared to have "depraved" the woman for the pair embarked on some type of scheme and, as a result, they had to leave Chicago. After arriving in New York, Martin was arrested for robbing a man and sent to jail for two years. Through Martin's attorney, Howard was introduced to Herman Cohen and they began a partnership that started with the organization of the fake firm of Deming & Company and ended with the arrest of the pair. In her confession, reportedly, she estimated she had swindled New York merchants out of over $50,000 worth of goods.[11]

Carrie E. Hayes

Described as "an attractive woman about thirty-six years of age, the wife of Dr. C. E. Hayes, a manufacturer of Louisville," Mrs. Carrie E.

Hayes spent the night of July 7, 1901, in jail at the House of Detention in Washington, D.C., after she was arrested on the complaint of the assistant postmaster in Newport, Virginia. Hayes had been collecting money from many prominent Washington women in connection with an enterprise known as the Monte Vista Mission Association, a reform movement for the free training and education of girls in domestic science. A partial list of Washington members of the enterprise included 50 women, many of them socially well known. From five of them she received a total of $150 toward the work of the mission.[12]

Apparently no complaint had been made about Hayes by any of the people who had contributed money to her proposed institution, and her plan to educate and supply competent household domestics had "met hearty endorsement." To those who donated $25 or more she gave a printed receipt admitting them to life membership in the mission association, the privileges of which entitled each subscriber "to a one-quarter acre lot at the Monte Vista resort," which was to be established about two miles from Newport, Virginia, and to "receiving from the mission trained household help without further cost." Washington police had received several letters from A. L. Payne of the firm Payne & Snider of Newport (he was also the assistant postmaster of the town) in which he declared there was no such institution as the Monte Vista resort and who used the word "fraud" in connection with the enterprise. When a reporter interviewed Hayes she told him she had an option on a piece of land owned by E. P. Williams that fell through at the last minute but she had recently secured an option on a piece of land in Roanoke and had been in the process of going there to secure the deal just about the time she was arrested. She complained the postmaster was a relative of Williams and "I attribute my predicament to his enmity." During the past couple of years while she had lived in Washington, explained Hayes, she had devoted her entire attention to the solution of the servant question. With respect to the Monte Vista project she said, "The idea was to give each subscriber a lot. I expected the subscribers to build cottages, thus establishing a summer resort, which would make the mission school self-sustaining."[13]

May H. Wilson

A man and wife had been in Washington, D.C., for only a week in July 1904 when police arrested them. During their brief time in the nation's capital, Francis K. Wilson (40, also known as George J. Dexter and Walter Williams) and May H. Wilson (27, also known as May H. Dexter and May H. Robertson) had been prolific advertisers in local newspapers. Arrest came after the police got a tip from the police of Trenton, New Jersey, after a man was arrested there. In his possession were several letters to him from F. Wilson detailing some of the couple's scams and giving a Washington address. Thus the police arrested the pair at an Indiana Avenue boarding house. Among their belongings were found a large number of ad clippings from newspapers in New York, Philadelphia, Boston and other cities, of the following general type: "BUSINESS CHANCE—LADY WANTS PARTNER. real estate business; $75 cash required; $18 a week guaranteed." Also found in the possession of the couple was evidence such ads had been inserted in many newspapers and a number of letters evidently written by people who had replied to the ads. And in some cases the letters asked for the return of the money the letter writer had advanced on the propositions made by the Wilsons or the Dexters. Following the arrest of the pair, detectives made the rounds of the newspaper offices and took possession of a number of letters written in reply to ads the Wilsons had placed in the Saturday and Sunday issues of the papers. One said: "STEADY YOUNG MAN WANTED FOR PARTNER, show business; $150 required; $15 a week guaranteed." Another ad read: "YOUNG MAN WANTED FOR PARTNER, REAL estate business; $200 required; $18 a week guaranteed." Since the arrests were made before any of the replies could be answered by the Wilsons, there were no victims in Washington. It was thought by the police the pair were wanted in a number of cities. With respect to May Wilson's behavior upon arrest, a reporter observed, "The woman took matters coolly when taken to headquarters, and declined to answer any questions. She is tall, good looking, and well dressed, and talked slang with the officers."[14]

Euniez Livingstone

Given the choice of being prosecuted on a charge of grand larceny or of getting out of town, a woman described by a journalist as "Pretty as a picture, well educated, the daughter of a well-to-do family residing in Chicago, but still a thief, one of the most dangerous female crooks with whom the police have had to deal in years" left Los Angeles in December 1903. If she returned to the city she faced prosecution. Euniez

(Nuce) Livingstone was said to be "beyond reformation, from a police standpoint and the officers believe that it is easier for them to force her to leave the city than to convict her." A few nights earlier she had been arrested on the complaint of Tom Newland, a Terminal Island saloonkeeper, whom she allegedly had swindled out of $560 after he had pitted his wits against hers. Arrested a day later and taken to the police station, "She was attired in garments finer than most wives of wealthy citizens wear. Within a few hours after the robbery she had purchased the finest store-clothes which she could find to fit her and her appearance when she was taken into custody was not that of a thief, but of a woman of respectability, and she tried to make the detectives believe she was such." A police matron did a strip search of Livingstone and found $130 in cash concealed under the ostrich plumes of her "picture hat."[15]

Livingstone met Newland on the street, after which he took her to dinner, paying $20 for her food and drink; then he took her to his room. Fearing he might be robbed Newland placed $560 in his hat and hung it on a hook on the wall. Livingstone pretended not to have noticed any of that activity but she had. When his back was turned she got the money and then, saying she would be back in a moment, left the room. Newland waited for 30 minutes and since she had not returned he decided to look for her. Picking up his hat to start out, he realized his money was gone and called in the police. It took the police a day to find Livingstone, by which time she had spent all but $130. "More than $360 had been blown out for clothing, and the balance was squandered in hack rides, champagne dinners and presents to friends." A friend of the woman by the name of Hughes appeared after the arrest and offered to make good Newland's loss provided there was no prosecution. The saloonkeeper agreed but the police added a condition of their own to the deal — that she must leave the city. Once she agreed Livingston was escorted to the Southern Pacific railroad depot and placed on a train going out of town. From looking up her record the police learned Livingstone had gotten money out of men in similar circumstances in amounts ranging from $20 to $100. None of them had pressed charges against her due to the embarrassing nature of the incidents.[16]

Belle Wilson

Charged with conducting a fraudulent concern Belle Wilson, head of the Wilson Sign Company, 603 Walnut Street, Philadelphia, was arraigned before U.S. Commissioner Bell in Philadelphia in April 1905 and held for a hearing. The U.S. District Attorney's office recommended the issuance of a fraud order against the firm. Post Office Inspector James Wardle testified, "The Wilson Sign Company is a work-at-home swindle, victimizing girls and women all over the country." At a cost of $1.10, applicants were supplied with material for making small cardboard signs. If the signs were satisfactory the company agreed to purchase them at a rate of $2.50 a hundred. Of course, none of the signs produced by those home workers were ever accepted by the company.[17]

Elizabeth C. Campbell

About 200 people went to the New Rochelle (New York) Theatre on October 28, 1906, with the tickets they had purchased in advance for $1.50 expecting to hear a concert of "high class" music presented under the management of Miss Elizabeth C. Campbell. Many of the ticket holders were said to be prominent members of high society. When they arrived at the venue they found the doors locked, the place in darkness, and no sign of a concert. Also in the crowd were many local merchants who had paid $5 and $10 for advertising space in Campbell's non-existing programs. Later in the evening theater manager William Gray appeared to say he had received a telephone message from the Bridgeport, Connecticut, police to the effect Campbell had been arrested there for using the name of the Young Men's Christian Association (without their knowledge) in connection with a show she planned to stage there. None of Campbell's promised and advertised artists appeared in New Rochelle that night. Campbell was described as a 30-year-old brunette from Canada who had lived in the New Rochelle area for several years, where she sometimes staged concerts at summer hotels.[18]

Campbell was arrested in West Chester, Pennsylvania on August 17, 1907, on a charge of obtaining money under false pretenses and arraigned the next day in Philadelphia at the Central Police Court. Her arrest came after a two week chase through much of Pennsylvania. "Miss Campbell, who is young, pretty, well dressed, and a persuasive talker, is charged with having swindled unsuspecting storekeepers out of considerable sums of money by an entirely new scheme," said an account. According to the police her scheme was to rent a hall and announce that an entertainment was soon to be given. She would then solicit advertisements from local storekeepers with which to fill her program. Around the middle of July Campbell rented a venue in Frankford, Pennsylvania and announced an entertainment would be given on July 29. Then she got ads, cash in advance. Once her program was filled she announced the show would not be held until August 14, and promptly left town. It was the change in date that aroused suspicion and caused the police to be called in. Held on $600 bail she was sent to Moyamensing Prison as she could not raise the money. Indignantly denying all charges and allegations in court she declared, "I make my living by giving elocutionary entertainments. I do literary work, and have written a little poetry."[19]

Mrs. Don Seymour

As she was leaving the Fort Pitt Hotel in Pittsburgh on July 20, 1910, a woman using the name of Mrs. Don Seymour of Chicago (she was also known as Mrs. R. L. Porter of Denver and Mrs. Ralph Stanning of New York) was arrested on a complaint by the Chicago police. In her room at the hotel were found letters indicating she had recently operated in Los Angeles, San Francisco, Chicago, St. Louis, Cincinnati, Philadelphia, and New York, and that she was about to operate in Pittsburgh. Her scheme was to collect money in advance on the pretext she produced and exhibited motion pictures of "great value." She was said to have taken $800 from her recent Chicago fraud and when arrested by the Pittsburgh police to have offered them $500 for her release, explaining she was due in New York in a day or two.[20]

Jane Doe

Deputies from the Sheriff's office in Santa Barbara, California were said to be looking for two women in January 1911, a mother and daughter who were alleged to have swindled many women in America on fake sales of silk material. To add insult to injury the pair also stole a policeman's rig, which that official had loaned them as part of a plan to effect their capture. Arriving in Santa Barbara from San Luis Obispo, the pair swindled a number of women (the pair solicited door to door) who ordered silk and paid half the cost in advance with the order, which was to come by mail, but never appeared. Next, the swindlers moved on to

Santa Maria. Police there were warned before their arrival to be on the lookout in case they showed up there. When they did arrive a policeman in Santa Maria wanted to gather solid evidence so he formulated a plan (details not reported) that involved loaning the pair a buggy while he telegraphed to the firm they named as employing them. The women drove away in the rig and promptly disappeared.[21]

Lena A. White

Mrs. Lena A. White, the head of a shorthand school in Los Angeles that taught a supposedly new method, found herself on trial in Judge Chamber's division of police court on a charge of obtaining money under false pretenses. Called "human voice" stenography, White claimed the new method could be mastered in a very short while, and that it thoroughly upset all the "staid principles" of Pittman, Gregg and other standard, established shorthand mentors. Complaining witness Mrs. Claire Hayward said she paid $15 to the White school to learn that she could master the new system in 45 minutes, but characterized the method as a fraud, as nothing new, and as an agglomeration of the shorthand characters and cabalistic signs. Hayward charged on the stand she had discovered one character that could be used to stand for any one, or all, of 16 different words. When she called that fact to the attention of White, the latter called her a "know-nothing."[22]

Walter H. Rammage of Pasadena, who invested $2,000 in the school to become a partner in the business with White and later agreed to buy textbooks and catalogs and assume the management of the school, was charged jointly with her, as he was the one who actually received the $15 from Hayward. White ran her "human voice" school on South Hill Street in Los Angeles and advertised the wonderful possibilities of its instruction. When she responded to the ad Hayward was told by White that anyone with ordinary common sense and $15 could master the new shorthand method. White claimed to be able to school a student so thoroughly in the new method that foreign languages might be dictated and transcribed from the shorthand notes with ease. A remarkable adjunct to the instruction, White was said to have told Hayward, was that of a mind cure, "which would straighten the mentality and restore vigor." After Hayward had learned the system in 45 minutes she went back to the school for more instruction the next day only to be told she had received all the instruction. Rammage took the stand to say he heard White tell Hayward that she could teach her how to take dictation in any language and transcribe it just as it was dictated.[23]

After the prosecution finished presenting its case, and before the defense presented its side, Judge Chambers interrupted the trial to instruct the jury to return a verdict of not guilty, declaring there was no evidence upon which to convict. Eleven of the jurors were willing to follow those instructions but one juror held out for two hours against a verdict of acquittal before he joined with the majority. Testimony during the last day of the trial indicated the human voice system was nothing more than the Pittman system. The judge, sustaining a defense objection, did not allow the prosecution to show a graduate of White's system could not take notes in a foreign language and read from those notes afterward, when the note-taker had no knowledge of that other language.[24]

Nellie Higgins

On July 3, 1916, Mrs. Nellie Higgins pled guilty in United States District Judge Trippet's court in Los Angeles to the charge of using the mails in a scheme to defraud. It was charged that she advertised for women to do work at home, lace-making, and promised large monetary rewards. She agreed to buy the lace from these women at so much per yard. As part of her scheme Higgins furnished a book of samples showing the sort of lace she would purchase. For that book she charged her prospective workers $2.50 a copy. When completed work was sent to her she refused to buy it, claiming it did not meet standards; then she cut the lace up into bits in order to create more sample books with it that she could sell to others. Reportedly, she victimized many women all over the country before the scheme was broken up, in the wake of numerous complaints made to post office inspectors who eventually launched an investigation that led to her arrest a couple of months earlier. In her defense Higgins said she was the sole support of two children. Higgins was fined $80, $20 on each of the four counts of the indictment, by Trippet.[25]

Ethel J. Cayce

Toward the end of 1918 an indictment with a charge of using the mails to defraud was issued against four people: Edwin R. Crocker, his brother Harry L. Crocker (both of Los Angeles), Frederick W. Sterling (Oakland), and Mrs. Ethel J. Cayce (of San Francisco, where she was arrested on November 16). Those four were said to be the directors of the Domestic Utilities Manufacturing Company of Los Angeles. They were charged with using the mails to defraud through the sale of contracts for the right to sell in certain districts washing machines and stove flues manufactured by the utilities company. Also charged in the indictment was that the four represented to purchasers of contracts that they could sell similar contracts (for smaller areas within their territories) making the plan "a variation of the endless letter chain." Edwin Crocker, company president, reportedly fled to Europe after the indictment was issued. It was estimated that 9,000 agents in the U.S. lost more than $1 million. Following her arrest, Cayce admitted she had profited to the extent of $54,000 in 116 days.[26]

8

Commercial Interests — Marion La Touche

Sometime during the fall of 1887 a shingle was hung at 165 West 23rd Street in New York City that informed passers-by that Marion La Touche (sometimes spelled Latouche, and also known as Marion Dow and Carrie Morse) "banker and broker" had an office there and for several weeks thereafter New York Police Inspector Byrnes had to listen to scores of women who complained that her business methods were those of a swindler. They had been lured to her office by ads offering employment and/or tempted by her promise of interest on deposits at the phenomenal rate of 20 percent per month. Complainants had invested from $300 to $800 each but when asked if they would prosecute all declined; either they wanted, thought Byrnes, to use his office to collect their money or they were too embarrassed to prosecute, not wanting the public exposure a police court appearance would bring. Finally, a Mrs. Clara Johnson consented to file an official complaint. From that a warrant was prepared and La Touche was arrested on December 7. According to Byrnes, "She is now 35, and a pretty and fascinating brunette" and was said to be well known to the police in many cities.[1]

Back in 1870 Marion was married to a man named Warren and living in Boston, where both were arrested on a charge of swindling but both escaped conviction. When Warren died Marion married a man named Dow and the couple started a fashionable boarding house in Boston's Back Bay. Soon, though, Dow left her a widow and Marion returned home to live with her father. However, she found herself in danger of being arrested for trying to negotiate a certificate for one share of

Michigan Central Railroad stock, which had been raised to indicate it was a certificate for 60 shares. Along with her father she fled to St. John, New Brunswick but was arrested there for trying to pass a forged check for $1,700. The next time she came to the attention of the police was in 1881 when she opened a "banking" office in Union Square in New York, but it was said she was so much under surveillance from the police that she decided it would be better if she went to Philadelphia. Apparently things did not go well for her there because, reportedly, she was arrested there, convicted of swindling and served a term in Moyamensing Prison. In 1882 she returned to New York and opened a broker's office on West 37th Street.[2]

Mrs. Carrie Morse was arrested in New York in October 1882, charged with fraud on a complaint from Annie L. Linton, who had also begun a civil suit to recover $1,000 from her. According to Linton, in July of that year she saw in a newspaper an advertisement in which Morse called for a partner with capital. After responding to the ad, Morse called on her at home and moved the conversation away from any reference to an ordinary business investment to one whereby Morse pitched that if Linton gave her $1,000 she, Morse, would invest it for her in the stock market and make her a great deal of money. Unconvinced, Linton declined the offer initially but Morse kept up the pressure by writing to her and stopping in to visit on several more occasions.[3]

Over time Morse embellished her own circumstances, telling Linton she owned two houses in Boston and held some mortgages on valuable real estate in that city. Finally, she induced Linton to give her $1,000 to invest in stocks with the understanding that Linton would receive all the profits from the speculation and the principal sum would be returned upon a call of three days. A few days later Morse sent Linton $131 in "profits" but when Linton called for the return of the $1,000 not long thereafter Morse at first evaded repayment and then refused altogether. When the police got involved her Boston real estate claims were checked out and found to be false. An inspector for the telegraph company identified her as a person who, some two years earlier, carried on in New York a stock speculation bureau that went under the name of McIntyre & Company. Police officers from Boston came to New York with an arrest warrant for one Marion E. Warren (Morse), charged with fraudulent stock operations in that city but when they arrived at the McIntyre offices they found the place closed and that the woman (Morse had called herself Marsh when she ran McIntyre) had disappeared. Among the affidavits in support of Linton's application for the order for Morse's arrest was one from Mary A. Brink, who asserted Morse had also defrauded her out of $1,000.[4]

It was not until April of 1884 that Morse was examined in the Tombs Police Court on a charge of swindling Brink out of her money, and at that time she also faced a separate complaint from Miss Helen Wilson. A Newark, New Jersey dressmaker, Wilson had a female friend, Hattie Herder, who was looking for work. Wilson replied to an ad Morse had placed, requesting a clerical employee, in October 1883. In a discussion of the job Morse told Wilson that she wanted a $1,000 security deposit as a guarantee of the proper performance of duties from any clerk she might engage for the position. After haggling a bit over that issue, Wilson deposited $600 cash on behalf of her friend for the job. However, when Herder showed up for her first day on the job she discovered the premises to be empty and that Morse had disappeared. Another complaint had been lodged by Mrs. Mary De Witt, a widow with five children who had a little shoe store in Harlem. According to her, Morse had gone under 13 aliases in as many months. Morse rented rooms at De Witt's house in July 1883, representing herself as M. E. Dowell of the M. E. Dowell Publishing Company at 261 Broadway; she also said she owned real estate worth $22,000 and had other valuable interests. De Witt added that Morse convinced her to sell her store to invest through her in the stock market. First she gave her tenant $600 in cash to invest and then $2,000 more after the sale of her property. Morse promised she would double De Witt's money but after giving her a worthless $125 check for rent that was due Morse vanished.[5]

The examination of Morse in court was well attended by the public and in the words of a reporter, "A number of women handsomely dressed in silks and furs, sat on a bench in Justice Duffy's private room yesterday morning and cast withering looks at Mrs. Carrie Morse, a rather fine-looking blonde, who divided her time between returning the looks and turning to her handkerchief whenever her counsel became pathetically eloquent." Brink testified that Morse had represented herself as the head of the Ladies' Investment Bureau of New York and also told her she owned dwellings in New York, Boston, and Philadelphia and was endorsed by three members of the Stock Exchange. Counsel for Morse argued all these complainants had simply given money to Morse to invest as people did all the time to brokers, and they had lost money just as many others did every day that played the market. Judge Duffy ordered her detained for trial with bail set at $3,400. She was convicted and sent to prison for two years. At the time of her arrest in December 1887, she had been out of jail only eight months. Marion told Byrnes she married a man named Royal La Touche in Philadelphia in 1881 and that in 1883 he was convicted of bigamy and sent to prison for three years.[6]

At La Touche's arraignment hearing on December 8 at the Jefferson Market Police Court, Clara Johnson, widow of a railroad conductor and struggling to support a child, told her story. On October 7, 1887, she saw an employment ad that induced her to call on La Touche. According to Clara, Marion said if Clara gave her $300 as a security deposit she would be hired to work as a clerical at La Touche's office at 40 Lexington Avenue and her salary would be $20 a week. Clara replied she had only $150 so La Touche condescended to accept that sum as the deposit, but reduced Clara's salary to $10 a week. Johnson worked for two weeks as a clerical but received no salary. Finally, worried she had been conned she asked for her $150 deposit back but testified she received nothing but contempt. After Justice Gorman ruled Marion be held for examination La Touche refused to give the court her birthplace, residence, or occupation and also refused to talk to the press. Although no other witnesses appeared against her, Clara said that in her tenure on the job many women had called on her employer and "invested" money at "fabulous rates of interest." Detective Harry Weyl of Philadelphia, who happened to be in New York at the time of the arraignment, told reporters he remembered the prisoner as a "commonplace swindler" in Philadelphia, where she worked with a "male adventurer, but the authorities made short work of them." With respect to La Touche's court demeanor and appearance a reporter observed, "When she was not defiant or insolent she was sour and snappish" and "Mrs. Latouch's wardrobe indicates either parsimony or financial embarrassment."[7]

As time passed more information on her background became known. She was the daughter of Jacob Gratz of Wassis, New Brunswick and was also known as Mrs. Marion E. Warren of Philadelphia, and as Mrs. M. S. Ware of 822 Wabash Avenue, Chicago. At the latter place she was arrested in 1875 on a charge of forging a draft of $1,964 on Charles E. Fuller, a banker in Boston. That check was cashed in St. John and Mrs. Ware, after remaining in jail in Boston from July 28 to September 28, 1875, was taken to St. John, where she remained in jail two months, and by a "disagreement" of the jury was acquitted. N. H. White, a Boston swindler who was once a friend of hers, was said to have swindled $700 out of La Touche after her return to Boston from St. John. Marion had reportedly been arrested in Boston on various charges but had always managed to escape conviction.[8]

Court examination of La Touche was held on December 9, 1887. Johnson elaborated that the $150 was given to La Touche (then going under the name of Mrs. Dow) with the understanding that Dow could use the money to trade in stocks on her own account and at her own risk but that Clara could have the money back at any time. A new witness was Emma Grenier, who told the court that on November 17 she gave $300 to Marion for the purpose of stock speculation. Grenier was assured by Dow, she said, that the money was as safe with her as if it was in a bank and that Grenier could have it back on demand at any time. When she made such a demand, however, she did not get her money back.[9]

Detective McManus testified that he obtained a letter, dated November 1, 1887, that Dow had sent to a Miss Eaton, with regard to a possible job. In that letter she said she remembered Eaton when she had called on Dow (in response to another matter) and she explained to Eaton that her business was in dealing with stocks and that she remembered Eaton having mentioned she was looking for a job doing light office work. "I am now in need of a young lady assistant here in my office, as I am very busy. I had intended to advertise for an assistant, but happening to recollect your address I thought I would drop you this line to say that if you are not otherwise engaged I might arrange to give you a position in my office during the Fall and Winter months, and perhaps longer if mutually agreeable," explained Marion in the letter. It continued, "I should require you here every day, except Saturday, from 10 A.M. to 3 P.M. The position would be a responsible one, as I should authorize you to receive and pay out money the same as myself, and you would take the entire charge of my affairs at all times during my absence, under my instructions. Of course, I should require some security of you and pay you a good salary... [signed] Marion L. Dow."[10]

In September 1902 she was arrested again, as Marion La Touche, for grand larceny but again she was discharged. Later in 1902 a nurse by the name of Jennie McKenzie entrusted $2,100 to her to purchase stocks on her behalf. When she failed to receive any stocks she had La Touche arrested but, once more, she was discharged.[11]

At the end of July 1917, Marion La Touche, then 66, was arrested on suspicion of fraud for promoting a get-rich-quick scheme among women. When she was arraigned in General Sessions Court Judge McIntyre held her on $35,000 bail, on an indictment charging her with the specific misappropriation of $200. As she was unable to furnish a bondsman La Touche was committed to the Tombs prison pending trial. Assistant District Attorney Weil declared her to be one of "the most noted of women swindlers." The complainant was Mrs. Anna M. Fitzgerald of Brooklyn, who alleged she gave La Touche $200 to invest for her and never received anything in return, although she said she made several demands.[12]

According to Weil, there were several other women who reported to him that they had been swindled by the defendant. One complainant declared she had lost $11,000 while two others in the courtroom said they had been swindled out of smaller sums. Weil asked McIntyre to set bail at $50,000, explaining, "Her career extends back to 1875. In her lifetime she has swindled hundreds of women out of millions of dollars. When she takes their money she disappears and does not show up again for a year or two. She has been indicted for grand larceny at least twice in the past and has served time in prison." When she was arrested this time, on Fitzgerald's complaint, the arrest took place just as she was leaving the Tombs Police Court, where she had been discharged by Magistrate Murphy on a similar complaint made by Mrs. Alice Hutchinson of New York. Hutchinson had charged La Touche with the grand larceny of $2,000, which she said had been given to Marion to invest for her. Murphy decided the complaint was a civil action instead of a criminal proceeding. She was sent to Auburn prison for 18 months.[13]

An almost identical complaint to the Fitzgerald one was made against Marion by Mary Hocke in 1921. Upon conviction she received an indeterminate sentence to Welfare Island. Yet another, and similar, complaint was made in 1926 by Anna Blackschmidt against La Touche, then known as Mrs. Marion Dow. As a result, she went back to Auburn, this time for three years. On an August day in 1931 Marion, then 85, was arrested again, as she walked along a New York Street. Her former landlady, Edna Mattke, alleged that on September 10, 1930, La Touche told her of all the money to be made on Wall Street by purchasing stocks. So persuasive was her pitch that Mattke gave La Touche $400 to buy some stocks for her. However, she never got any stock nor did she get her money back. When she spoke to her boarder about it, La Touche simply moved away and disappeared. Because she had three felony con-victims in her past, La Touche stood in danger of going to jail for life if convicted. Under a four strikes and out provision then in place — known as the Baumes law — any one who was convicted of a felony for a fourth time had to be sentenced to life in prison; the judge had no discretion.[14]

When she was arraigned on the Mattke complaint Edna declared she had received no stock and had not even gotten a receipt for her money. La Touche insisted she had given Mattke a receipt and the agreement was that she would invest in the stock market for her landlady and do her best to make money. When District Attorney Charles Pilatsky asked the prisoner if it was true she had been sentenced to Welfare Island in 1884 she replied it was so long ago she could not remember.[15]

La Touche was indicted by the grand jury on a charge of grand larceny in the second degree. Assistant District Attorney Henry Alexander revealed that several other women had been victimized by the prisoner, besides Mattke, in the same manner. Investigation revealed that La Touche had bought stocks with the money her victims gave her but kept them for herself. Police records showed Marion, over the 47 years from 1884, had been arrested nine times on larceny and theft charges and had served four prison terms after convictions under various names.[16]

On August 31, 1931, Judge Donnellan allowed Marion to escape a life sentence by letting her plead guilty to a misdemeanor. The women swindled besides Mattke had all lost amounts less than $500. When first arrested back in 1884, Marion told police she had been born in Canada and had married her first husband, a dry goods merchant, soon after the Civil War. He died in 1879, after having introduced her to the lure of the stock market, she explained. In 1917, aged 71, she was convicted on a fraud charge in New York and sentenced to an 18-month term in Auburn State Prison for Women. Two years later she received another sentence to Welfare Island for a theft and that was followed in 1926 by another three-year sentence to Auburn.[17]

On September 9, 1931, Judge Donnellan first sentenced La Touche to a term of six months to three years but then suspended the sentence, giving the woman her freedom. She was placed in the care of Staff Captain Agnes McKernan of the Salvation Army. That institution had taken an interest in her and volunteered to provide her a home for life "in the proper environment."[18]

Faking wealth was another well-used scam practiced by confidence women. The idea seemed to be that if you pretended to have a lot of money yourself, and/or you faked connections to people of wealth, it would all work to your advantage when you tried to scam other people. And it did seem to work. Financially, the most successful female fraud artist of this period was Cassie Chadwick, who used the fake wealth background to full advantage. No matter that the lies she told of her background were so exaggerated and impossible as to, one would think, break the credulity of any but the most outrageously naive listener.

Faking Wealth

Annie C. Kley

Mrs. Annie C. Kley was arraigned before Justice Duffy at the Tombs Police Court on March 13, 1876, charged with having swindled various merchants and individuals out of sums of money, rent bills, and so forth, by representing that she was awaiting a remittance of $3,000 from her husband who was employed, she claimed, in Washington, D.C., by the U.S. Treasury Department. Police said that Kley was a "clever adventurer of the Hortense P. Watson type," and that she had been living for some time at the rate of $1,000 a month, "obtained by her ingenuity in victimizing merchants." Some 18 of those victimized people were listed by name in a news account, with amounts swindled from them ranging from $29 to $5,000. A reporter commented, "Mrs. Kley is about fifty-three years old, and a native of South Carolina. It is said that her husband in Washington sends her $100 every month on condition that she does not go near him."[1]

Mary Hansen

Later in 1876 Mrs. Mary A. Gibson, alias Hansen, alias Klink, was charged with having defrauded Samuel Garretson, Horace Farrier, and others, out of large sums of money by falsely representing that she was heir to an estate in Germany bequeathed to her by Archbishop Wolf of Freiburg and that she was to acquire that money through the intervention of Cardinal McCloskey, of the Roman Catholic Church. At her examination before Justice Keese in Jersey City, New Jersey, Cardinal McCloskey was there as a witness for the prosecution and denied the woman's story completely. He said he did not know Gibson, there was no Bishop Wolf of Freiburg and there was no such dignitary in his church. Garretson testified he would not have made the large and numerous advances of money he made to her if he had known her story about coming into an inheritance was untrue. Gibson's lawyer argued the complaint should be dismissed on the ground that as her inheritance story had not been made for the purpose of inducing the advances made by Garretson, she should not be held. Gibson stated she was born in Baden-Baden, Germany and was 39 years old. Remarked a reporter, "She is a coarse vulgar-looking woman, with no attraction of person, of manner, of address." Keese committed her for trial.[2]

Apparently nothing came of the swindling done on the basis of the McCloskey story, for it was reported that in the latter part of 1879 New York City police detectives Handy and Fogarty arrested her for obtaining goods from about 20 different firms in the wool business. Among the victims were Bernstein & Company of Canal Street and Franklin & Company of Howard Street. Reportedly her total take that time was about $12,000. A couple of years after that the Jersey City Rogues' Gallery description of her was as follows, "Mary Klink, alias Mary A. Hansen, alias Gibson, aged 48, hair brown and gray, eyes hazel, weight about 190 pounds, height 5 feet 1 in., German, but speaks good English." On January 15, 1886, Frederick Bohmet of New York went to the police and told them that in September 1885, a long-time friend of his, Julius Klink, informed him he had just married a wealthy widow named Hansen and because she was very wealthy he, Klink, would never again have to work—he was a shoemaker. According to Klink, Mary had just inherited $750,000 left her by an uncle with the money being due to be paid to the woman in a few days, after a few minor problems had been ironed out. Of course, the problems dragged on until Mrs. Klink asked Bohmet if he could advance her some money to deal with lawyers' fees, and so on, involved in the estate hassle. Asked what security they would put up, Mr. and Mrs. Klink said Bohmet would have his money paid back in full in a matter of days and as a bonus they would give him a four-story tenement house and lot. He advanced them $2,316. Later Bohmet discussed his situation with a lawyer who, sensing a con job, advised him to go to the police; he did. Around that time a woman by the name of Mary Mesam complained to the police she had been swindled out of

$2,500 by a woman named Hansen. Mary Klink was arrested in Jersey City in January 1886 and taken to New York where she was held under $8,000 bail. A week later her lawyer got her discharged from the Bohmet complaint on the grounds the money was loaned and no evidence had been introduced to show her representations were false. As she left the court she was arrested again and taken before Justice Duffy on the complaint of Richard Perry of New York, who charged her with obtaining $300 by representing the Sheriff of Philadelphia held $11,000 of her money and she needed to go to Philadelphia immediately to retrieve it. Additionally, she was charged with obtaining $500 from Mesam by representing that she owned a number of houses in Philadelphia but she needed some cash to deal with small legal problems involving those houses. A detective checked out her story in Philadelphia and found it to be bogus; she owned no property and there was no such lawyer as she had named. Thomas Byrnes, an NYPD inspector, listed by name 16 people who had been swindled by Mary at this time, including Bohmet and Mesam. Individual amounts ranged from $90 to $2,900 and totaled $15,231. Byrnes said there were a number of others who had also been victimized. Hansen was committed to Ludlow Street jail on a judgment obtained in the civil case by Mesam, but the complaint in this case was withdrawn and Hansen was discharged from the jail on August 30, 1886. She was then rearrested on a warrant issued by a Philadelphia magistrate, charged with swindling a party in that city some years previous. The Grand Jury, though, refused to indict her in that case as her husband had already served five years in prison for it. Mary Hansen was discharged in New York City on September 10, 1886.[3]

A decade went by and then it was reported that Mrs. Mary Hansen, charged with swindling the late Dr. Lott out of $10,000, gave herself up in July 1897 to Brooklyn police. She had been sought for some time. "Mrs. Hansen is big and buxom," said an account. "Her hair is iron grey, and through a pair of heavy gold-rimmed spectacles twinkle a pair of gray eyes. She is sixty-four years old, but her manner and movements are those of a woman of forty. Her general appearance is that of a well-to-do German housewife." Brooklyn Police Chief Murphy said of Hansen's career that she had made $250,000 from swindling since 1876 and her victims included businessmen and others in Brooklyn, New York, Philadelphia, and other places. What she had done with all the money was a mystery to the police as it was considered then to be a certainty she had little money in 1897. For the previous few months she had scratched out a living as a midwife and nurse. Murphy added, "She always spent money lavishly." Elaborating on the McCloskey story of 20 years earlier Murphy stated, "The story was spread far and wide and on the strength of it Mrs. Hansen secured thousands of dollars. A number of people asked the Cardinal when the money would be turned over, and he was so annoyed by the repeated inquiries that he told the police, and Mrs. Hansen for a time disappeared. She turned up in Philadelphia under another name and swindled wealthy men there right and left." Harry Parmenter, a hatter, fell under her wiles and lost $1,000. In Brooklyn she was said to have defrauded A. D. Matthews & Company out of $2,000 "and in addition, numerous tradesmen are regretting they ever met her." Indictments for grand larceny and for fraud had been issued against her.[4]

Catharine Waters

Also in 1876, George Phelan told the story of Catharine A. Waters, described by a news account as follows: "She is attractive, of medium height with black hair and eyes and of dark complexion; she is under thirty years of age, and is said to be a terror among house owners and agents." On April 13 of that year a woman calling herself Catharine Waters presented herself to Phelan saying she wanted to rent the premises at 438 West 23rd Street, owned by Mrs. Phelan, George's mother. Waters said she was worth $50,000; her husband was a lunatic and she referred Phelan to a Doctor Drake who, she said, would vouch for the truth of her story. Mrs. Phelan's daughter visited Dr. Drake, who agreed that Waters was all that she represented herself to be. Then Waters told Mrs. Phelan she would pay half a month's rent to cover up to May 1, but somehow managed to take possession of the apartment without paying anything at all. On May 3 Mrs. Phelan spoke to Waters about the rent only to be told boldly by the latter that she had no intention of ever paying any rent and that she would not vacate the premises until she was paid a certain amount of money for vacating. Mrs. Phelan pleaded her case but to no avail.[5]

Following that skirmish, Waters affixed a large tin sign, which contained her name and occupation of dressmaker, to her flat, even though the lease expressly said that no business signs were allowed to be displayed on the building. Even though Mrs. Phelan was upset over the sign and complained about it, Catharine simply laughed it off. One morning it was discovered the sign had been painted black, which caused Waters to become angry and to accuse Mrs. Phelan of defacing her sign. She procured a warrant for the arrest of Mrs. Phelan. Also, Waters tried to force a newspaper carrier to testify that he was hired by Mrs. Phelan to deface the sign, but the young man refused, as he knew nothing about the incident. Appearing before Justice Smith, Mrs. Phelan was discharged. Later, when Waters was finally evicted, she took with her, it was alleged, about $1,000 worth of clothing and other items that belonged to Mrs. Phelan. Then Waters was arrested. In tracing some of her background George Phelan discovered that in the year before she resided in his mother's house, Waters lived at six different addresses in New York City and was evicted from all of them except the last, wherein the owner paid the $200 demand of Waters as her price to vacate, the same amount she had requested from George's mother. Among her aliases had been Kate Shandley, Mme. La Manche, Mrs. Sinclair, and Mrs. Walters. The goods allegedly stolen from Mrs. Phelan by Waters were found in a pawnshop. Earlier Waters had been arrested for pawning the property of some of her servants but was not punished. Also learned about her past was that through advertising for a position wanted as a housekeeper "she has secured money from elderly gentlemen who proposed marriage to her, and one who threatened to have her arrested was told that she would make New York too hot to hold him" if he did complain.[6]

Kate Laird

On May 20, 1884, police arrested what they, and hotel people, referred to as a "hotel beat." Reportedly, for some time past the woman had been living at the expense of the proprietors of first-class hotels in New York City. Her method was to send her maid to a hotel and to order that a "splendid suite" of rooms be prepared for her mistress. On the following day the mistress arrived, with her maid, to take possession of the suite. No baggage usually came with her but she told the hotel staff her trunks would arrive in a day or two. In the meantime the bills she ran up from shopping, carriage renting, and so on, were all charged to her hotel bill. When the payment of the bill became a pressing necessity she quickly disappeared. According to an account, "In this manner she successfully swindled the proprietors of the Coleman, Ashland, Everett, Belvedere, and a good many other hotels out of sums varying from $75 to $200. The Hotel Keepers' Association, however, finally became aroused, and sent an accurate description of her to every hotel of any note in the city."[7]

In the middle of May a woman drove up to the Brevoort House hotel in a closed carriage and presented a letter to the clerk, from her mistress. In that note Kate Laird ordered an expensive suite of rooms for herself to be ready for occupancy later that day. She did take possession but was recognized from the description that had been circulated and was arrested. When confronted by the police she was said to have made a full confession. Laird explained to the police that she did have money but it was in the hands of a downtown broker. However, due to legal complications she could not touch that rather large amount of money and had thus adopted the method of living she had been employing. The maid, who was not arrested, gave the same story as had her boss. Laird, at various time and places, had used the names of Knox, Bernsley, and James, registering at some hotels as a married woman, at others as Miss. She was arraigned for examination.[8]

When she appeared in court for examination the first witness to testify against her was Samuel Smith of the Morton House hotel. He identified the prisoner as Mrs. Boyd, who had occupied a suite of rooms at his hotel from April 14 to April 23 and who left abruptly without paying the $86 bill she had run up. Samuel White of the Everett House testified the prisoner, calling herself Mrs. James, owed him $121.75 for room and board for a week. According to Joseph Wahrie, manager of the Belvedere Hotel, she ran up a bill there for $77.45 before disappearing. At some of the hotels she left a trunk behind that contained nothing of value; at others she brought no baggage at all. After she took the stand Laird told the judge she was 18 and had an $8,000 inheritance held in trust but the man in charge had suddenly become evasive and was not giving her money as he had in the past. Thus, she said, she couldn't pay any of her bills. Justice Smith asked her why she used so many false names when she registered at those hotels. Laird said, "I use no false names, all that I use are my own. I am now just studying for the stage, and have at times and in different places used the names of Mrs. Boyd, Mrs. Knox, Mrs. James, and Miss Benchley." The judge dismissed most of the complaints against her on the ground no false pretenses had been used. Kate was arraigned for swindling on the complaint of H. H.

Brockway, manager of the Ashland House, for running up an unpaid bill of $6.85 for room and board for herself and her maid for one day. However, that too was thrown out of court.[9]

Bertha Stanley

An arrest warrant was issued in San Francisco for Bertha Stanley (Big Bertha), the "confidence queen," on the complaint of a jeweler of that city named Henry Parsons, in April 1888. He became acquainted with her through his aunt, at whose house she boarded. It was alleged that Stanley defrauded Parsons out of $1,500 worth of diamonds belonging to his firm. Parsons gave her the jewels for no payment in advance after Stanley suddenly became interested in the jewelry business and declared she would launch her alleged son Willie into that trade and to that end deposited a $5,000 check (it was worthless) with Parsons, as the jeweler and his firm were to be involved somehow in getting Willie into the business. Bertha was to later invest $75,000 in the business after her return from Los Angeles. On that trip she was accompanied by Parsons, at her invitation. On reaching Los Angeles Stanley discovered that she needed several thousand dollars, which she alleged she had on deposit at the Anglo-California Bank. She gave Parsons a power of attorney to draw $20,000 from that bank but when the jeweler went there he was surprised to find there were no funds there to her credit. When he returned to the address where the group was staying he found Bertha and Willie had disappeared. As part of the supposed wealth she represented herself to Parsons as having a bank account in San Francisco.[10]

Within a month or so Bertha was arrested, with a court proceeding for grand larceny held in June 1888. Another main witness against her at the trial, besides Parsons, was William Gruhn, who testified that he met Stanley at the Reverend Dr. Messing's house in San Francisco and fell in love with her. She represented herself to him as being wealthy, saying she had $80,000 in the Anglo-California Bank, and the finest house and horses in La Salle, Illinois. When they became engaged he gave her a diamond ring worth $250; she gave him a ring that she told him she bought from Parsons for $285, but when she left on her trip to Los Angeles she took the ring back from him, telling him it was not in keeping with her wealth, and that she would replace it with a costlier one. Gruhn added that Stanley claimed she was worth $600,000 or $700,000 in total and was on intimate terms with Jay Gould and the Vanderbilt family. Allegations were made at the trial — but not substantiated — that her real name was Bertha Herman and that Willie was not her son but her husband. Other witnesses included shoe dealer J. Lesser and retailer Gordon Taylor, who each told of several unpaid bills they held against the accused. Bertha and Willie were held on charges of obtaining money from Gruhn under false pretenses. The judge held the evidence did not warrant a committal on the charges of grand larceny brought by Parsons, but it was sufficient to indicate fraud with the result the judge reduced that charge to one of obtaining goods on false pretenses.[11]

However, on November 28, 1888, the trial on the charge brought by Gruhn ended with a judgment in favor of Stanley and her son. Early in 1889 Bertha was acquitted on the remaining charge and, as a reporter exclaimed, "Mrs. Stanley is now at liberty."[12]

Anita de Bettincourt McMurrow

For a long time Mrs. Anita de Bettincourt was a prominent figure in the social circles of Philadelphia, with a supposed fortune of $32 million behind her in Spanish bonds. However, she was arrested in Philadelphia late in 1892 for obtaining money under false pretenses. William G. Taplis, a Georgetown druggist, complained she scammed him out of $2,500 based on the strength of that phony fortune. Her arrest occurred on a train from Washington that was bound for New York. Around 60 years old, Anita claimed a connection with the de Bettincourt family of Spain. It was back in 1873 when she first established herself in style in a great mansion in Philadelphia. Patrick J. Brennan, a Philadelphia produce merchant, said he was victimized to the tune of several thousands of dollars due to the unlimited credit he extended to her, on the representation of a lawyer that she was indeed rich. Brennan said, of her method, Anita would invite prominent merchants to her house when she was entertaining distinguished guests and then on the strength of the Spanish bonds negotiate a loan, usually of from $1,000 to $5,000. Anita represented herself as the only heir to the de Bettincourt family, one of the wealthiest of the noble families of Spain.[13]

Also involved in Anita's story were various Spanish diplomats. The suicide of the Spanish minister, Senor Barca, which occurred in New York in 1883, was attributed to an entanglement with the "Countess de Bettincourt." Senor Dupuy de Lome, first secretary of the Spanish legation back then, said Barca believed her stories of great wealth and that she promised to reward him handsomely if he would assist her to get access to the millions of dollars that were supposedly on deposit in Spanish banks (part of her story was that because of legal technicalities she could not access the money, but was working to resolve those hitches). Barca got into some sort of financial difficulties as he tried to aid the woman. When he appealed to Anita to help him she refused. He shot himself to death but first wrote to Dupuy — then away in the Catskills — that he had been deceived by her. Senor Segrasio, first secretary of the Spanish legation later on said Anita besieged the legation in 1884 for information about Spanish finances and showed him a bank book with an alleged $32 million on deposit in Spain. When word was received from Philadelphia that she was using the replies from the legation to her enquiries as evidence as to her wealth in order to fleece Philadelphia merchants, she was dropped by the legation, which no longer believed her or offered her any assistance. One of the unconfirmed stories from Philadelphia was that in reality Anita had been a chambermaid in a sailors' hotel in that city 20 years earlier and that her husband was a sail maker named John McMurrow, who had been fired from his job for drunkenness around the time of Anita's arrest.[14]

Anita died suddenly in January 1906, in Philadelphia. In the wake of her death her son John McMurrow was arrested because of statements by neighbors that he had ill-treated his mother and had argued with her shortly before her death. However, when the coroner's jury rendered a verdict that Anita died of heart disease, her son was released from custody.[15]

Sophia Caroline Smith

Mrs. Sophia Caroline Smith, charged with swindling dry goods firms by representing herself as the wealthy Mrs. Collis P. Huntington, or a friend of hers, was arraigned in Jefferson Market Police Court in New York in November 1895 and held by Magistrate Mott for trial. While only two complainants were in court to testify against her, it was said that more were ready to come forward if the first two fell through.

Sarah Switzer, owner of a dress shop at 424 Fifth Avenue, alleged that Smith obtained from her shop a black dress trimmed with blue silk and lace, valued at $195, on the strength of her representation that she was a great friend of Huntington and also that she was about to marry a wealthy man named Fletcher. A day or two later Smith took the dress to Jackson's dry goods store on Sixth Avenue, where she told the clerk she wanted alterations in the dress, which she said she had bought in Paris, and purchased articles of clothing costing a total of $104.99. With the announcement that she was Mrs. Huntington of 65 Park Avenue, she ordered the goods charged to her account and drove away in a carriage. The owner of Jackson's explained to a reporter, "Though we did not know her, she was such a good talker, so haughty and well dressed, that we thought it was a straight transaction. Had I seen the woman myself, however, I should have been suspicious, for I know Mrs. Huntington by sight."[16]

As soon as the store learned the real Huntington was in San Francisco the police were called in and Smith was arrested. According to a reporter, "She is forty-six years old and has three grandchildren. She is 5 feet 3 inches in height. Her face is strongly marked, with a straight nose and a firm jaw, and her dark-brown eyes are forever shifting and restless. She was continuously smiling with no apparent cause, and though quite calm and self-possessed, there was a certain strange nervousness in her manner that all who observed her closely attributed to an unbalanced mental condition." Continuing with the description it was reported, "Mrs. Smith is a very glib and witty talker. Her manner is engaging and calculated to inspire confidence. She is a very determined woman, and occasionally assumes an imperious manner which by no means invites interference." Her vanity was noted because during the court proceedings she called across the courtroom to the sketch artist not to draw her as she did not look her best and then she offered to provide him with her picture.

Another of Smith's victims was John Walker, who kept a livery stable at 58 West 15th Street. She had taken him for $14 worth of cab hire. For two days she had rented carriages from him, representing herself as Mrs. George Wolf, wife of a butcher at 630 Sixth Avenue. When the bill reached $14 he asked for payment. Smith left, saying she would return in a moment with her checkbook but never came back. Wolf the butcher was swindled for $7 worth of meat when she ordered meat from him, posing again as Huntington. Explaining an address discrepancy Smith told Wolf to send her order of meat to her rooms on 28th Street because she had an Irish cook at her mansion at 65 Park Avenue with whom she could not get along.[17]

Mrs. H. J. Giddings

When Mrs. H. J. Giddings came to Los Angeles in May 1901 she stayed only a little over a week, but in those eight days she took the city by storm: she passed worthless checks, she bought a business block on Spring Street and a beautiful residence on Adams Street, she bought jewelry, she jumped a hotel bill, she rented offices for her "enormous" oil business, she hired men to work for her at fabulous wages, she rented a cottage by the sea for the summer and she had her teeth fixed by a dentist to whom she tendered a bad check. Not all of her fraudulent activity cost her victims money; some could only be characterized as bizarrely inconvenient for the dupes. A reporter called her "one of the cleverest adventuresses and swindlers who ever tarried in this city." At the Natick House in Los Angeles she paid her week's bill with a bad check. She did leave her trunk behind saying she would be back that day. Of course, it contained nothing of value. Giddings told people she was formerly a telegraph operator at Bakersfield but when the oil excitement started in that area she got involved in it and made her fortune. Now she had come to the Los Angeles area to expand her oil business to that area and even to move her oil empire headquarters to Los Angeles.[18]

As far as was known the first appearance of Giddings in Los Angeles was on Wednesday morning, May 22, when she registered at the Natick House (it had a reputation as the hotel in Los Angeles used most often by people in the oil business). "She is a slight woman, rather tall, of pleasant demeanor and fair to look upon," said a journalist. "She wears glasses, dresses in fashion, talks fluently, particularly about oil, and walks briskly." On the Saturday after her arrival she placed an ad in the *Los Angeles Times* wanting to hire men to work as superintendents in her new oil fields. She received over 90 applicants and hired two—at salaries of $350 and $400 a month. Both were to start work within a few days; one had been working at a salary of $5.50 a day. Then she met businessman George Couch. His house was for sale and she agreed to buy it, without asking the price. Giddings was having all her money sent down from Bakersfield and since she was going to move her oil empire headquarters to Los Angeles she decided to also buy Couch's office block for the asking price of $60,000. Later she learned his house was listed at $16,000 but that was fine with her. Arrangements were made whereby she would return to Couch's office in two days to sign all the necessary papers to buy the two properties and to pay a deposit. But on the day before the scheduled appointment, Giddings showed up at Couch's office without an appointment to say that while buying a pair of shoes in a downtown department store her purse was stolen (it contained, she said, $98 in gold). As her money had not yet arrived from Bakersfield and she was temporarily penniless, could Couch lend her some money to tide her over until the morning? She only wanted $5; Couch lent her $7. That was the last Couch ever saw of her.[19]

Next she went to Dr. Schiffman, the dentist, to get some work done. After he finished she told him her purse had disappeared from his office (she said she had left it under a chair). Schiffman assured her she must have left it somewhere else as it could not have been removed from his office. Then she told him her story about her money coming the next day from Bakersfield and could she come back the next day and pay. He said no; she paid him with a $30 bad check. Going to a jewelry store, Giddings bought $450 worth of jewelry and paid by check. Explaining her money would arrive in two days she told the jeweler not to cash it until then. In the meantime, she told him, he could keep the check and the jewelry. She never returned. Giddings went upstairs to see the woman who ran the office building above the jewelry store, where she told her story about moving her headquarters and thus rented an office suite above the store. While she promised to return the next day and pay the rent she was not seen there again. At the Natick House she struck up a friendship with another guest, Mrs. G. N. Spragins, who was looking for a house to rent for the summer near the ocean. Telling Spragins that was just what she wanted to do as well, the pair found a place they liked in Santa Monica and agreed to rent it together for the summer, each paying half. Spragins never saw her again. After an eight-day stay Giddings paid her Natick bill to that point, $7.50, with a bad check and vanished from Los Angeles.[20]

Just a few weeks later, on June 17, a *Los Angeles Times* reporter happened to be at the train station in San Diego where he saw the Reverend R. B. Taylor, pastor of the first Presbyterian Church there, bidding goodbye to a woman the reporter recognized as Giddings. After she had left the reporter went over to Taylor, who told him he first met Giddings (calling herself Mrs. A. E. Hooper) at his church a few days earlier when she told him she had been a missionary in India under the Presbyterian Board. So convincing was Giddings in telling that story that Taylor asked her to give a talk of her experiences in India at his church the following week. When she got the train that day (supposedly to Los Angeles) she told Taylor she would be back in plenty of time to give her talk. Although she gave the impression in San Diego of being financially well off she borrowed the money for her train fare to Los Angeles. Even then she got Taylor to ask for a half-rate fare for herself as a missionary, explaining she had lost her credentials. Taylor did try and arrange the discount but failed.[21]

Grace Anton Vanschaack-Smith

When Mrs. Grace Anton Vanschaack-Smith killed her husband and herself in New Rochelle, New York, in November 1907 it was felt to have been a direct result of her career as a swindler. One account suggested she may have been another Cassie Chadwick. She had claimed a relationship to the former Lieutenant-Governor of Connecticut and that she had been bequeathed money in his will. With the estate of that individual almost cleared up it meant Grace would not take much longer in paying back money she had been loaned on the strength of the bogus inheritance story, or so she told her creditors. But instead, Grace shot her husband, set fire to the family home, and then shot herself through the heart. "There can be no doubt that the woman was always more or less insane," remarked an observer. Reportedly, the last five years of Grace's life were given up to a systematic wholesale swindling of merchants, although it was also stated that "her experience in the business of getting something for nothing began early in her life." Beginning with the fall of 1902 and continuing almost to the time of her death, she looted various business houses in New York, always professing great personal wealth that just happened to be inaccessible at the moment, with discovered transactions totaling $20,000 worth of goods under false pretenses.[22]

Anna Minuth

Mrs. Anna Minuth, who said she was formerly the wife of Baron von Hatzfeldt of Germany, was arraigned before Magistrate McQuade in the Yorkville Court in November 1915 on a charge of passing a worthless check in a transaction in which she posed as the representative of the wealthy and socially prominent Mrs. Elsie French Vanderbilt. New York City architect Benjamin Levitan was the complainant. Minuth, in the guise of being Vanderbilt's agent, went to see the architect, explaining that Elsie had commissioned her to negotiate for plans for the construction of a theater on a plot adjoining the Astor theater on Broadway. Allegedly, Minuth told Levitan that Vanderbilt had obtained a sub-lease from the Shubert Brothers and desired him to prepare plans for a theater costing $200,000. In reply to a telephone message from the architect, the Shubert offices informed him that Vanderbilt had taken an option on the sub-lease and on that basis Levitan started work. A few days later Minuth appeared at the architect's office accompanied by a bogus Vanderbilt. They discussed details for a while and later Anna got Levitan to cash a $68 check for her; it bounced. Worried by that transaction he went personally to the Shubert offices, where they phoned the real Vanderbilt who denied all knowledge of her "agent" and proved she was not in New York on the day of the visit. That prompted a visit to the police, and Anna's arrest. She told the police she was 42; had married Baron, or Count, Edmund von Hatzfeldt 25 years earlier but later divorced him and married architect F. A. Minuth (then deceased) in 1899. She also told the police she would make all her checks good as soon as she was in receipt of a legacy of $35,000, which was then in the process of being settled.[23]

In court a couple of days later Deputy Assistant District Attorney Spies said he understood Anna had swindled nine others, besides Levitan, three of whom were in court. At one point in the proceedings Minuth became hysterical and cried out, "I didn't do it. It was all a frame-up against me. I didn't do it." Among other victims was Dr. James Ward, an art collector who met Minuth three years earlier when she asked him to appraise two paintings in her home (a fancy apartment). He pronounced them genuine works of Reubens and Franz Hals and said they were worth $20,000 each. Ward was then hired by Minuth as the agent to sell those paintings, at a commission of 15 percent and $50 a week. After five weeks she gave him a check for $150; it bounced. Later when he found a buyer, Ward learned Anna had only an option on the paintings and that she had allegedly borrowed $2,000 on the paintings by posing as the owner. During his dealings with Minuth, Ward was also introduced to the bogus Vanderbilt, who assured him he would be well compensated for any services he might render to the "baroness." Hughes Brothers, grocers, and Nicholas Anson, butcher, also were victims of Anna. Before all those people, said Spies, Minuth was accustomed to posing as an intimate friend of Mrs. Vanderbilt. A representative of the Pinkerton detective agency told Spies the woman had also posed as the wife of the late Dr. Francis Delafield of New York City. Minuth was held for trial on a charge of obtaining money under false pretenses.[24]

Faking Wealth — Sarah Casselman

Mrs. Sarah Casselman (alias Banker, Lee, Ackerman, and Sutherland) was arrested on November 20, 1876, in New York City at Mrs. Hungerford's boarding house, where she resided. That facility was said to be one of the finest establishments of its type in the city. After introducing herself to Hungerford as Mrs. Sutherland, daughter of Judge Wisner of Elmira, New York, she let it be known she was a person of ample means and of high social standing and that she was also friendly with a lot of Hungerford's friends. When she had boarded there for about one week the landlady happened to read in the newspaper an account of the recent exploits of a confidence woman (using a different name) at the establishments of Mrs. Bishop and Mrs. Putnam. Struck by the fact the description of the woman matched that of her new tenant, Hungerford contacted the police. They arrived at the boarding house with Bishop and Putnam in tow and the entire group confronted Casselman in her room. It was the same woman and she was promptly arrested.[1]

After some questioning she acknowledged that her name was Sarah C. Casselman and that her husband had left her about two and a half years earlier. According to her she first married a man named Sutherland and after his death she went under the name of Lee and then Ackerman. She insisted her maiden name was Wisner and that she was from Elmira. A search of her person by the police discovered a clipping from the New York *Sun* of a few years previous that detailed an exploit of that time. It related that under the name of Casselman she had obtained room and board for herself and her husband at a lodging house run by Mrs.

Gleason. Next she called at Kinney's livery stable where she arranged to have a carriage always in readiness for her use. Sarah told Kinney her first ride would be on the following day when she planned to go to the Chatham bank to cash a check for $7,000. Before that time, though, she asked Gleason to cash a check for her for $150, drawn on the same Bank. Failing that, she asked the owner of the house, Mr. Browne, to cash it. He said he would but then her carriage arrived and she said she was off to consult with her cousin Judge Sutherland. A few days later Gleason asked for a settlement of the board bill but received only "marvelous stories of wealthy relatives and high social connections." Eventually the landlady employed a private detective who learned that Casselman was not known to Judge Sutherland and that she had prepared to repeat her exploits at another boarding house in New York, where she in the process of negotiating her accommodation. As a result of the investigation a piano Sarah had installed for herself at Gleason's was taken back by the dealer, and one requested for her next boarding house was denied.[2]

Some five years earlier, it was reported, Casselman had been busy in Jersey City, where she succeeded "in swindling several aristocratic families." There she rented an elegant house, fitted it out in style and then proceeded, said an account, "to ingratiate herself into the good grace of her neighbors. In this she succeeded so well that in the 18 months she remained there she fleeced several wealthy families out of large sums of money, and the landlord out of the rent." One night Casselman mysteriously disappeared and nothing more was heard from her for a long time. After a prolonged absence she returned to New Jersey, apparently giving a satisfactory explanation for her absence with the story that a wealthy uncle of hers had died, leaving her a large sum of money with the result that she was then wealthier than ever. Sarah told that story to a man (one of her earlier victims) and said she so loved her Jersey City location that she was going to buy not a house, but a mansion there, and settle permanently. Believing her story, the unidentified man agreed to let her remain in his house as a boarder until the negotiations for the purchase of the house were completed. Those negotiations took five weeks and at the end of that time Casselman went out one day to pay the first instalment on the purchase. None of the people in Jersey City saw her again.[3]

On November 21, 1876, Sarah Casselman was arraigned before Judge Bixby at the Washington Place Police Court on the charge of defrauding boarding house keepers and of having stolen diamonds and jewelry from Mrs. Bishop. The "adventuress" was remanded to the Tombs prison for a couple of days.[4]

Casselman generated enough notice and attention that the *New York Times* was moved to publish an editorial about her, under the title "The Boarding-house Ravager." With regard to women and crime in general, the editor declared, "To be sure there is something in the sight of a woman in distress, whether as Juliet in the tomb of the Capulets, or an adventuress in the toils of the Police, which touches the manly heart.... But the stoutest masculine spirit softens whenever the wickedest woman comes to genuine grief." Nevertheless, the editor argued, since confidence was one of the principal foundation stones of society, "we must say that it is well that Mrs. Casselman, with all her aliases, has been caged at last." Since society was built on confidence and society, to a large extent, was also built of boarding houses then Casselman, "an enchantress, a sort of female Cagliostro, who was engaged in the business of ravaging boarding-houses," it followed, "was ravaging society. She was a public enemy. So long as this dreadful person was at large, suspicion lurked around the numberless boarding houses where middle-aged ladies, who had seen better days, dispense mild coffee, baker's bread, and all other well-known comforts of a house."[5]

Distrust thus fell on all boarders, thought the editor, due to the exploits of Casselman since the "adventuress has for years carried on her nefarious trade with impunity." However, the editor thought it was the first time, as far as he knew, "that sheer audacity has been able to deceive worldly-wise women with stories of possessions and aristocratic connections which never existed. Mrs. Casselman's horses and servants that were always coming but never came, her baggage that existed only in her imagination, her remittances that were checks on the bank of fancy, and her relationships that were marvels of invention, are abundantly imitated, after all, for thousands of people are living from day to day on their talent for keeping up appearances."[6]

Tombs physician Dr. David Brekes examined Casselman on November 22 with respect to a "writ of lunacy." After that interview he told the press he thought she was rational enough to know what she was doing and that she had told him an "incredible" story of her early life. In that story Sarah claimed she had married at the age of 12 when she was a "well-developed grown-up woman" and that she was a mother at 13; her first husband was 35 when he married her. A man from New Jersey who said he was a friend and neighbor of a man whose daughter was married to Casselman's son contacted Brekes. To his knowledge Casselman had attempted to buy a $20,000 house not long before with all the preliminaries completed only to have the deal fall through because she had no money at all. Another time she had extensive stables fitted up for the horses she claimed to own but also in this case it was discovered she had no money, and no horses either. Brekes told reporters he had found Sarah in conversation and appearance to be rational and coherent. He also declared her as being physically sound and, "That she is a lady of refinement and education and good physique cannot be denied." However, he felt if the statements of the man mentioned above were true it might indicate Casselman was laboring under the hallucination that she was wealthy—"in fact, it would prove she is a monomaniac." In conclusion Brekes remarked, "It is hard to determine, without knowing the antecedents of a person, his line of life, habits, training, and social conditions, whether abnormal conditions are the result of lunacy, eccentricity, or shamming."[7]

After Brekes's examination and statements Casselman told reporters, "The public press is teeming with my alleged offenses, but I am not conscious of having been guilty of any serious breach of the law. If I have not paid my way in a few boarding-houses, and left owing a few weeks' board bill, where is the great harm in that.... I am only a poor, defenseless woman, and therefore I am a fit subject for persecution and slander." As she bemoaned her fate to the reporters and reproached the public for a while she worked herself into such a state "that she became hysterical and subsequently fell into a long swoon," from which she fully recovered. On November 23 Brekes announced his conclusion to the examination of the prisoner; she was not legally responsible for her acts and that she was the victim of chronic monomania, accompanied with the delusion of possessing imaginary wealth. Thus, if that conclusion was accepted by the court it would mean the acquittal and discharge of Casselman to friends who were willing to care for her or, if none were available, the Commissioner of Charities and Corrections would take her in charge.[8]

Although Brekes's "certificate of lunacy" was sent to the District Attorney's office, her examination in Court before Justice Bixby continued. One who testified was Mr. Casselman, who said he first met her eight years earlier and that she had represented herself to him as being very wealthy. Among other items, she said she owned two houses in Fifth Avenue, New York, and gold mining stock in California. "When

I married her I was surprised to see her dressed so shabbily, believing that a woman of her reputed wealth would wear better clothes," Mr. Casselman explained. "Later I was told that she was poor, and that her boasted wealth was all a sham to get a husband to support her. This and other reasons influenced me to leave her. We could not live happily together and we finally agreed to a mutual separation."[9]

Eleanor Bishop told the court she first met the defendant two years earlier, with Casselman again representing herself as being wealthy and speaking often about her fortune. Then, on October 22, 1876, Sarah came to her house to say she wanted to arrange room and board with Bishop. As evidence of her wealth she presented her with a bogus receipt for $150 for professional services, purportedly signed by Edward Wilder, a lawyer. Believing the story, and knowing Wilder, Bishop rented a suite of furnished rooms to Casselman, with board, where Sarah stayed until November 2 when she suddenly disappeared leaving a bill of $175 unpaid. A sworn statement from Wilder was introduced to the effect he never gave the prisoner a receipt at any time, never did any professional services for her, and never knew her. Ebenezer Balch testified that Casselman stole several articles of value from his house when she boarded there during July and August 1876, worth $125 in total, including clothing and jewelry. Balch said he had her arrested on that charge and the stolen articles, he claimed, were found in her possession.[10]

On November 25, 1876, Judge Lawrence in New York Supreme Court issued a writ of habeas corpus and certiorari in the case of Casselman — unexplained but presumably based on the certificate of lunacy. At that point a new history of Sarah was released, although there was no mention about the source of the new background. She was born in the town of Starkey in Yates County, New York, where her father George Miesner and mother still lived. The family lived in "humble circumstances" with the father employed as a farm laborer. When quite young Sarah left home to go into domestic service in a neighbor's family where she was given the opportunity to acquire a fair education. Her personal beauty and her "superior grace and address made her a belle" in the neighborhood. While still a young woman she came to New York City and worked as a servant before she married a wealthy German importer of wines and liquors named Sunderlin. From that union came one son, said to then be a practicing physician in Syracuse. After living with Sunderlin for several years the couple separated with the father retaining custody of the boy.[11]

When next heard of, Sarah was the wife of a man named Casselman and around that time she was said to have entered upon her career as a Congressional lobbyist at Washington, D.C. In that career she was said to have been successful. While she was engaged as a lobbyist she became acquainted with many prominent people, something that stood her in good stead while on her travels as an "adventuress" through the Southern and Western United States. In February 1876 she returned to her home at Starkey to attend the funeral of one of her sisters. She remained there several weeks and bought a rig from a livery stable owner whom she paid with nothing but promises. As well, she began negotiations with the owners of several large farms in Starkey, ostensibly for selecting property for a residence, but she followed through on none of them. Around May 1, 1876, Sarah Casselman left Starkey and traveled to New York City "her route being marked with numbers of unpaid hotel bills."[12]

11

Faking Wealth — Bertha Heyman

Twice arrested at the New York Hotel in September 1880 was Mrs. Bertha Heyman. Her accusers were Edward Perrin and his wife Tilly, who had begun a suit against her to recover money that they said she procured from them under false representation. Perrin worked as a conductor on a Pullman railroad car and lived in Chicago. In the affidavit upon which he procured an order for the arrest of Heyman, he declared that when he first met her in April 1880 she told him she had a large estate and that she paid a lawyer $6,000 a year to manage that property. Desiring to find a competent man to do the job for a lesser amount, she offered the job to Perrin along with a salary of $2,500 a year. He said he accepted the offer and resigned his job as a conductor with a promise to start work for Heyman on May 1, 1880. She told him, Perrin continued, that $29,000 was almost due her from her estate but before she could obtain it from her agent she needed some money for various purposes. As further evidence of her wealth Bertha took the conductor to see a house she owned, at 814 Lexington Avenue, New York. Influenced by all of this, Perrin said he loaned her $1,035 to help her out, selling his household furniture to raise the money and accepting her assurance that she would repay him as soon as she got money from her agent, or when her inheritance problems were settled by the Executor Robert Bonner who, she said, was also her guardian.[1]

Perrin declared that he discovered Heyman did not have a large estate, did not own the house at 814 Lexington Avenue, that Robert Bonner was not her guardian or her Executor, and that the man named as her agent, Edward Lauterbach, was not her agent. Those revelations prompted Perrin to take action against the woman. When Heyman was taken into custody in this action she procured her release by depositing $500 with the Sheriff. Tilly Perrin, who had begun her own suit against Bertha to recover $905, next procured an order for her arrest. Tilly added that Bonner had told her indignantly that he did not know the woman at all and that she knew Heyman maintained a "luxurious" apartment in the New York Hotel, employed several servants, "and she avers upon information and belief that Mrs. Heyman has imposed upon many persons by her false pretensions." Bertha was arrested again.[2]

Another complainant against her at this time was a lawyer named Henry C. Botty, who initiated his own lawsuit against her some six weeks after those launched by the Perrins. His story was that he met her in the New York Hotel on July 26 and she told him she was worth $20 million in her own right, but that she wished to conceal that fact from her husband — a dissolute person — who, if he found out she had inherited such immense wealth, would ill-treat her until he got control of it. At her request Botty drew up a number of legal papers for her, advised her how best to manage her mythical wealth, and defended her in some of the fraud suits then already underway against her, presumably including those of the Perrins. After having procured for her a loan of $500 and having had much trouble in getting that money back he became worried. Thus, he initiated his own lawsuit against her for $1,500 for legal services rendered — she had not paid him anything.[3]

Bertha was next heard from in London, Ontario, where she was reportedly arrested on February 8, 1881 in company with a Dr. J. E. Cooms, charged with defrauding a Montreal commercial man out of several hundred dollars by a confidence game (not described). Nothing came of the arrest as she was back in New York within a very short time. According to police records she was born Bertha Schlesinger in about 1851, a native of Koblyn, near Posen, Germany. Her father served five years in prison there for forging a check. She was married twice, first to a Fritz Karko when she first came to America in 1878. After living in New York a short time they went to Milwaukee, where she was afterwards married to a Mr. Heyman, although her first husband was still living and no divorce had been obtained. Bertha stood 5' 4" tall and in the late 1880s weighed 245 pounds. Around the same time as her brief trip to Canada, Heyman induced the father of Lena Schwartz, a maid in her employ, to draw his lifetime savings from a bank and give that several hundred dollars to her as a loan. That was the last he saw of it or her.[4]

Early in 1881 Bertha was arrested on Staten Island and held in jail for several months on a charge of stealing a watch from Mrs. Pauline Schlarbaum, an elderly lady with whom she lived on Staten Island. By the time she came to trial on that charge, in June 1881, she had been accorded the title of "the Confidence Queen." During her incarceration she received what was said to be unusual attention from public officials, being permitted to vary the monotony of her prison life by carriage drives and visits to the theaters in New York City. In prison she was also known as "the Princess" while numbering many people in high official positions among her friends.[5]

When Bertha moved in with Schlarbaum, who lived in Southfield, Staten Island, she represented herself as being immensely wealthy. By her professions of kindness and repeated declarations of the possession of great wealth she succeeded in inducing Schlarbaum to give her two watches and $250, which the latter had in the bank, promising as a reward to purchase handsome new furniture for her, and to present her as a gift with the house and lot of which she was the tenant. In pursuit of her schemes she called on Theodore Morris — an old friend of Schlarbaum's husband and the owner of the Staten Island property that he rented to the widow Schlarbaum at a nominal rent. Heyman explained she wanted to buy it for Schlarbaum and he agreed to sell it for $2,500. To pay Morris she gave him a $13,000 draft from a Milwaukee bank out of which he was to pay himself. However, before a response was received from the Milwaukee financial institution Bertha called on Morris again, telling him that a stepson was suing the widow and had placed the Sheriff in possession of Schlarbaum's home. The son, she said, would settle for $500 cash and as a lawyer had recommended a settlement be made Bertha wanted to arrange it by paying the money but she was just then short of cash while waiting for Milwaukee to cash her draft. On the strength of her story Morris gave her $500 with Heyman promising to keep an appointment to repay the money in three days. Bertha failed to keep that appointment and disappeared. It soon was revealed the Milwaukee draft was worthless and the story of the house seizure was completely false. Heyman was acquitted on the charge of stealing Schlarbaum's watch.[6]

However, Heyman's taste of freedom was brief for she was arrested as she left the courthouse on June 29, 1881 (after the Schlarbaum acquittal) by New York City police and taken to that city on a bench warrant. She was arraigned in the General Sessions Court on June 30 on two indictments for obtaining money by false pretenses from Charles Brandt, a liquor dealer, and from Theodore Morris (two separate incidents) with respect to the $500. She was alleged to have obtained $960 from Brandt on the representation that she had become heiress to the estate of a George Courtis, of Poughkeepsie, valued at several million but she needed money in order to defray the necessary expenses and pay her hotel bill at the Gilsey House. Brandt at one time had some business relations with Fritz Karko, the then deceased first husband of Heyman. One reason Brandt had for helping Heyman get her money was that some two years earlier Bertha had fleeced Brandt out of a couple of hundred dollars by giving him a similar story. This time around Heyman promised she would also repay that earlier amount. Recorder Smyth committed her to the Tombs prison without bail.[7]

The trial took place in October 1881. On the stand Heyman denied all allegations and said Schlarbaum made up the house possession story and sent her to Morris to get $500—she just functioned as a messenger. Observed a reporter, "The jury showed their appreciation of Bertha's story by finding her guilty after deliberating about five minutes. On hearing the verdict the Confidence Queen made a terrible outcry and held her handkerchief to her eyes, from which, however no tears could be seen to flow." Just before she was tried she ran up a bill with the dentist used by Judge Cowing, who presided at her trial. When asked for payment, Bertha sent word that the dentist "need not trouble himself about so trifling a sum as she had fourteen millions on deposit in a trust company, but could not spare time to go down town to cut off the coupons." Heyman was sentenced to two years in the penitentiary, in October, and served her sentence at Blackwell's Island.[8]

While incarcerated at Blackwell's Bertha was visited by a German named Charles Karpe, who said he knew her in the old country. Then Karpe charged that Heyman had swindled him out of $900 during her time in prison, all the money he had, in order to bribe Warden Fox in order to receive special privileges at the prison. Called in to investigate that story were Commissioners Jacob Hess and Mr. Porter of the Department of Charities and Corrections. According to Karpe, Bertha told him she would come into a lot of money as soon as she got out of prison and would reward him handsomely for whatever sum of money he might loan her. He finally decided to make a formal complaint after Heyman continued to make financial demands, through a series of letters to the man. Hess and Porter took Karpe and his letters to Blackwell's Island where they confronted Heyman and Fox face to face and placed the letters before her.[9]

Bertha admitted having written the letters but denied she had paid Fox anything, and said that she had received only $10 from Karpe, which she spent on herself. When one of the Commissioners asked her why, then, she wrote the letters, Heyman said, "I am a swindler as you know, and I wrote those letters because it suited my purpose. I lied in them. If it should suit my convenience tomorrow to tell you another story I should do so." Fox denied all the charges, but admitted he had detailed Heyman to his own house to work as a servant, which he had the right to do under the rules. Promising a full investigation would follow, the Commissioners, in the meantime, did instruct the Warden to put Heyman back into the regular prison population and directed that hereafter no prisoners should be detailed to the Warden's house. With respect to Bertha, Hess remarked, "This woman is utterly untrustworthy. She is as bad as bad can be, and would not scruple to swindle her associates in the prison if she could get a chance."[10]

Upon her release from the penitentiary Bertha went to New York City and established herself at the Hoffman House under the name of Mrs. Richards. While there she made the acquaintance of a New York stockbroker named Edward Sanders. On the representation that she had a check for $10,000 and a lot of stocks and bonds deposited in the safe at Hoffman House, she borrowed various sums of money from Sanders totaling $255 and a valuable diamond from him, and $200 from his partner. In the course of negotiations Bertha showed Sanders a sealed package said to contain those securities (later it was found to contain only waste paper) worth $87,000, and she claimed she was worth $8 million in all. When the fraud was discovered Sanders laid a complaint and a warrant for her arrest was issued. Early in July 1883 Bertha was arrested in Paterson, New Jersey. Taken first to Jersey City, she told Police Chief Murphy there that she had been out of prison only two weeks "but during that time I have succeeded in getting over $2,000, and from people who thought they were sharp, too. I take no pride in overvailing a fool. The moment I discover a man's a fool I let him drop, but I delight in getting into the confidence and pockets of men who think they can't be skinned. It ministers to my intellectual pride." She added she did not care for money alone but she liked to get it.[11]

Heyman's trial for swindling Sanders concluded before Recorder Smyth in the Court of General Sessions, on August 22, 1883. In this case, said a reporter, "The jury promptly returned a verdict of guilty within four minutes" after retiring. According to this reporter, "Bertha is a stout, gross-looking woman, and it is difficult to imagine how she has succeeded in ensnaring so many victims by appeals to their confidence." And, it was also reported, "During the charge and the arguments of counsel, Bertha employed her old tactics of weeping copiously, but for once they failed in their purpose, and the verdict of the jury was promptly rendered." She was sentenced on August 30, 1883, to five years in the penitentiary, and was released in the spring of 1887.[12]

Out of prison for something less than a year, Bertha Heyman was arrested on March 31, 1888, in San Antonio, Texas, while she was on board a Southern Pacific Railroad train. Heyman and her companion were found to have on their persons a quantity of diamonds, jewelry, gold watches and cash; she was charged with obtaining goods under false pretenses.[13]

New York City Police Inspector Thomas Byrnes summed up his impression of Heyman in 1886 while she was still incarcerated. "This remarkable woman used to lodge at the leading hotels, and was always attended by a maid or man servant. At the Windsor and Brunswick Hotels in New York City she had elegant quarters," Byrnes wrote. "When plotting her schemes she would glibly talk about her dear friends, always men well known for their wealth and social position. She possesses a wonderful knowledge of human nature, and can deceive those who consider themselves particularly shrewd in business matters."[14]

12

Faking Wealth — Cassie Chadwick

Things began to unravel for Mrs. Cassie Chadwick at the end of November 1904 in Cleveland, by which time a lawsuit had been initiated with respect to Chadwick's biggest scam. As a result of investigations undertaken in regard to that legal proceeding, Cassie's past misbehavior, unknown to her associates in Cleveland to that point, surfaced. When Cassie married Dr. L. S. Chadwick in Cleveland in 1896 she was Mrs. C. L. Hoover, a West Side (Cleveland) woman and a reputed widow. After her marriage she moved into the Chadwick family home on Euclid Avenue in the most aristocratic part of the city, where she reportedly had her own automobile and carriages along with a retinue of servants. If the Euclid Avenue home was plain on the outside it was said to resemble an Oriental palace on the inside, thanks to the decorating touch of Cassie. During her time in Cleveland Chadwick was well known to the merchants as a woman who spent thousands of dollars at the stores, buying the costliest gowns and furnishings and paying many thousands for jewelry and plate. It was stated that Chadwick imported more valuable articles than any one else in Cleveland.[1]

Litigation then underway against the woman revolved around a loan of $190,800 to Chadwick from Boston banker Herbert Newton. A source close to the deal said the loan was made purely as a business proposition and, "Mr. Newton's judgment, it will be alleged, was influenced by the certificate of Ira Reynolds, Secretary and Treasurer of the Wade Park Banking Company of Cleveland, that he held securities belonging to Mrs. Chadwick to the value of $5,000,000." If that was not enough collateral, a note for $500,000, payable to Cassie and bearing the signature of Andrew Carnegie (one of America's wealthiest men) as the note maker, was presented by Chadwick as further evidence that her credit was unimpeachable. Explaining how she came to possess such a note, Cassie said that on one of his trips to Scotland Carnegie carried with him a block of her Caledonian Railway stock, which she wanted him to sell for her, feeling a better price would be achieved with a sale in Scotland. In lieu of a receipt for the stock, Carnegie gave her his note for $500,000, or so went her story. When payment on the $190,800 loan was not forthcoming, Newton began legal proceedings. On November 29 a rumor circulated that a woman named Mme. Devere (sometimes De Vere), who had been convicted of forgery nearly 15 years earlier and served time for the offense, was also once known as Mrs. Hoover, the same name under which Cassie married Dr. Chadwick. Immediately Cassie stepped forward to emphatically deny the insinuation she was Devere. President Beckwith of the Oberlin Bank in Ohio also came to her defense by declaring she was a woman "of spotless record" and that there must have been two Mrs. Hoovers.[2]

During the 1850s Daniel Bigley lived on a small farm in Eastwood, Ontario, where he scratched out a meager living and had a large family, eight children in all. His fifth child was a daughter born in 1857 and christened Elizabeth but who came to be known to all the family members as Betty. Never a particularly beautiful girl, Betty Bigley suffered slightly from deafness from a very early age, as well, she spoke with a lisp. She was said to be very bright and an academic leader in her classes at school but she was not popular socially with her schoolmates, who branded her with the label "peculiar." They thought her strange. From an early age she had a mania for fine clothing and for jewelry, although these were items far beyond the financial reach of her father. According to her sister, Mrs. Alice M. York of San Francisco, Elizabeth always seemed absorbed in thought, and would sit in silence by the hour. She seemed to be in a trance and would not pay attention to any one during those periods. Coming out of those thinking spells, added York, she seemed bewildered but would never discuss her strange actions or the many scrapes in which she found herself involved.[3]

The first brush with the law for Cassie took place in 1879 when she was a young woman of 22 or 23, who was arrested at Woodstock, Ontario for forgery. Even then stories were in common circulation to the effect that she was an heiress and they were said to have undoubtedly had their origin in the "designing brain of the young woman herself." The offense of which Bigley was acquitted on the ground of insanity was the forgery of the name of Reuben Kipp, a farmer of East Oxford, Ontario, to a note for $300. Edward George Thomas, an organ manufacturer, testified Betty bought an organ from him on October 6, 1878, paying him $25 in cash and giving him a note for the remaining $125. When the note became due Thomas said Betty put him off several times until she finally came to his store with two notes, one for $300 signed by Kipp, the other for $150 signed by Charles Hayward. She wanted Thomas to get the $300 note cashed for her and take his $125 out of it. He refused but he did take the note as security for Betty's debt.[4]

After the Woodstock affair, Betty left home and went to live with her sister, Mrs. York, then in Cleveland. Soon she ran into trouble with moneylenders there when she tried to borrow money on York's furniture, apparently without her sister's knowledge. Forced to leave the York home by her brother-in-law, she moved to another part of Cleveland, where she became acquainted with Dr. Wallace S. Springsteen. They were married in December 1883 but just 12 days later the doctor applied for a divorce. Following that she lived in various boarding houses and was known under various aliases, such as Mme. Rosa. One time in 1884 while she was stopped at the Reed House in Erie, Pennsylvania, Cassie pretended to be very ill. It was reported, "Through a trick of extracting blood from her gums she led persons to believe she was suffering from a hemorrhage, and the kind-hearted folks went down into their pockets for money to get her back to Cleveland." When those good folk in Erie wrote to her for the repayment of those loans — Cassie having posed as wealthy but temporarily embarrassed — they received in reply letters saying, "Poor Mari [the name she was using there] died two weeks ago" and that announcement was followed by a tender tribute to the deceased from the deceased herself. Gaps, of course, existed in Carrie's recorded history. After living for a time as Mme. La Rosa, and claiming to be a clairvoyant, she disappeared from Cleveland and, it was later learned, married a farmer named Scott. A divorce was said to have soon followed. After that, according to Cassie's sister, the woman married a man named Hoover, who left her a fortune when he died.[5]

The next stop was Toledo, Ohio, where Elizabeth Bigley appeared in 1890 as Mme Devere. Cassie lived in an extravagant and lavish style there, riding in fine carriages and spending money freely. Reportedly, she secured large sums of money from various men, but her career was suddenly cut short by her arrest on a charge of forgery. Notes to a total of $40,000 and bearing the forged signature of a Mrs. Blythe of Cleveland were the problem. Joseph Lamb, a married express clerk with five children, said he met Devere and visited at her Toledo home. Soon she mentioned to him that she needed $1,500 to go to Philadelphia. Lamb raised it by giving her his savings of $1,000 besides $100 cash he had in hand, and his note for the balance. After being away for a week Cassie returned to Toledo and began asking Lamb for more money. "I really am Mrs. Florida Blythe of Cleveland," Lamb swore she told him. The real Mrs. Blythe was a very wealthy woman, and when she asked him to obtain money on notes purportedly signed by Mrs. Blythe, he did not hesitate. Some $40,000 was raised that way before the pair were arrested in 1890 after the notes were determined to be forgeries. During the trial Lamb told everything he knew and was acquitted by the jury on the ground he was merely a dupe. Devere was convicted of forgery and sentenced to 9.5 years in the penitentiary; she served 3.5 years before being paroled by Ohio Governor McKinley. As a condition of her parole Cassie was required to report to prison officials regularly. Her first two reports came from Woodstock, Ontario. "I am living quietly with my mother, Mary Ann Bigley, at Woodstock," said her 1894 report. For 1895 her report said, "I am stopping with my sister Mrs. Alice York, at Cleveland." At that point Mme. Devere disappeared permanently.[6]

Doctor Leroy S. Chadwick, member of an old family and well known in Cleveland, was suffering from a form of rheumatism, and a Mrs. Hoover advised him to try massage. Her advice was followed with beneficial results and Chadwick's gratitude grew into admiration and the couple married in 1896. They were married in Pittsburgh by a relative of the doctor's and later the ceremony was repeated in Canada. Apparently Cassie lived quietly with her new husband for some seven years, albeit spending money lavishly. However, that money seemed to have come to her honestly — from Hoover's death and the well-off Chadwick family. Cassie seemingly had no money problems or any need for extra funds. But in 1903 it was back to scamming. Banker Ira Reynolds, secretary and treasurer of the Wade Park Banking Company of Cleveland, was a lifelong friend of Dr. Chadwick and had met Cassie at the doctor's home, prior to the marriage. Sometime in 1903 Cassie visited Reynolds with a package she wished her husband's friend to keep for her at his bank. It contained, she said, securities worth $5 million. She did not want her husband to know of her great wealth, she explained to Reynolds, and would he guard the package for her and on January 1, 1907 pay her the accrued interest of some $350,000 a year. There were some problems involved that prevented her from getting the full benefit of those stocks until 1907. According to Reynolds, Cassie submitted a list of securities in the package, to which she asked him to sign his name (which, of course, would have implied he had inspected the contents of the package and verified the list of securities Cassie claimed it contained). When Reynolds hesitated to sign, as though he wanted to check the contents, Cassie became indignant that he would doubt her word. Placed in that position Reynolds did the courteous, gentlemanly thing by not doubting her word. He signed the list. That meant the package could not be opened without breaking the seal, and the banker had no right to do that until 1907.[7]

And that was the start of Cassie's big scam. Reynolds himself became one of her victims by lending most of his personal fortune to her. Things went along smoothly for Cassie as she borrowed larger and larger sums until Herbert D. Newton, a Boston banker, got worried and started his lawsuit that showed "how banks had been worked for loans all over the country ... and the showing of notes bearing the signature Andrew Carnegie had been used as the bait," besides the package of mythical securities. Reverend Charles A. Eaton, pastor of the Euclid Avenue Baptist Church of Cleveland (of which John D. Rockefeller was the leading member), was the man who made it possible for Cassie to become acquainted with banker Newton of Boston. That introduction came about indirectly through a member of a Boston law firm who was a relative of Eaton. Cassie introduced herself to Eaton and asked him for advice on her business affairs, especially as to where she could raise money. Eaton suggested she try Cleveland bankers but Cassie explained she did not want them to know of her temporary financial embarrassment, so could Eaton recommend bankers in the East? She promised, "I will pay them back and reward them well." Next Cassie gave to Eaton's Boston lawyer relative a $500,000 note signed Andrew Carnegie and the list of securities. Armed with those documents the lawyer called on one banker to get Cassie a $200,000 loan, but he declined, not believing Carnegie would have floated such a note to such a woman. But Newton succumbed, after he made several visits to Cleveland to personally meet with Cassie. Newton made the first loan of a few thousand dollars; others followed and soon the total was $190,800. Later he became worried as his suspicions grew, so he launched his lawsuit, and that stirred up trouble for other of her creditors in Oberlin, Ohio.[8]

Into the spotlight was thrust C. G. Beckwith, president of the Citizens National Bank of Oberlin, Ohio and the bank's cashier A. B. Spear. Those two were arrested on the charge of embezzlement around the same time Cassie was arrested. Beckwith lent the woman his private fortune of $120,000 and $240,000 of the bank's funds. Sixty-five-year-old Beckwith had been one of Oberlin's most respected citizens and was believed to be a shrewd, hardheaded banker. He began his career with the bank when he was just 18 and worked his way all the way up to become its president. Bankers in Elyria, Ohio had informed him that Cassie was anxious to arrange some small loans and that the bonus she gave "was of such proportions that it made an excellent investment for an individual or bank." Those Elyria bankers told Beckwith they held about $10,000 of her paper, and they considered the security "gilt-edged." Immediately Beckwith arranged a meeting with Cassie and, when she produced her list of securities, lent her $5,000. And, "For this loan a bonus was given the amount of which is unknown." It was paid when due and another loan was granted, for $10,000. It too had a "good bonus" attached to it and was paid back. Around this time Oberlin College lent Cassie $75,000 with the bonus attached to that loan said to have been about $5,000. Soon thereafter, Oberlin officials became suspicious about the transaction but Beckwith stepped in to assume the note, and received a $5,000 bonus on that deal.[9]

When the truth about Cassie's frauds was revealed, Beckwith said, with respect to the loans he made to the woman, "I thought then and I think now that in some respects she was the most remarkable woman I had ever seen. She was a splendid conversationalist, and there was no subject that seemed foreign to her. All stories of hypnotism [speculation existed that was the source of her power over people] are the vilest bosh. She said that she needed money, and I thought from what she said that I was not assuming an unusual risk by letting her have it." He added, "I have seen three chests full of jewels owned by Mrs. Chadwick. There were diamonds worth a king's ransom. Apparently she took great delight in displaying them. She would hold them in her hand and fondle them. Her jewels alone must have been worth $500,000." After Beckwith became suspicious he made efforts to make good on the loans, alerting bank directors to the problem. As a group they made a few visits to Cassie during that stormy month of November 1904 to try and retrieve their money, but to no avail. A last trip by the men to Cleveland was made on the day before Thanksgiving to settle the debt. She promised to do so, but did not. In any case it was then too late and the bank went out of business, forced to close its doors for good on the Monday after Thanksgiving. When informed that the securities held by Reynolds were simply worthless scrap paper, Beckwith was said to have suffered a mental and physical collapse.[10]

During November, also, several meetings were held between lawyers representing Newton and Cassie. She argued the securities were controlled by another party whose name she withheld, as security for a loan that she had negotiated and thus, as a result, she was unable to touch the securities. Lawyers for Newton confronted Reynolds in an attempt to make him open the package. However, he steadfastly refused doing no more than to release the list of securities originally submitted to him by Chadwick, and signed by him. According to the list the securities in the package consisted of some United States Steel stock, some shares in an American railroad, gold bonds, and an "immense" block in the stock of the Caledonian Railway of Scotland. Reynolds said if Newton's lawyer could obtain Cassie's consent to inspect the securities he would offer no objection. Of course, Chadwick refused.[11]

As December 1904 began the controversy over Cassie's identity as Devere remained unresolved. Reporters located her sister, Mrs. York, then living in San Francisco, and interviewed her. York spoke briefly of their background in Ontario and that Cassie married Hoover in 1880 and went to live in Cleveland. When Hoover died in 1887 he left her an estate worth around $50,000. Over the next 10 years, said York, Cassie lived on that money and also was employed as a traveler for a wholesale millinery establishment. Newsmen then asked about the period in question, the early 1890s, when Devere was in prison. To those queries York replied, "There was some trouble. Mrs. Hoover got into difficulty and I would sooner not discuss that portion of the story. You know what I mean. I am not denying any of the reports that have been spread broadcast about her, nor am I endeavoring to hide anything. There was trouble." York added she knew of no acquaintance her sister had with Andrew Carnegie "nor any one of the wealthy people of that stamp." Cassie's only response to the interview given by her sister was to declare that Mrs. York was not her sister.[12]

Identity problems were resolved dramatically in Cleveland on December 15 when Mrs. L. M. Kissinger and Mrs. Flora Kissinger, who were formerly employed in the Ohio Penitentiary at Columbus during the time Devere was incarcerated therein, identified her as the woman jailed there for forgery as Mme. Lydia Devere. Later the same day Beckwith of the ruined Oberlin bank called to see Cassie in her cell, accompanied by his wife, who had stood by him through "the avalanche of reproach that is being heaped upon him by his fellow townsmen." All the depositors in his bank, of course, had suffered losses when the bank collapsed. Even though Chadwick's frauds had destroyed his bank, as well as his own private wealth, he said to her that day in the cell, "You've ruined me but I'm not so sure yet you are a fraud."[13]

Just a few days earlier President Beckwith of the failed Citizens' National Bank of Oberlin provided his own confession, said an account, "concerning the monumental transactions of Mrs. Chadwick that taxed the credibility of the few who heard it, but documentary proof compelled belief. The unequivocal statement is made in the confession of President Beckwith that the means by which Mrs. Chadwick secured the immense loans was by a written promise delivered into the hands of the banker that the Citizens' Bank would be made the trustee of the $5,000,000 estate which has just been revealed to the world as an absolute myth." The written promise given by Chadwick to Beckwith was to the effect that her affairs would be turned over to the Oberlin bank on July 1, 1903. In consideration thereof, Beckwith and Cashier Spear were to receive $10,000 a year each for their management skills.[14]

To further smooth the way between herself and Beckwith, and to soothe any fears that might arise, she told the banker a story during one of his visits to her Euclid Avenue home. On one of the walls was a picture of an elderly man. She told Beckwith it was an uncle of hers who, while not wealthy, regularly kept the Chadwick family supplied with money. For a long time she did not know the source of his wealth until he took sick and called Cassie to his side on his deathbed, to tell her a secret. And the secret was that the family was related to Andrew Carnegie, which explained Cassie being worth $5 million. That claim of a relationship with Carnegie had been made for some time before the notes signed with the name of Andrew Carnegie (one for $500,000, the other for $250,000) were ever seen by the Oberlin bankers. In fact those notes were not produced until Beckwith became insistent that something be done to pay back the loans.[15]

Chadwick was never short of excuses as to why she could not repay the loans. She once told Beckwith her massive estate and wealth were then managed by three trustees, all New York men, one of whom she said was William Baldwin. According to this story she could not get hold of any of her money except through Baldwin. After repeated and unsuccessful efforts by Beckwith to get in touch with Baldwin he concluded he was a mythical person. As Beckwith's bank was more and more pressed for ready cash because of all the money given to Cassie as loans, bank directors put more pressure on the president to straighten out the bank's financial position. Out of the blue Chadwick presented an excuse for not paying that she had not used before. It seemed a Pittsburgh banking firm held a power of attorney to manage her estate and in order to fulfill her promise to the Oberlin bank to let them manage her estate, it was necessary to satisfy the demands of Pittsburgh. And that would take some time to do, she explained. More and more the Oberlin banker came to see it all as a sham, but he was in too deep by then and caught in a trap.[16]

In his confession Beckwith revealed how Chadwick dealt with her victims. She had the servants in her house coached in how to behave and help out. On one occasion when Beckwith, Spear, and two of the bank's directors called upon her in one of their periodic visits with the purpose of getting the loans paid back, Cassie "kept calling them from the room, singly, to converse in private. She promised both personal rewards and rewards for the bank for the accommodation that had been extended, and artfully explained that to rush things might spoil everything." Also noted was, "Every few minutes a maid would come into the room saying that Madame was wanted on the telephone or that a telegram had just been received — all calculated, as the banker now sees, to assist in the attempts to allay suspicion and bolster up the hope that relief was at hand."[17]

Because she seemed to scam so many supposedly shrewd financial men so easily, stories sometimes spread that her power must come from somewhere else, such as through hypnotism. To that point a reporter wrote, "Mrs. Chadwick didn't have to hypnotize anybody, if she knew how, for she understood her quarry. She knew that to get something out of the shrewd banker the banker must be made to believe that he is getting a big thing…. In return for a loan Mrs. Chadwick was willing to give a large bonus…."[18]

To this day the full extent of Cassie's fraudulent takings remain unknown. Most contemporary observers believed many who were victimized never came forward. Debts that were known, as of December 25, 1904, were reported to be as follows: Citizens' National Bank, Oberlin, Ohio, $240,000; C. T. Beckwith and A. B. Spear (personal loans over and above bank indebtedness), $107,000; Herbert Newton of Brookline, Massachusetts (bank unnamed), $190,000; Euclid Avenue Savings and Trust Company, Cleveland, $38,000; American Exchange National Bank, Cleveland, $29,000; Savings Deposit Bank, Elyria, Ohio, $10,000; Woerster the jeweler, Elyria, Ohio, personal, $10,000; J. D. Chadwick, Franklin, Pennsylvania, personal, $9,000. Those sums aggregated to $633,000.[19]

Lending credence to the idea that many had not come forward was an article that appeared in November 1907, datelined Pittsburgh. When papers were introduced into litigation surrounding legal proceedings involving a man named W. C. Jutte, the public got a greater glimpse of the extent of Cassie's scams. Documents showed that Chadwick obtained from two wealthy Pittsburgh men, James W. Friend and Frank N. Hoffstott, respectively the President and Vice President of the Pressed Steel Car Company, $798,200 in loans for which she put up as collateral her $5 million worth of mythical securities. That brought the known total of her takings to $1,431,200.[20]

Perhaps one of the more unbelievable parts of her story had to do with her claim of holding those notes from Andrew Carnegie. As a reporter suggested, that Carnegie "should have his notes of hand for vast sums hawked about by a woman like Mrs. Chadwick was unbelievable." When the report of the notes was first brought to his attention (after the frauds were over and Chadwick was in jail) Carnegie's secretary gave out the following statement, "Mr. Carnegie wants me to say that he does not want to be bothered any more about this Chadwick woman. He is quite angry over this persistent use of his name and wishes it to cease at once. Once and for all, he never knew Mrs. Chadwick or any other such woman, and he never signed any such paper as the reports credit him with. That is all." One of her favorite tactics was to pick out a lawyer of high standing who handled the business of banks and tell him she was a woman of great wealth but that she was temporarily embarrassed and needed an immediate loan. Further, she explained, she did not wish to tell her husband and in fact he did not know how much she was really worth, "At the same time you will readily see I don't care to sacrifice any of my securities. I am willing to pay a handsome bonus for the loan." When the banker asked her just what securities she had she pulled out her $5 million list (signed by Reynolds) and the Carnegie notes. Despite the obvious suspicion that should have attached to those items, the banker, said a reporter, "can see only the possible $10,000 bonus for himself for lending the money of the bank."[21]

Where did all the money go? A receiver was appointed who had seized all of the woman's assets at the end of 1904 and those assets were said to be negligible. Reportedly, she spent money extravagantly and eccentrically. During the Christmas season in 1903 she bought eight pianos at one time, which she gave to friends. Also, a couple of years earlier, she took seven society girls from Cleveland to Europe, paid all their expenses, and bought valuable presents for each one. Even when purchasing the smallest toilet articles she insisted top price be paid, and she judged everything by its price. "If a thing didn't cost enough to suit her she would order it thrown away," observed one account. Before traveling to New York City on one of her shopping expeditions, Cassie would order a suite reserved for her at the pricey Holland House but when she arrived she stopped at some other hotel for the week. Nevertheless, she retained the rooms she was not using and sent a check in payment for them when she left the hotel she did occupy, to return to Cleveland.[22]

Chadwick had a ring set with gems (worth $14,000) and a pearl necklace ($10,000). When they were delivered she decided to wear them at once. Although it was in the morning, she dressed in a Parisian gown (worth several thousand dollars) with a long train and the new jewelry and swept into one of the hotel dining rooms, sat down at a table and ordered something to eat. Of course, the other patrons all stared at her with amazement. She was said to have been pleased with all the attention she received. On the next morning the hotel manager went to Cassie's suite to ask if she had lost some jewelry. She said no. Then the manager showed her the ring and necklace she had bought just two days earlier. Cassie agreed they were hers and she must have mislaid them. Apparently when she had taken a bath the previous day she had pushed her stockings into her shoes as she undressed and in those stocking she placed the jewelry. One of the maids, who was unaware of the contents of the shoes, put them out in the hall for the boy to pick up and polish. It was that hall boy who discovered the jewelry and turned it in to the manager. Dressing up at unusual times apparently was a regular habit with her for it was reported, "She would walk into the dining-room of a hotel at noon dressed as if she were ready to go to the opera. She would wear evening clothes, and her fingers and throat would glisten with jewels." At home in Cleveland she would order valuable Parisian rugs thrown out because, she explained, she had seen so much of them she was tired of looking at them. Another favorite habit was to order three cabs at once because she would only ride behind bay horses and, fearful that a black or gray animal might arrive if she ordered only one cab, she ordered three to increase her chances. One of her fears was of redheaded people. One time she contacted an employment agency and asked them to send a maid to her residence. A maid was sent but because her hair was red she was told by Chadwick that her services were not wanted. A second request for a maid to the agency brought a second red-haired woman. "Go away! Get out of my sight!" Cassie screamed at her. "Go back to the agency and tell the manager not to send any more red-headed girls. I won't have them around."[23]

Spear, Beckwith, and Cassie were indicted for a variety of offenses involving fraud against the national banking system. Beckwith died before coming to trial; he was truly a broken man. After he pled guilty Spear was sentenced to seven years in the penitentiary and served out his time at Columbus, Ohio. Cassie Chadwick came to trial on March 6, 1905 and two weeks later was found guilty of conspiracy to defraud a national bank and was sentenced to 10 years in the penitentiary.[24]

Cassie arrived at the penitentiary in Columbus, Ohio on January 12, 1906, from Cleveland, to begin her 10-year sentence. There was a lot of interest in the event with 10 police officers at the train station to keep the crowd back while three other officers escorted the woman in a carriage, and plainclothes officers were also scattered around. At the penitentiary Chadwick was compelled at first to sleep on a cot in a corridor of the prison because the women's section was full with every bed in every cell occupied. If she was found to be in good physical condition she was to be occupied in doing washing or other heavy work; if not, she was to be placed in the sewing department. The entry from the prison book was as follows: "Mrs. Cassie L. Chadwick, alias Mme. Devere — ten years — conspiring to wreck a national bank — Cuyahoga Country — received January 12, 1906, expires January 12, 1916 — good time — November, 1912."[25]

A follow-up article published one year after Cassie's arrival in the penitentiary described her as having been broken in spirit and body. Declared to be only a shadow of her former self, a Cleveland reporter reflected, "Less than three years ago Mrs. Chadwick was living in a palatial home. She was driving about the streets of this city in an automobile, and borrowing immense sums of money, as though it were water."[26]

By October 1907 Cassie was reported to be in very poor health in the woman's hospital ward at the Ohio Penitentiary, with unexplained medical problems. Her first severe problems arose some three weeks earlier when she collapsed and was unconscious for a time. At first it was thought she was faking it to gain sympathy but within a few days it was known her case was serious, and she was placed under the constant care of the prison physician. Speculation arose that her troubles were caused directly by indulging in rich food. "When she first came to the prison, Mrs. Chadwick sent to a fashionable restaurant in the city for her meals, and ate the richest viands," commented a journalist. "Finally, the prison officials ordered that she be compelled to eat the regular prison fare, but she still complained of her stomach, and gradually became worse." Cassie died in that hospital ward at the Ohio Penitentiary at 10:15 P. M. on October 10, 1907. She had been comatose for many hours before the end. No friends or relatives were at her bedside. Emil Hoover, her only child, was summoned but did not arrive before his mother's death. Upon her death Cassie was about 50 years old.[27]

A few years later when a journalist gave a brief summary of her career he raised a point that would often arise over time. He observed that no one questioned the representations of Chadwick. A simple letter to Andrew Carnegie would have exposed her lies and ended her scams, "but no one dreamed of writing to him."[28]

Pension Fraud and Imposters

Mary Ennis and Ann Leonard

At the beginning of September 1869 a complaint was made before United States Commissioner Shields by John J. Ring, a clerk in the Pension Office in New York City, charging 13 female pensioners then drawing federal pensions due to husbands who had been killed in the Civil War with having committed perjury. All 13 were widows of deceased soldiers. Perjury was charged since all swore an oath the previous March when pension payments were last made to them that they had not remarried and were continuing to live in a "state of widowhood" for the purpose of procuring pension money. Two of the 13 were arrested within a few days, Mary Ennis and Ann Leonard. Mary admitted she was living with a man named King and was known as Mary King but said she was not married to him. Leonard admitted she had been married to a man named Mitchell for the past seven months but claimed that she was not aware she had committed any offense in swearing the opposite before the Pension Agent.[1]

Yet a reporter who was obviously sympathetic to the difficulties people often had in obtaining pensions remarked those problems "are so great in many instances pensions are never obtained." The process was described as an exceedingly slow one and was frequently so expensive that the sums finally obtained would hardly pay the cost of getting them. First there were lawyers to whom fees had to be paid, "and who in many cases cheat their clients out of their claims. Then there is the unwinding of red tape in Washington, a most laborious, expensive, complicated and all but everlasting labor, the result of which is often an announcement that technicalities stand in the way of a final settlement." Claimants were described as generally poor and unable to pay the expenses of such proceedings, "and the consequence is that many are compelled to forego altogether the rewards to which they are justly entitled."[2]

Joannah Kennefick

Joannah Kennefick was arrested in February 1876 on perjury charges laid by the United States Pension Agency in New York City. She was the wife of Michael Kennefick, a solider in the 62nd Regiment, New York State Volunteers, who died in Baltimore May 5, 1864 from disease contracted in the army. Since his death his widow had been drawing a pension of $8 a month, payable quarterly in New York. Her offense consisted of continuing to draw the pension after having been twice married since her first husband's death. Since October 1868 when the first of her two remarriages took place Joannah perjured herself regularly four times a year. Every three months she appeared before the Pension Court and swore that she was still the unmarried widow of Michael, and twice each year, as required by law, she had brought two witnesses with her to swear her affidavit was true (which illustrated the difficulty of the pension procedure).[3]

The first hint of Kennefick's perjury came to the Pension Agent, Jacob M. Patterson, in February 1876. Information came to him that she had married Alexander Murphy in October 1868 and that he died in 1872. Next she married Samuel Crocker. Copies of the marriage certificates were obtained and Patterson waited for the next quarterly swearing period to confront her; that occurred later in that month of February. On the day of the quarterly payment she showed up as Joannah Kennefick, swore the oath and affixed her signature to the form. She also had with her two witnesses to substantiate her oath. Patterson then questioned her closely but she maintained she had not perjured herself and continued to do so until the marriage certificates were produced, whereupon "she was forced to confess, and at once entered the plea of extreme poverty." Joannah explained she was a poor woman who had remarried twice in the hope of getting a home and comfortable support but had on each occasion been disappointed. She related her story from jail to a

New York Times reporter. Nova Scotian by birth she came to New York as a young girl and at the age of 16 married a man named Darcy, with whom she lived until his death, having three sons by him, one of which was then living. Left a widow when she was 20 she married Kennefick in 1860. After Murphy died she rented a room and eked out an existence solely by means of the monthly $8 pension. When she married Crocker she soon found out he was not the man of means he said he was and feeling, therefore, deceived she obliged Crocker to leave. Since the separation Joannah had been living in Jersey City and then Newark and "She had taken in washing and a little needle-work, had profited by charity in a measure, and had filled up the gaps with the United States pension."[4]

Harriet N. Kingsbury

Another woman caught in a pension claim fraud was Mrs. Harriet N. Kingsbury, who was tried in the U.S. Circuit Court before Judge Benedict and a jury, in January 1880, after being indicted for forgery of the name and false impersonation of her niece in making out an affidavit to be used by Kingsbury in the pursuit of a bogus pension claim. The niece in question, Mrs. Evadne Brady, testified the signature purporting to be hers on the affidavit was not her handwriting. Also testifying was the notary who declared Brady was not with Kingsbury at the time the latter made the affidavit representing herself to be Evadne Brady.[5]

Sarah C. Sadler

At the end of October 1890 Mrs. Sarah C. Sadler of Stoddard County, Missouri was arrested on a charge of filing a bogus pension claim. Vincent Ditmore of the 128th Illinois Regiment died during the Civil War and not long after his widow Sarah married a man named Poplin. When he died Sarah married a man named Sadler. In 1890 Sara submitted an application for a pension as the widow of Ditmore. In support of that application and under the name of Poplin (using disguised handwriting) she swore she was personally acquainted with Mrs. Ditmore and that Sarah had not remarried since Ditmore died. A pension was duly granted and Sarah received a $2,700 back pension (it was a quarter of a century since the war ended) in one payment. She bought a farm with that money but once the fraud was discovered the U. S. government attached the property.⁶

Matilda Brayfield

In the Federal Court in Springfield, Illinois in June 1895, Mrs. Matilda Brayfield, "an aged woman of Percy County" was fined $1,000 and costs, amounting in total to around $2,000, for presenting a false claim for a pension, alleging her husband had served through the Civil War, when evidence presented in court showed her husband had never been in the Civil War or in any army.⁷

Sarah Flynn

Civil War pension claims continued to be filed, even after the beginning of the twentieth century. In U. S. court in Sioux Falls, South Dakota in October 1901, Sarah J. Flynn of Lake Preston, South Dakota, pled guilty to making a fraudulent application for a pension and was fined $1,030 by Judge Carland, an amount she immediately paid. Flynn, in her application, alleged she was the widow of Silas J. Flynn, a member of the Seventh New York Infantry. However, Flynn's real widow testified in the case and the U.S. government was able to produce other evidence, which the applicant did not attempt to dispute.⁸

Mrs. Diaz

Another group of con artists were the women who took on the identity of someone else usually still then alive — imposters. Sometimes they took on the identities of women with means, but not always. On November 9, 1872 a woman entered Earle's Hotel in New York at Canal and Center Streets with a request to see the head clerk, Mr. G. Lansing. She gave her name as A. M. Dyas, informing Lansing she was the author of the *William Henry Letters*, published by Osgood & Company of Boston, and that she was also a regular contributor to the magazine *Hearth & Home*. Suitably impressed, Lansing placed an elegant room at her disposal. At the end of the week Lansing sent a bill for $21 up to her room. In response, Abby asked for a day or so of grace until she could get to see her publisher and get some money. Although Lansing said okay he was leery enough that the next day he called on Mrs. Chase, editor of *Hearth & Home*, and asked about the financial condition of Abby Medora Dyas. Chase declared it was first class and that she would advance her $500 or $1,000 any day. A satisfied Lansing returned to his hotel, still believing the real Dyas was stopping at his hotel. A day later the bill was still not paid and then Lansing discovered the woman had disappeared. As a next step he wrote to Osgood & Company asking for Dyas's address and received in reply, "Plymouth, Massachusetts." He forwarded the bill to her at that address but in return got a note from Dyas declaring she had never been in Earle's Hotel in her life. And furthermore, she said that for over a year she had been annoyed by a woman who impersonated her throughout the U.S., and who left in her wake unpaid bills in every town. From the description of the imposter that Dyas supplied in her note, Lansing knew the woman who stopped at his hotel was the imposter in question. Police were notified; they traced her to a Manhattan address, and arrested her there at the end of December. From a cell she told a reporter she was 35 years old, had been born in Philadelphia and then moved with her family to St. Louis. She married Juan Henrico Diaz, who died in March 1863, and came to New York.[9]

A day later it was reported that her real name was Dyce and that her arrest was a major topic of conversation in church circles as she had for several months past been "working" the various aristocratic churches and ingratiating herself into the good graces of leading members of different congregations. "She is particularly adapted for this system of swindling, being apparently possessed of a modest, unassuming manner, and knowing every line in the Bible at heart," observed a reporter. "She is, to use the stage expression, letter perfect, and is constantly quoting from Scripture." Over the previous month she had attended every church service at Trinity Church and became so well known among the congregation that the pastor, Dr. Middleton, believing her to be an honest and hard-working woman, offered to pay the amount she owed to Earle's Hotel. One of the members of the congregation, a Mr. Depew, met her six weeks earlier when she was supposedly trying to raise money to return to her family in St. Louis. Depew gave her a total of $50 to $60, over time. Abby was able to secure board at a lodging house by giving the names of Mr. and Mrs. Depew. Suddenly Abby vanished, leaving behind many unpaid bills. After being brought up to date on her various activities Depew pronounced her "a finished and dangerous confidence woman."[10]

Jane Doe

Newark, New Jersey police were looking for a woman swindler, in the first couple of months of 1899, who had been defrauding Newark storekeepers out of goods by pretending she was Mrs. David Young, wife of the General Manager of the North Jersey Traction Company (the public transit system). The latest victim was a phonograph retailer. A woman drove up to the store in a cutter, explained she wanted a phonograph, and casually mentioned that he probably knew that she was Mrs. Young. The cost of the phonograph and accessories came to $59.95 and after getting the articles she drove off. Storeowner Mr. Petit explained later that he never thought of asking for the money. He sent off a bill to Mr. Young but it was returned with a note that Mrs. Young had made no such purchase. After making a visit to the Young residence and seeing Mrs. Young in person, Petit knew he had been scammed. "The swindler was well dressed, a fluent talker, and had no regard for the price of the articles she ordered," remarked a news account. "The police believe that the swindler had been making a study of the habits of the genuine Mrs. Young and that this enabled her to successfully carry out her plans."[11]

Anna D. Smith

A woman who said she was Mrs. Anna D. Smith, daughter of the late Governor Dennison of Ohio (he was also Postmaster General in President Abraham Lincoln's cabinet), was arrested in New York in May 1904, charged with defrauding the Hotel Navarre in that city. An executive at the hotel, Charles Dabb, said Smith left the hotel suddenly some five weeks earlier, owing $271 for room and board and money loaned. He added that she left a trunk behind but it was filled only with discarded clothing. Smith declared her arrest to be "an outrage" and that she had left the hotel because of a "difference" with Dabb and she was waiting for a remittance from Columbus, Ohio in order the pay the bill. Since she left the Navarre, said the police, she had stopped at the Gilsey

House and the Hotel Aldine. At the latter hotel the woman owed $200 for five weeks board.[12]

Jane Doe

Several Los Angeles merchants were the victims of a woman fraud artist in 1905 and lost goods ranging in value from $25 to $150. Those frauds were conducted by a woman calling herself Mrs. Eva B. Duncan and purchases included everything from fancy groceries to finishing materials and paints for building. A complete set of furniture was also swindled from a retailer. Duncan was a widow who lived in Attica, Indiana. She had relatives in Los Angeles and near the end of 1904 she inherited a property in Los Angeles when one of those relatives died. Duncan came to Los Angeles, staying for six weeks at her newly acquired house. Then she went back to Indiana, intending to settle her affairs and to move permanently to Los Angeles in a few months. After her return to Attica, there appeared at various Los Angeles stores a woman representing herself as Mrs. Duncan and she freely ordered goods, asking credit for a short time and citing her home ownership as collateral. Usually credit was granted. All purchases were delivered to the Duncan house (then, of course, unoccupied). No delivery person ever caught on to the fact the house was empty and always the delivered goods, left at the front door, disappeared soon after they were delivered.[13]

Elinor Beattie

Elinor Lorraine Beattie, accused of having stolen $1,500 worth of silverware from the Gorham Manufacturing Company, was brought to New York City in October 1909 by Detective Bernard Flood of the District Attorney's office on the White Star ocean liner *Baltic*. Flood went over to London, England about four months earlier to bring back Beattie, who had been arrested there when her whereabouts were discovered through the work of the Gorham Company's detectives. By fighting extradition as hard as she could Beattie had kept Flood waiting around in England since June. Of the return trip, observed a reporter, "Miss Beattie is a large masculine-looking woman. She is said to have interested her fellow-passengers during the voyage by smoking cigarettes."[14]

Earlier in 1909 a woman who said she was Mrs. Charles Stearns, wife of a former Attorney General of Rhode Island, rented a flat at 111 West 104th Street. That woman, said the police, was Beattie. Mrs. Stearns, then Mme. Perugini, wife of the Italian Charge d'Affaires in Peking, once was a patroness and close friend of Beattie. Established in her apartment Beattie asked the Gorham firm to send some silverware to her home that she might select from. The selection sent over by Gorham was valued at $1,500 and was left with her overnight. When the firm's salesman called back the next day he found Beattie had vanished, along with the silverware. Detective Larkin, of the company, soon discovered she had pawned the goods for about half the value at various pawnshops in Manhattan, and had then boarded the liner *Carmania* and sailed for England. Soon international cables were sent and she was followed from the time she landed in England and trailed for several days until enough evidence was obtained and she was arrested. Just before boarding the *Carmania*, Beattie went to a department store and ordered a $40 dress to be sent to her on board the ship. When the store's delivery boy arrived with the dress he gave it to Beattie and asked for the $40. Beattie said she had already paid for it at the store. That caused an argument to break out, with Detective Mallon (of the store) called in to settle the matter. He ruled in favor of the delivery boy.[15]

Frances Hollander

Posing as the daughter of Governor Foss of Massachusetts, as the wife of various prominent men such as famous vaudeville comedian Lew Fields, and "acting other bold roles," a young woman in her early 20s swindled Boston and New York firms out of several thousand dollars' worth of finery, according to a confession the police said the woman made to them in September 1912. She claimed to be Frances Hollander, daughter of wealthy parents and "a pupil in a Baltimore convent." Although she said she originally came from Chicago she would not tell police the names of her parents. Later she amended her story to the police by admitting there was no convent in her background but adding that she had done a stretch at a reform school in Lancaster, Massachusetts, and had used at least half a dozen aliases. Police investigators found 50 expensive gowns at a well-known New York hotel, where the woman had been staying. Upon that discovery she was alleged to have made her confession. Only six months earlier, she said, she had been released on probation from a term in the Lancaster Reform School for obtaining from a Boston jeweler two diamond pendants by representing herself as one of the twin daughters of Governor Foss. After she ran away from her probation officers she came to New York, where she represented herself as the wife of a prominent resident of Lynn, Massachusetts and thereby obtained expensive gowns and other finery. "I came to this city," said Hollander, "because I wanted to see life and excitement. I did get all those pretty things without paying for them, but I thought I would be able to pay some time; I did not think it was stealing."[16]

Within a month the story had changed and she was said to be Vera Dowling, daughter of George Dowling, an aged and respected resident of a suburb of Boston. After her arrest in Boston some two years earlier for stealing jewelry she had been disowned by her family. In June 1910, according to her latest story, she met a Harvard student who, with a promise of marriage, persuaded her to go to Baltimore with him. Frances lived with him for several weeks using money derived from the sale of stolen jewelry to live on. She blamed her love for the student as much as her love of finery for her situation. When she was deserted by the student she returned to Boston, registered at a hotel and resumed her larcenous ways. On August 15, 1912, Frances came to New York where she operated for about a month before she was arrested. Her favorite method was to have store clerks sent with her from shops where she had made purchases to her hotel, for payment for the goods. Once in the lobby, under one pretext or another she persuaded the clerk to let her take the articles to her room, and to return immediately to the lobby with the payment. Of course, once out of sight of the clerk Frances vanished from the hotel through another door and when the clerk, after waiting a reasonable amount of time, asked at the front desk he learned no such person was registered at the hotel.[17]

Jane Doe

Los Angeles police, under personal instructions form Police Chief Sebastian in May 1913, had started a major search for an aged woman who was posing as the widow of the late General Alcorn, a Confederate veteran and one time Governor of Mississippi. She was branded as a fraud by relatives of the historic statesman and warrior. Reportedly,

Daughters of the Confederacy and other Southerners residing in different parts of the country had been victimized out of large sums of money through the woman's claim of a relationship to the late Alcorn. The general's real daughter, Mrs. E. W. Rector of Hot Springs, Arkansas, wrote a letter to a Los Angeles contact outlining the fraud. The contact went to Sebastian and explained the situation; Sebastian then ordered an immediate search for the woman. In her letter Rector explained her mother died November 22, 1907, and that "the aged adventuress has been posing as Mrs. Alcorn for months."[18]

Jane Doe

A woman was locked up in New York City in July 1915, charged with fraudulently obtaining $4,435 from Frank J. Mahoney, representing herself to be the widow of the late Standard Oil executive and railroad builder, Henry M. Flagler. Investigation brought out the fact that the woman had lived in luxury for some time in Washington, D.C., under the name of Mrs. John Henry Johnson and had contracted large bills and borrowed money there while representing herself to be the Flagler heiress. In explaining the use of the name Johnson the woman told the police that it was the name of her daughter's husband and that she had assumed it to keep away beggars who might be attracted by the name of Flagler. In Washington, it was learned that under the name of Johnson she had rented and furnished elaborately a house at one time occupied by the Russian Embassy, and that S. E. Stonebraker, a real estate agent, held claims against her for $4,000, about $2,000 of which was said to have been advanced to her to buy furniture.[19]

Then there were the various frauds too difficult to categorize as a single group or happening too infrequently to do so. They ranged from the confidence women who swindled goods on nothing but nerve, to women who faked injuries to collect damages, to women who tried to con customs agents, to mention a few.

14

Various Frauds

Kate Clifford

On a February night in 1873 a woman entered the establishment of C. G. Gunther & Company in New York and asked for a set of furs that she said she had left to be cleaned. The person who was temporarily in charge of that department in the store was about to hand them over, apparently satisfied with the matter of identification. Then one of the storeowners, Mr. Gunther, happened by and he said he would have to send for the woman who had charge of that department, to identify the claimant whom she knew by sight. Kate Clifford then remembered some urgent business in another part of the city that required her attention and she rushed off, promising to call again for the furs. A few days later, by chance, Gunther saw her again on Broadway and became convinced she was on a swindling expedition. He called a policeman over and Clifford was stopped as she left Keeping's jewelry store. It was then learned she had secured a gold watch and chain from the store clerk on the representation that she had left it to be repaired. Before going into the store she had been able to see the watch she wanted through the window. Taken before Judge Cox at Jefferson Market Police Court, she pled guilty to larceny with respect to the watch. Clifford was sent to the City Prison for four months.[1]

Caroline Davis

An official from McCreery & Company dry goods store in New York called at police headquarters in August 1883 with a letter placing an order he believed was bogus. That note requested that an evening dress not to exceed $75 in price be selected and sent immediately to Saratoga to Mrs. Louis de Jonge, the bill to be sent to her husband, a merchant in New York City. Upon investigation it was discovered the note was a forgery by some unknown person who, during the preceding 14 months, had swindled McCreery more than once and had victimized other dry goods houses. A dress such as requested was given to a police detective who went by train to Saratoga. When he arrived at the address he asked for Mrs. De Jonge and was received "by a handsome, fashionably dressed woman about twenty-six years old." She said the dress was for her, complained about the amount of time it took to arrive and signed for it as Mrs. De Jonge, whereupon the detective arrested her. After being allowed to change her clothes she returned to New York City with the detective on the midnight train. At the police station she was said to have made a full confession to the "numerous swindles attributed to her." It was learned she was Mrs. Caroline G. Davis, daughter of Alexander Greer, a tobacco merchant of Albany who died a rich man a few years earlier. Caroline married R. E. Davis when she was 18 but was divorced from him in April 1883. According to a reporter, "Mrs. Davis's relatives are all wealthy and she is also understood to be possessed of means."[2]

Mrs. E. S. Hudson

A news account from Boston in early 1885 detailed the operations of Mrs. E. S. Hudson, a widow, who was said to have succeeded in swindling hundreds of victims in Boston, including many leading business firms. Surprisingly, she reportedly never worked under an alias, and was assisted in her swindling by her daughter Amy. "Their prepossessing manners and winning ways completely captivated their victims," remarked a newsman. She was the widow of Dr. E. S. Hudson, formerly a practicing physician in Medway, whose death, the newspaper said, was believed to have been caused by the "disgrace" brought upon him by his wife's conduct. Summarizing her career the newsman wrote, "She has swindled hotel keepers, furniture dealers, jewelers, dressmakers, and even a cook and laundress of various amounts. It is estimated that their swindlings in this city will reach $30,000. No criminal action has yet been brought against Mrs. Hudson." Her past was said to have been fully investigated by the newspaper and it was discovered that similar practices by the woman in Philadelphia and New York led to her hasty departure from those cities.³

A month later, in March 1885, Emma Hudson was arrested on two separate occasions and charged by police in New York City with two separate offenses. In one instance she was charged under the hotel act for swindling the proprietor of the Coleman House hotel out of the amount of her hotel bill. Hudson was also charged with larceny after five small pieces of silverware were stolen from a doctor's office and later pawned. A servant at Dr. Janvrin's office identified Hudson as the person who came to see the doctor but left the office soon after when the physician did not arrive at his office. Shortly after the woman left, silverware was discovered missing from a pantry just outside the waiting room. Police discovered the silverware in a pawnshop and later happened to find the tickets in Hudson's room at the Coleman House while investigating the earlier charge.⁴

Mrs. Hill

Before outlining a particular swindle in June 1888, a reporter for the *Los Angeles Times* made a general comment on the number of female sharpers, or fakirs, in the area, by saying, "They are not numerous, but of late several of the smiling she rascals have made their powers felt in this city." Some days earlier, a pretty woman who gave her name as Mrs. Hill visited Doc Lewis at the Empire Stable and convinced him to rent her a horse and buggy as she urgently needed to get to Pasadena; she said she would pay upon her return. Hill was gone all day and when she returned to the livery stable late in the afternoon she handed Lewis a bundle and asked him to keep it for her until the next day when she would come to collect it, and pay for the buggy. But days went by and the woman never returned. Finally, he opened the bundle only to find it contained nothing but old stockings and old underwear. Lewis then started out to make a thorough investigation only to learn, said a reporter, "that he had been taken in by one of the sharpest confidence women in the State."⁵

Belle Clark and P. M. Seaman

A three person team of F. K. Clark, his wife Belle Clark and her sister Miss P. M. Seaman worked at defrauding merchants in Pasadena before moving on to do the same in Los Angeles and the trio, said an account, "succeeded in swindling almost every merchant in Pasadena and quite a number in this city [Los Angeles]." Usually the way it worked was that the two women went into a store and ordered some goods. When the clerk asked for payment they told him to charge it. If the clerk balked at that idea the women sometimes said they were property owners, which sometimes worked by itself, but more often they gave a character reference with Clark filling that role, as in saying Clark the lawyer knew them and would vouch for them. One firm victimized in Los Angeles was the Parisian Cloak and Suit House at 119 South Spring Street, where they managed to swindle $54 worth of goods out of the store using the above ruse. When store manager J. L. Salkey could not collect on the bill he swore out a complaint and arrest warrants were issued. Clark was quickly arrested but the two women saw the authorities coming and barricaded themselves in their Pasadena residence so that service of the warrant could not be made. Police set up a round-the-clock vigil at the house, in order to arrest them the moment they stepped outside. It was a full day before the women surrendered with all three then brought to Los Angeles, charged with conspiracy to defraud.[6]

At their trial in May 1890, a shoe dealer, M. S. Hewes, testified that on October 3, 1889, the three came into his store to buy shoes. Clark explained he wanted credit, declaring Seaman owned real estate in Pasadena and giving as a reference a firm in Los Angeles, Sanborn & Vail. One of the clerks at the shoe store was dispatched to the offices of Sanborn & Vail, which happened to be only a block or two away, where he learned the trio had gotten pictures on credit but had never paid for them, with the pictures ultimately being recovered by Sanborn & Vail, but only after a lawsuit. Hewes, of course, told the three that they could not have any credit from him but by that time each of the three had on a new pair of shoes they wanted to buy. After closing and locking the store's doors, Hewes invited the group to take the shoes off. The two women did surrender the shoes they had tried on but Clark ran and jumped out of a back window still wearing the new and unpaid-for shoes. After evidence in the case had closed Clark asked for, and received, a continuance for a week in order to file a brief. Clark then asked the Court to direct the court reporter to transcribe the testimony for him but was told he would have to make his own arrangements — that is, if Clark wanted a transcript of the trial he would have to pay the court reporter for one. His next move was to go over to his wife and get a "cut-and-dried" dispatch from her that spoke of money coming to her from the East, the same dodge the group had often used in the past. Showing this dispatch to the court reporter — in the face of all the evidence on that point taken down by that very court reporter — Clark asked him for credit on the transcript until the money from the East arrived. Not surprisingly, the court reporter declined. At that point Belle Clark was acquitted on the ground there was no evidence she had conspired with her husband or with Seaman.[7]

Kate Bradford

In May 1894, opinion in the Williamsburg section of Brooklyn was divided as to whether Mrs. Kate Bradford of 658 Bedford Avenue was a suicide or a fugitive. Her two young sons played in the street with the neighborhood children as they usually did but when Bradford disappeared she left her family penniless. All of her furniture was mortgaged and her home was reportedly pledged as security for some investments. Kate had induced many of her neighbors to invest money with her and it, too, had vanished. The heaviest loser was Alfred Squires of 656 Bedford Avenue, who lost $30,000 in cash and his house, which he had mortgaged to raise money to invest with Kate. Squires also persuaded a number of other people to invest money with Bradford: Mrs. Walter Locke of 651 Bedford and a Mrs. Elder of the same address. It was said, "The neighborhood of Bedford Avenue and Rutledge Street is peopled with her dupes." Bradford conducted her business quietly. She did not advertise but solicited customers through neighbors and personal friends. She accepted any amount of money to invest, from $10 upwards to thousands with the inducement being she paid $1.50 per $10 per month to the people who invested with her. Sometimes she paid as high as $2 per $10 per month. It was believed she paid back money due to old investors with some of the money received from newer investors — a simple Ponzi scheme. Bradford was about 40 years old, well liked in the neighborhood, with a "winning" personality and was a prominent member of Christ Church in Bedford Avenue. Many of its parishioners were among her victims.[8]

Six months later, W. H. Bradford obtained a judgment in the New York Supreme Court against his daughter-in-law Kate for $3,573.73. He was the first of her dupes to sue for the money had had given her. However, Kate was still a fugitive.[9]

Ellen Field

Around the beginning of 1895 Mrs. Ellen Field went into the store of Mrs. Sullivan on North Spring Street in Los Angeles and told a pitiful tale about a poverty-stricken family, for whom she said she was soliciting donations. Touched by the story, Sullivan gave goods to the value of $8 as a donation and Field departed. A few weeks later she returned to the store and said she wanted to make some purchases for herself. Based solely on that past interaction, Sullivan allowed Field to take a number of expensive goods on credit. At the time Field lived in rented rooms where it was said she failed to pay her landlord, but collected rent from sub-tenants she admitted to the rooms, without the landlord's knowledge. Suddenly, Ellen Field vanished, leaving a number of unpaid bills behind her, including Sullivan's.[10]

Mabel Blannon

Mabel Blannon was released from the penitentiary in October 1898 after having served a term of three years for petty larceny in Washington, D.C., having robbed an old soldier. Not quite one year later Mabel was arrested and charged with defrauding merchants after numerous complaints had been made to the police and several of the merchants had identified Mabel as the fraud artist. One victim was V. M. Balderson, who owned a grocery store at 900 Sixth Street in Washington. A woman entered his store and stated that her employer, Mrs. Holden, wife of Dr. Holden, who lived near by, wanted to secure goods on credit. He refused to grant any credit without a signed order and, after going away for a short time, Mabel returned with an order bearing Mrs. Holden's signature — Mrs. Holden later pronounced it a forgery. Blannon was then allowed to take the goods (valued at $3) away. Several other merchants in the same area had also lost goods to the same woman tendering false orders, ranging in value from $1 to $5. Among those who gave her goods on credit were Reuben the confectioner and McMahon the grocer. But some merchants were suspicious and efforts by Mabel to secure goods from Charles Butts, grocer, and from Nace's oyster house failed. Two policemen on bicycles received information that Blannon, for whom they had been on the lookout, was loitering on the grounds of the Soldiers' Home and they went there and arrested her. A small basket that she carried contained 10 bottles of beer and a bottle of whisky, which the police think she had been offering for sale to the veterans.[11]

Mrs. E. Ernshaw

A confidence woman who gave her name as Mrs. E. Ernshaw was arrested on November 1, 1907, in Stockton, California after a lengthy search in numerous stores. For several weeks small storekeepers had reported that a woman would place an order for groceries or dry goods and give an address, with the goods to be paid for on delivery. Then the woman would return to the store later the same day, saying she was in a hurry for a few articles and would take them with her. When the delivery truck arrived at the given address the driver was met by bewildered householders who had placed no such order. Reportedly, "The woman made the rounds of a number of stores and secured a considerable quantity of provisions in the last two months." Her arrest came when her description and method of operation were so widely circulated that she was recognized. A store clerk, recognizing the method, refused to allow her to take any items from the order in advance of payment. Then he notified the police who launched a search in the neighborhood.[12]

Annie Rowland

Among the women who allegedly defrauded their employers was Annie Rowland. She was the matron of Dr. William Hammond's sanatorium in Washington, D.C., in 1889, who, after running up bills with merchants amounting to some $2,000, allegedly pocketed the cash given her to pay those bills and fled Washington, being on the run for almost a month before she was arrested in Minneapolis by Detective Mahon of the Washington police. When Mahon was given the task of finding the runaway woman he went to Philadelphia, where Rowland had previously worked as a matron in a couple of medical institutions. He did learn there she had been friendly with a Lizzie Kessler, an orphan at one of those institutions. From Philadelphia Mahon traced them through a few other states before running them down at the home of Kessler's brother in Minneapolis, where Rowland was arrested. Dr. Hammond said at the time of her arrest that he had never authorized his matron to run any bills whatever, and that he always supplied her with money to pay for supplies each week as needed. That cash she got from him she had appropriated to her own use, putting off the payment of the bills she got until they reached figures that caused the dealers to demand payment, whereupon she disappeared.[13]

Another three weeks passed before Rowland, charged with embezzling, was returned to Washington. She was described as "about forty years of age and appears to be both refined and ladylike." Specifically she was then charged with embezzling $60 but the prosecution said the real total would likely reach $3,000. Rowland, as matron, had exclusive control of all money spent for the supplies for the maintenance and running of the institution. Hammond left it all to her and supplied her, in cash, with whatever sums of money she needed. Denying all charges, Rowland explained her flight by saying she went to Philadelphia with the intention of returning to Washington in a day or two, but at the urgent request of a friend she consented to go out to Minneapolis, intending, however, to return immediately.[14]

A day later at a court appearance her lawyer, C. C. Cole, explained her flight differently by saying she left Washington to spend her vacation with friends, with Hammond's knowledge and consent, and that she knew nothing about the charges against her until her arrest. While Rowland was matron of the Sheltering Arms, an orphan asylum in Philadelphia, it was said she was especially kind to Lizzie Kessler, a young orphan who had inherited $1,200 and, said a news account, her "conspicuous attention to the girl aroused the suspicions of the managers of the asylum." They concluded Rowland was interested in Lizzie because of her inheritance and was laying plans to gain possession of the money. To prevent that the child was sent to live with a Chester County farmer but apparently Rowland and the girl kept in touch through letters, with Lizzie disappearing around the same time as did Rowland. The pair linked up in Philadelphia before moving on together. Kessler traveled to Washington with the police and their prisoner Rowland and it was believed she would be returned to the Philadelphia orphanage.[15]

During the hearing Hammond, a physician and retired surgeon-general of the U.S. Army, testified he gave Rowland $60 on July 30 to purchase supplies for the following week. He did not know what happened to the money but soon got bills from Waltham (a butcher) and Cook Brothers (grocers) showing him the supplies had not been paid for as he supposed. According to him he had not only never authorized his matron to run any bills, but had specifically prohibited the practice, yet the Waltham bill had then reached $1,424.20 with the Cook Brothers tab at $1,260. Hammond believed Rowland had never paid those merchants and that the bills extended over the entire period of her employment as matron, from January 8, 1889 until July 31, 1889. During that time he estimated he had given her $1,800 in cash for the purchase of supplies, which he was led to believe was all she required. With respect to Rowland's flight, Hammond said she left on July 31 and was to return the next day but he never saw her again until after her arrest. After her departure the bills suddenly turned up and he placed the matter in the hands of the police. W. T. Waltham, on the stand, said that when he had spoken to Rowland about the bill Rowland informed him that Dr. Hammond was too busy to attend to bills and that he would have to wait for payment until the doctor's new house was built. Mr. Cook, of Cook Brothers, told a similar story and both of them were sure that Rowland had never paid for any supplies during all her time of the job.[16]

Apparently there was no trial in this case, or there was an acquittal, because about one year later there was a report that a suit was filed in circuit court by Annie Rowland and her husband Adolph, against William Hammond, in the sum of $20,000. The suit charged that on August 5, 1889 Hammond charged Rowland with having embezzled the sum of $60 and that she was afterward arrested and indicted, and that the charge was false.[17]

Susan Macomber

Forty-two-year-old Susan Macomber stood in the dock on March 10, 1911, in West Side Court in New York City charged with forgery in the third degree in misappropriating money which, according to her employer, amounted to between $14,000 and $15,000 but which she acknowledged amounted to $8,000 or $9,000. Macomber lived with her parents in East Orange, New Jersey and she was employed for about two years, up to January 12, 1911, as a bookkeeper at $19 a week for the John Lane Publishing Company of New York. She was dismissed by Lane on January 12 after the company books were found not to be in order; she had allegedly diverted funds for her own use. Placed in evidence was a long letter to Lane in which Macomber gave a list of checks diverted to her own use and the letter made a confession to the Lane company. In the letter she said she used all the money she took in keeping a good home for her aged parents. According to the story the parents supposed their daughter earned a salary of at least $50 a week. Described as a woman of deep religious feeling, it was also reported she had never speculated in stocks or gambled.[18]

Executives at Lane Publishing believed Macomber stole money for less than half of the two years she worked for them and what baffled them the most was expressed by Benjamin Maupin, Lane treasurer, who said, "What she did with all the money is puzzling us. Although I understand that she has established a comfortable home in East Orange and has provided many comforts for her parents, it does not seem possible that she could have spent so large a sum in that way. In fact it could cost her but a fraction of the amount taken." Nevertheless, Macomber stuck to her story that every cent she diverted was spent on her parents' living and upkeep. Reportedly, some 10 years earlier she had graduated from the New York University Law School. Prior to that she was employed in one of the city's big department stores and had also worked as a drug store clerk at one time. Macomber moved herself and her parents into the comfortable home in East Orange in May 1910, at a rent of $70 a month. Mr. Macomber, 74, served in the Federal Army during the Civil War as an officer. He was then employed in one of the railroad offices in New York City and to save him the half-mile walk uphill home from the station his daughter had provided him with a carriage ride every evening. With respect to Susan's lifestyle, Mr. Macomber said, "She lived quietly and made no investments or property purchases. She had no expensive habits of dress, and was not identified with any of the local societies, nor did she entertain."[19]

Rose E. Bowers

Mrs. Rose E. Bowers, accused of swindling the Fitzgerald Music Company of Los Angeles out of a considerable sum of money in the sales of pianos consigned to her as the company's manager in San Diego, was arrested on September 5, 1911. Actually she had been apprehended in Oceanside a week earlier and since then had been detained under guard by private detectives, apparently employed by the Fitzgerald firm. Bowers arrived in San Diego as Mrs. Dunbar, a widow. Some months later she married a music dealer named A. F. Bowers. When Mr. Bowers left his wife she took over his music business. One account estimated Bowers made over $50,000 from her swindling of the Fitzgerald company but George Barnes, business manager of the firm, said the company loss was more in the neighborhood of $2,000.[20]

Bowers's scam involved contract manipulations. She obtained pianos from Fitzgerald by means of forged contracts that appeared to show those pianos had been sold to various individuals on the installment plan. When the pianos arrived at her premises in San Diego, Rose sold the instruments for cash and kept the money. Meanwhile she made a number of installment payments on each of the phony contracts, at least for a time.[21]

Gertrude McCrimmon

Horse trader David B. Low of Los Angeles saw an ad in the newspaper in late 1905 for the sale of a team of draught horses. When he answered the ad he was shown the animals in a South Hill Street stable by Harry Ashton and F. R. Doyle, stablemen. Low was told the horses were owned by Gertrude McCrimmon, a "handsome young woman" of 25. She wanted $275 for her horses but after some dickering, during which time McCrimmon was coy for a few days, a deal was struck for $240 with Low putting down $15 as a deposit. On November 9 Low met Gertrude at the stable by appointment and asked to be allowed to drive the team before the final payment was made. Stableman Doyle, listening in, butted into the conversation to say the horses could not be taken out of the stable until their board bill of $130 to the stable had been paid. McCrimmon pleaded with the stable boss to make an exception but the stable stood firm. At that point Low gave up and paid over the full $225 outstanding, anxious to close the deal. After paying the stable its $130, and giving Low a verbal guarantee the horses were sound, Gertrude pocketed the rest of the money and left the stable. Low departed driving the horses but found, after they went a few blocks, they could hardly walk (they had been doped and that allowed them to pass muster for a short time). Ashton and Doyle laughed as they told the luckless Low what a bad deal he made, when he returned to the stable. Low said they told him the same horses had been sold half a dozen times and they were always returned to the stable, and were always sold back for around half price. Ashton then proposed to buy the horses for $125. Although he had paid $240 just a couple of hours earlier, Low agreed.[22]

Later that same month, Charles Fishel, a rancher from Tropico, California, told the police a woeful story of how McCrimmon had sold him a couple of "wind-broken, spavined and diseased" bay horses similar to those sold to Low. She used the same general method and when he went back to demand his $150 be returned Gertrude gave him nothing but derisive laughter. Fishel also answered an ad offering two horses for sale and when he met McCrimmon at the location where they were stabled (a place different from that used for the Low transaction) Gertrude verbally guaranteed the pair of horses to be sound and said, "You needn't take my word for it, though; see Dr. Crandall the veterinary on Washington Street, he has just examined them." Fishel took her advice and went to the vet's office where he met a man claiming to be Crandall who attested to the glowing health of the animals. Thus, Fishel paid in full and drove the horses away. However, their wind began to fail only a few blocks from the stable. The horses tried to lie down in the street. A stranger just happened to show up then, declared he was a lawyer and offered to return to the stable with Fishel and adjust the matter legally. Accepting his new friend's advice the pair returned to the stable. Fishel demanded his money back but McCrimmon declared, "You've been skinned and you deserved it all. Run along now and don't holler any more. I know my business and I know you can't do a thing with me. Take the beasts away, they are eyesores." Then the "lawyer" suggested a compromise by proposing that McCrimmon pay Fishel $50 and take back the animals. But Fishel held fast to his demand for a full refund, also realizing that his new friend was really a McCrimmon accomplice. When a reporter for the *Los Angeles Times* visited Gertrude the next day she denied knowing Fishel, "Never heard of the man in my life. Oh, yes, I deal in horses and if the suckers will bite they deserve to get skinned." Also, she told the journalist she did not know any Dr. Crandall or any David Low.[23]

Mary Mayer

One who used the fake injury scam was Mrs. Mary Mayer. Authorities in New York were said to be searching, in March 1893, for the relatives of a mysterious old woman. Mayer appeared in Brooklyn about one month earlier and claimed to have been accidentally thrown from a sleigh in which she was driving with her son. "She was refined and lady-like in appearance, was well dressed, and apparently about sixty-five years of age," said an account. A Mrs. Lent took the woman and gave her room and board for a time and afterward Police Matron Elizabeth Barling of Brooklyn took her home to live with her for a time. Seemingly somewhat demented, it was thought her reason might have been impaired by the injuries she received when thrown from the sleigh. A letter was sent to Rochester to an address where she said her son lived — but it turned out to be a post office. Mayer said she resided in St. Louis but no such person was known there at the address she gave. Continued investigation by the police produced a letter from Mrs. E. L. Mix of West Hartford, Connecticut, in which the writer said a woman answering that description had come to her with the same story, and was taken into her home. Later Mayer disappeared from that home with several items and $10 cash. Mix said her guest had a scar over her right eye and a broken joint on the third finger of the left hand, which matched the physical characteristics of the Brooklyn guest. Barling went to Justice Haggerty and showed him the letter. He told her to bring Mayer to court and committed her to jail for further examination. During her court appearance, observed a reporter, "She made a great outcry and almost went into hysterics."[24]

Jane Doe

Police in Cleveland, Ohio were on the watch in late 1897 for a swindler working the injury scam in that city. One night she showed up at a Denison Avenue home late in the evening, claiming to have fallen out of her carriage and injured her leg. She remained at that house for a week, as a guest, and then, after borrowing $50 from the householder fled. She was reported to have operated the same con in several northern Ohio towns, including Seville, Worcester, Doylestown, and Median. Invariably her introduction was to represent that she had injured herself in a mishap with her carriage and was in need of temporary relief. Among the many aliases she had used were included Mrs. Anna May, Mrs. Mary Kock, Mrs. General Poole, and Mrs. General Whitaker.[25]

Maude Myrtle Johnson

Mrs. Maude Myrtle Johnson stood trial in Seattle in December 1909 accused of obtaining $600 from the Seattle Electric Company by false pretenses, and who was described as a "professional damage claimant." John Ferron, a claims agent with the Oakland California Traction Company, took the stand to say he knew the defendant as Mrs. S. T. Brown who sent for him on July 4, 1909, relative to an injury she said she had sustained in that city. A reporter commented, "In the courtroom here, Mrs. Johnson carried a baby boy, which the police say she bought from an incubator company here, but which Mrs. Johnson declares is her own child, born in Kansas City, December 7, 1908."[26]

Many years later a news account reported Johnson had been arrested and placed in jail in Portland, Oregon in May 1922. "Known to police and railroad claim agents throughout the United States a few years ago as Queen of Fakers, Mrs. Johnson is said to have swindled railroad companies out of thousands of dollars through her ability to fake injuries while riding on railroad trains," said the account. "According to the police, she is able to throw her joints out of place, tear ribs loose and cough up blood at will." One of her tricks, it was alleged, was to place a bottle against one of her ribs and then to throw herself on it at any sudden jerk of the train, tearing the rib loose. Not only could she seemingly injure herself in that fashion, but the trick would also cause a hemorrhage. Using such scams, she was estimated to have received damage claims to the total of $200,000; the smallest claim granted her was $2,800, the largest $32,000. Reportedly, she had fleeced 19 railroads in that manner. Johnson used over $150,000 of that money to produce female theatrical road shows and motion pictures in the northwest United States. But, with respect to those endeavors, failure followed failure and loss followed loss. A final theatrical endeavor was launched by Johnson but it too ran out of money with the troupe becoming stranded in Portland. Entirely out of funds, a series of bad checks totaling $232.50 were passed on local stores, allegedly, by Johnson. Her arrest quickly followed. Prison, though, did not seem to suit Johnson because, said a journalist, "A nervous breakdown from remorse requires constant medical attention upon her. Extreme leniency will be dished out to her."[27]

Anna A. Sturia

When Mrs. Anna A. Sturia was arraigned in General Sessions Court in June 1910 it was the climax of a series of distressing accidents that seemed to beset this "comfortable-looking, middle-aged woman of

Hazlet, N. J." According to the records of the Alliance for the Prevention of Accident Frauds, she had fallen down numerous stairways in the previous five years, so numerous that the District Attorney's office was inclined to think she made a business of it. Thus, an indictment was filed on June 1, charging her with grand larceny in the second degree in that she accepted $500 from the New York Central and Hudson River Railroad on November 17, 1906, as damages for an injury she said she had sustained in falling down the steps of the station at 125th Street and Park Avenue some weeks before. The indictment did not deny the fall, but asserted the injury was not caused thereby, and that Sturia was making use of a chronic complaint. In the original complaint by the Alliance their report pointed to some dozen claims initiated by Sturia, filed in various States, and covering the past four years. For the most part they were filed against railroad companies and usually for falls. Once it was a complaint against a department store (they settled with Sturia) and on another occasion it was a claim over a "severe jarring" on a ferryboat. Damages paid to the woman ranged from $50 to $1,000. Secretary Arnold of the Alliance commented that when Sturia ventured a second suit recently against the Pennsylvania Railroad, lawyers for the railroad pointed silently to the earlier proceedings, with the result the second suit was "hastily dropped."[28]

Ellis Glenn (Cora Alice Cunningham)

Cora probably faked her own death in order to collect on a life insurance policy and went on to commit various forgeries, but the bizarre circumstances of her life — posing as a man, passing successfully as a man even to the point of spending some weeks in a holding cell with her true gender undetected — overshadowed any criminal activities. Cora married Melville Rader in Addison, West Virginia. Later he sued for divorce but before it was granted he was murdered by William Cole, who later died in prison. Then she married Frank Palmer in Philadelphia, by whom she had a son who was then living with grandparents in Addison. After deserting him Cora married a railroad brakeman named Ross, in Parkersburg, West Virginia and later went to Florida where she was married to William Treadway in Cedar Keys. It was there in Florida that Cora Cunningham ceased to exist. Her death was a mystery to her family but her alleged husband at the time (Treadway, whom the family had never met and who likely did not exist, was likely a fictitious person invented by Cora) sent her trunk home, and in it were her clothing and various other personal items. Cora's mother Mrs. Martha Miller sent a tombstone to Cedar Keys to be erected over her daughter's grave there. Treadway was the person who informed the family of Cora's death. From the ashes of Cora's death rose two new people — E. B. (Bert) Glenn, a man, and Ellis Glenn, also a man.[29]

It was in the summer of 1898 that Ellis first appeared on the scene in Montgomery County, Illinois. She appeared in the guise of being an agent of a sewing machine company; Ellis was duly accredited by the company's representative in St. Louis and dressed like a man "and to all intents and appearances was of the masculine gender." She posed as a man and mingled easily with men to the extent that her sex was never questioned by her friends and associates. Selling sewing machines out of Hillsboro, Illinois, Ellis rented a room in the home of James Duke, who lived in the small town of Butler, four miles from Hillsboro, with his two daughters Ella 24 and Nellie 26. Within three months of her arrival at the Duke home Ellis was regarded as virtually a member of the family, with Nellie addressing him affectionately as "brother" while Ella had accepted him as a suitor for her hand. In presenting herself as a man Ellis drank a little, but not to excess, played cards and games of dice with the boys, used mild cuss words, told suggestive stories on occasion, with enough suggestion to please a male audience.[30]

In her role as sewing machine agent Ellis had plenty of opportunity to select her prospective fraud victims from among the wealthy residents of the county. She settled on two of Montgomery County's wealthiest residents, brothers John and Duncan McLean. Her scheme was an old one used by many confidence artists of obtaining signatures of prospective victims under some pretext and either using the originals or forging them to notes of large amounts. Ellis got the two signatures and forged them to a note for $2,000. It was her intention to discount the note and leave the area. However, the man she presented the note to in order to discount it was familiar with the brothers' ways of conducting their affairs. John signed all his business documents but his daughter signed his name to all other papers and correspondence, due to some slight physical problem her father had. Ellis had obtained John's signature from a letter not knowing he really had the daughter's signature of the name, and not the one that would be affixed to a note. That error led to Ellis being arrested and indicted for forgery. At the time of the arrest Ellis was engaged to marry Ella on October 8, 1899. Mr. Duke signed bonds for the court appearance of the alleged forger after her arrest, which got Ellis out of jail. She was taken back into the Duke home as a boarder on the same close relationship she had held with the family before the accusation of crime was made against her.[31]

Ellis remained with the Dukes almost until the day of the wedding. But on October 6, Ellis went to St. Louis saying she had business to do with her employer but would be back on October 7, the day before the wedding. However, on October 7, a letter arrived for Ella from a T. H. Terry saying Ellis had drowned when she fell from a barge near St. Louis. Terry claimed to be a friend of Ellis but said not to bother to try and contact him as by the time Ella got the letter Terry would be on his way to tend to a sick brother in Charleston, West Virginia. Due to the odd nature of the supposed death the Dukes investigated further. Contact with the postmaster in Charleston revealed that all Terry's letters came through Charleston, from Paducah, Kentucky. Duke contacted the police there and flyers containing a description of Ellis (who they believed to be Terry) were circulated. On October 20 the body of a floater was found in the river near Paducah and was promptly identified as that of Ellis Glenn, by a man who said his name was T. H. Terry. Recognizing her from the flyer, police in Paducah took Terry into custody and wired Hillsboro authorities. Sheriff Cassady went to Paducah and identified Terry as Glenn. Agreeing to return with the sheriff, Ellis was held in jail at Hillsboro for four weeks before she pled guilty to the charge of forgery and was sentenced to an indefinite term at Chester. Two days before the prisoner was to be taken to jail Ellis was visited by Duke, on November 23, and, said an account, "even up to that time there were no suspicions of her sex, even among her fellow-prisoners in jail."[32]

When Ellis was taken to prison at Chester she was there submitted to the customary prison regulations with her hair being clipped short. Then she was taken to the bathroom by the attendants for the usual preliminary bath whereupon her sex was discovered. Prison officials were shocked. The prison physician was called in and he officially proclaimed the prisoner Ellis Glenn to be a woman. As there was no accommodation at Chester for female convicts, it was necessary to send her back to Hillsboro to decide what to do. In the end it was decided she needed to be tried again, because a male person had been convicted. At first Ellis promised to again plead guilty, as a woman, and accept a light sentence. However, she changed her mind and entered a plea of not guilty. In the meantime the authorities in Parkersburg, where she was wanted on a forgery charge, had picked up her trail when the publicity and flyers with a description were circulated after the faked death of Ellis. Before she was retried in Hillsboro she was sent back to the West Virginia city.[33]

It was in June 1901 that Ellis came to trial in Parkersburg on a forgery charge with respect to a deed of trust that was then some two years old. Several people came forward to positively identify her as Cora Alice Cunningham, who was born and raised in Addison, West Virginia. Among those were B. D. Hutchinson, United States Commissioner in Addison and a prominent merchant. Ellis Glenn had a peculiarly shaped scar on the top of her head, as a result of a burn; Cora had an identical scar. Officials believed Cora faked her death to defraud insurance companies and took to male attire to more perfectly disguise herself and avoid detection. It was a theory that accounted for the fact Ellis, somewhat mysteriously, always had money at her command. However, those officials had no evidence on that point but were said to be contacting insurance companies. While she was in disguise in the Parkersburg area she went under the name of E. B. (Bert) Glenn.[34]

At the trial one that testified was Mrs. George A. Hoover, with whom Bert boarded for a time in Parkersburg, and whose daughter Bert was engaged to marry. Hoover said that once while cleaning Bert's room she found a gray dress, a woman's hat and some feminine underwear. When asked what explanation Bert gave for the garments she told Hoover they had belonged to his dead mother.[35]

Another witness was Ernie Byers, who had roomed with Bert Glenn all the time he lived in Williamstown (near Parkersburg) and who said he never knew Glenn was not a man. He had visited gambling dens, saloons, and other such places with Glenn many times and said Glenn always acted like a man in every way. Among the jobs she held while masquerading as a man in the Parkersburg area were house painter, sign painter, carpenter, bricklayer, butcher, barber, teamster, real estate agent, horse-trainer, paper hanger, and plumber. At the end of her trial in Parkersburg, in July 1903, the jury was split evenly, six to convict, six to acquit. She remained out on bail until June 1905 when the case was finally dropped. Glenn was allowed to depart free of bond.[36]

Less than three months later Ellis, again masquerading as a man, was arrested in Millington, Michigan on a forgery charge, allegedly having fleeced a local farmer out of $500. After her 1903 trial Glenn got a job clerking in a small store near Parkersburg, as a woman of course, and befriended a woman customer. Eventually, she convinced that woman to turn over a deed to a house and lot to her. Then Glenn went off to a town in Michigan some 200 miles from Parkersburg where she passed herself off as the owner of the house and lot, and also again pretended to be a man. She arranged to trade her property to a local farmer for his real estate, plus $500 in cash. Once she got the $500 Glenn disappeared and returned to Parkersburg, where she resumed life as a woman. Not long after that she returned to Michigan, where she was arrested when a sheriff identified her from a scar that formed part of her circulated description. Ellis Glenn was tried and found guilty and sentenced to the woman's prison in Michigan under an indeterminate sentence not to exceed 14 years.[37]

Louise Shaw

New York City police arrested Louise R. Shaw (also known as Bock, Collins, Pattan, Marie Michelet and Mrs. Grace Henderson) on November 24, 1882 after she fell into a trap set by police. Earlier that month she had been hired for the position of governess in the family of a Mr. Davis, seeming to be competent for the job and speaking several languages fluently. On November 14 the governess disappeared with jewelry, watches and other property of the Davis family worth more than $2,500. When police investigated they found she had left the Windsor Hotel, Jersey City, New Jersey, on November 10, where she had registered as Mrs. Collins, a supposedly wealthy Englishwoman. All the hotel owners had to secure a debt of $64 was a valise filled with dirty underwear. Information there led police to a publisher in New York where she had applied for a position as a translator of French and German. She didn't get that job but was hired as a book canvasser and given the district of Orange, New Jersey; she gave her name as Mrs. Grace Henderson of Tottenville, Staten Island. Then a letter for Marie Michelet came to the Davis home, postmarked Philadelphia. The writer was a well-known businessman who had a one-week fling with Louise and who promised to aid the police, when they contacted him and assured him he would not be exposed. He met her in August on an ocean liner coming to New York from Europe and they became intimate. After spending a week in New York he went home to his wife in Philadelphia but continued to correspond with her — he knew her as Louise R.

Bock. With the help of the businessman a set-up was arranged whereby Louise was arrested when she went to a predetermined post office to supposedly get a letter from him. In her possession when she was arrested was jewelry valued at $1,000 that Davis identified as belonging to his daughter.[38]

Her history, from her and from police records, revealed she was 27 years old, "swarthy, lady-like, and well educated. She speaks French, German, Spanish and Italian well, and knows the ways of good society." After getting married when she was young to a German named Bock she experienced ill treatment from him and left him. She claimed she was to receive a large sum of money but it was then tied up in litigation. Then she came to New York in July 1882 and soon thereafter called Knevals & Ransom, prominent lawyers in Manhattan. Louise told Ransom "a pathetic story" about her child being stolen from her in England and of her journey to America to try and retrieve the child. To support her story she gave Ransom a letter that appeared to be from an English lawyer well known to Ransom. In it Mrs. Bock was recommended as a desirable client; Ransom promised to interest himself in her case. As he was about to escort her out of the office she mentioned she was embarrassed because she had just lost her purse in a cab, which contained all her money and her checkbook. Courteously, Ransom loaned her $40. Not much later a messenger boy from Louise's hotel showed up at the lawyer's office with a note from her asking if Ransom could loan her another $50 as she urgently needed some new clothes. He did. Bock next used her charms on a gentleman connected with the White Star line of ocean steamers and, said an account, "on a spurious check and by plausible representation, backed up by a reference to Ransom, obtained $100." That man's wife was displeased with what she considered to be Louise's "undue familiarity" with her husband in the notes she sent him and went so far as to complain to the police. By then, though, it was too late as the police learned Louise had sailed for Europe on July 15. In addition, "They ascertained that she had lived as Mrs. Collins in West Twelfth Street and as Mrs. Pattan in two places in Brooklyn. In these places she was successful in petty swindles and thefts."[39]

No sooner had Louise arrive back in Europe than she turned around and came back to New York on the same line of steamers, arriving in September 1882. On September 19 she called at Mrs. March's home for working girls, representing she wanted shelter as thieves had stolen her money. That night a Mrs. Elliott and her daughter, just arrived from

England, were sent to March's for lodging but the place was full so they were sent on to another lodging house. Bock overheard the conversation and the next morning called on Elliott, pretending to be an envoy from March and that she had been asked to show Elliott every courtesy. Bock learned the newcomer had come to America to set up a business as a seamstress and that Mr. A. Wilson of Atlanta had control of her money. After obtaining Elliott's baggage checks Bock went to the terminal to collect the luggage, pretending to be Elliott and making enough of a fuss to insure recognition later. That done she telegraphed Wilson, as Elliott, in Atlanta to say she was sick and needed money. Wilson replied, directing her to a New York bank to get money. After presenting the telegram there they gave her a check for $100. Returning to the baggage terminal she induced an employee there to go with her to an office, and to vouch for her identity, thereby allowing her to cash the check.[40]

The next stop for Louise was to an employment office for servants from which she was sent to the home of banker Davis, whose wife wanted a governess. Bock went there under the name of Marie Michelet and gave as a reference Mrs. E. Collins of the Windsor Hotel, Jersey City. Louise had lived there as Collins and when she received the Davis letter of inquiry she gave herself a glowing reference. At her trial, for stealing the Davis family jewelry a plea of insanity or kleptomania was made by her lawyer and she was sent to the Utica (New York) Asylum where she remained for 20 months.[41]

On March 6, 1885, Mrs. Jeannette Vandarstain, a wealthy California resident, sailed for Europe. A fellow passenger, Louise Shaw, struck up an acquaintance during the voyage and upon her arrival had won Jeanette's confidence to the extent that in some fashion she got control of one or more of Jeannette's trunks and made off with them. Police in Liverpool, England conducted a search but found nothing. New York police were notified and Detective Golden groped in the dark until the mysterious disappearance from Busch's Hotel in Hoboken, New Jersey on April 23 of the "well dressed wealthy widow, Mrs. L. V. Black" came to light. Golden suspected the trunk left behind was Vandarstain's and with Bock's photograph established she had been Jeannette's fellow passenger on the ship. Some articles in the trunk were marked J. V. and they corresponded with the list sent by Liverpool police. Reportedly, Bock was once convicted in England on a charge of having obtained 80 pounds Sterling from the Lord Mayor of London. Her plea there had been one of insanity and she was sent to Camberwell Prison, said to be a "lenient punishment" that was "secured through the influence of her brother and friends."⁴²

Mrs. Frank Wiborg

Mrs. Frank Wiborg, wife of an Assistant Secretary of Commerce and Labor in President Taft's administration and a niece of General Sherman, appeared in Federal District Court before Judge Hunt in New York in October 1913 and pled guilty to the charge of having failed to declare dutiable goods worth $4,000, which she brought with her from Europe on the liner *Mauretania* on September 5. She was accompanied in court by her eldest daughter "and both women were heavily veiled. Mrs. Wiborg was required to remove her veil for the proceedings." Her lawyer, John Stanchfield, told the Court he was permitting his client to plead guilty against his better judgment. She was not all that strong, he said, and he did not believe she could stand the strain of a trial. After Wiborg entered her formal plea Stanchfield "introduced evidence to show that a prison sentence might endanger Mrs. Wiborg's life." When the defendant returned from Europe, explained Stanchfield to the court, she had with her 20 trunks and it was impossible for her to remember all the goods they contained; there was no intention to defraud. Stanchfield introduced a number of letters attesting to the high moral character of the defendant, including one from Henry W. Taft, brother of ex–President William Taft. Judge Hunt declared he knew Wiborg to be a woman of high moral character and he was convinced that imprisonment would not be necessary to satisfy justice in this case. The court then imposed a fine of $1,750, which Wiborg paid at once.⁴³

Mrs. Whitney Warren

The Collector of the Port of New York, Dudley Malone, announced at the Custom House on December 10, 1915, that he had ordered the baggage of the socially prominent Mrs. Whitney Warren, wife of the architect, who returned from Europe on November 15 on the French liner *Espague*, to be seized and forfeited. He also ordered the paperwork on the case be sent to the U.S. District Attorney for evaluation to determine if there was an attempt made to defraud the Federal Government by Warren and by Miss Evelyn Byrd Buren, who owned part of the confiscated luggage but was not a passenger on the liner. Upon arrival the declaration made by Warren and handed to the Customs official stated the total value of the dutiable articles in her possession, including those belonging to Buren, was $1,500. After an examination at the Appraiser's Stores 26 gowns in her luggage were valued at $6,148. The forfeitable value of the goods was $13,389, which was the home value plus the duty.[44]

Warren's gowns were contained in five trunks and were not itemized, nor were any bills shown for the goods purchased in Paris. After Customs Inspector Harry Pfeiffer had examined the baggage he did not feel satisfied with the amount declared by Warren, $1,500, and reported it to his superior. It was then after six in the evening and the trunks were ordered to be sent to the Appraiser's Stores for examination. On November 16 and 17 the 26 gowns were appraised by Charles Riotte, the government's "gown expert," at more than $7,000. Present at that examination of her gowns were Warren and her lawyer, James F. Curtis, a former Assistant Secretary of the United States Treasury, who took the matter up with the Treasury Department in Washington, where it was referred back to Collector of the Port Malone. After a conference at the Custom House the Collector ordered a second appraisal, at which the value was put at $6,148.[45]

Ida Miller Blighton

On October 2, 1915, Mrs. Ida Miller Blighton of New York, who said she wrote fiction under the name of Alvina Howels, was arrested on a charge of having obtained $6,000 from Mrs. Giles of the Hotel Iroquois and $300 from Mrs. M. L. Simons, wife of a British army officer, on the pretense it was to be invested in war stocks. According to police there were a number of similar charges against her. Simons told police she was introduced to Blighton in an uptown shop. During their conversation she mentioned her husband was with the British army in France, whereupon Ida ingratiated herself with Simons by casting the horoscope of the husband and declared he was safe and would go through the war unharmed. Other women with complaints against Ida also told of meeting her in shops or restaurants where she sought out women with money and once a conversation had been struck up with them explained how much money could be made by the judicious use of war stocks. Simons explained she was anxious to make money in order to pay a visit to her husband in France and therefore gave Blighton $100. On the following day, said Simons, Ida phoned to tell her the stock had soared in value and her first day's profits were $700. When Ida suggested another $200 invested might run the profits into the thousands, Simons quickly got $200 more from the bank and turned it over to Blighton. Since that time, Simons had been unable to locate Ida. Finally, she complained to the police.[46]

15

Various Frauds — Ellen Peck

Ellen E. Peck was described by New York Police Inspector Thomas Byrnes as an ordinary sharper whose small exploits in the area of fraud were scarcely worthy of notice prior to 1878. But when she managed to swindle soap maker B. T. Babbitt out of $19,000 that year she came to be looked upon as an operator of some talent. Babbitt had been robbed a short time before of something like $200,000 by dishonest employees — his bookkeepers Beckwith and Lewis. After their arrest Peck visited the soap manufacturer in the role of a private detective, representing that she was in the possession of valuable information concerning property owned by the clerks that could easily be sued for or seized. Falling for her story Babbitt advanced her the $19,000 Ellen demanded only to afterward discover her information was false and worthless. Later Peck was indicted for the Babbitt affair but every time the case came up for trial she was taken very sick, until the court lost patience and told her the next time the trial was scheduled she had to appear, or forfeit her bail. Then she suddenly became insane and was sent to an asylum in Pennsylvania. Her counsel was able to get the complainant to agree to sue her in a civil suit, with that suit to take precedence over the criminal charge. Once that agreement was in place Peck, with the same suddenness with which she lost her wits, recovered her reason, left the asylum and returned to New York City.[1]

On July 18, 1879, the confidence woman was tried and acquitted in the Kings County Court of Sessions, on an indictment charging her with obtaining several thousand dollars worth of diamonds and jewelry under false pretenses from Loyance Langer of New York. Peck was arrested again, on September 16, 1881, at her home at 307 Putnam Avenue, Brooklyn, having been accused of defrauding John H. Johnson, a New York jeweler, of items in the amount of $150. Johnson alleged that when Ellen selected the jewelry she paid $25 down and represented herself as Mrs. Eliza Knight, giving as a reference a bank in New York. On making inquiries at the bank Johnson was told that Knight had an account there and he therefore let her have the articles. Subsequently, though, he learned the Knight who had credit at the bank was an entirely different person from the one who bought his jewelry.[2]

Yet again, Peck was arrested at her home, this time on December 3, 1881, by New York police detectives, on a warrant issued by Justice Bixby at the Tombs Police Court, in which she was charged with obtaining money by false pretenses on a complaint made by Samuel W. Pinzer, a New York City patent pill manufacturer. Allegedly Peck defrauded him out of $1,050 by falsely pretending she could make a fortune for him by speculating in the stock market. Pinzer first met her in the summer of 1881, as Mrs. Elizabeth Knight, when she told him that by investing $8,000 in Chicago and Northwestern Railroad bonds, under her direction, he could realize in a few months more than $30,000. One of the reasons she could accomplish such gains, he said she told him, was that she was in the confidence of several large operators in these bonds with whom she planned to cooperate and by their combined efforts they would move the stock to such an extent that huge profits would be realized. Because of her own lack of capital, she continued, she was looking for two partners who were each able and willing to advance one-third of the money required, while she would supply the other third. After several interviews had been conducted with respect to the proposition she got Pinzer interested in the scheme and told him that a Dr. Fitch in Brooklyn had agreed to invest one-third of the needed capital.[3]

On August 18 papers were drawn up to formalize the agreement, with the three parties agreeing to form a pool of $8,000 to be used by Peck and her brokers in the manipulation of the stocks named. From time to time Pinzer advanced sums of money to Peck and received from Mrs. Knight a number of letters outlining encouraging results. When Pinzer had over $1,000 invested he began to make more demanding inquiries in regard to the manner in which the money was being invested. Peck responded that she was worried the scheme would not be a success and went so far as to accuse him of having revealed her plans to Wall

Street operators who had thereby been able to frustrate her plans. Such a response aroused Pinzer's suspicions and when he made inquiries at the brokers through whom Knight pretended to operate for the benefit of the pool he found they knew nothing about her. He then wrote to Peck and arranged a meeting with her at the Astor House where he demanded his money back; she laughed at him. Pinzer then went to the police to report a fraud. From his description of the woman one of the police detectives recognized Elizabeth Knight as being Ellen Peck, and she was arrested.[4]

Another swindle by Peck around this time involved her in obtaining $21,000 worth of diamonds from John D. Grady, a diamond dealer, by representing that she could find customers for the precious stones among the ladies of her acquaintance. She was arrested and spent some time in jail in Brooklyn on this charge before being tried and acquitted. Another charge made against her was for fleecing a wealthy Cuban out of $12,000 worth of diamonds by false pretenses. From Sohmer and Company she was charged with having obtained a piano on December 16, 1880, by fraudulent representation. Ellen Peck was about 50 years old in 1880.[5]

Early in March 1884, under the name of Mrs. Elizabeth Knight, she was introduced to diamond broker John Bough, by another broker. She represented herself to be a rich speculator in jewels who would be likely to call upon Bough to obtain precious stones that her customers might require. About a month later she called on him to say one of her friends wanted to buy a diamond ring. After going through his stock she selected one worth $75 and was allowed to take it away. Peck returned the next day and paid for the ring, steadfastly declining to accept the commission broker Bough felt she was entitled to. Ellen paid another visit to Bough on April 28, 1884 to explain that a very rich friend of hers was going to dine with her that evening and she wanted some jewels to wear and to show, in the hope of selling them to her friend. A pair of diamond earrings and two diamond rings, worth $400 in total, were selected. Also, she told him, if she could not sell them to her friend she would buy them for herself. With a promise she would be back the next day with the money she left the store with the jewelry. Bough never saw her again. When he went to the address he had on file for her he found it to be phoney. At that point he complained to the police, who once again recognized that Knight was Peck.[6]

Police found the jewelry had been pawned for $180 in July, by an unknown person. However, on August 1, a woman answering Peck's description went to Simpson's pawnshop where she told Simpson she was very rich and recently an unknown person had stolen some of her jewels. She described them, the ones taken from Bough. Her story continued that for inexplicable reasons the thief had mailed her the pawn ticket and presenting that to Simpson, demanded her jewelry be returned. Simpson refused. Peck then hired a lawyer and launched a civil lawsuit to gain possession of the items. When that case came to trial on September 11, New York City police detectives were among those in attendance. They listened to Peck swear she had bought the diamonds in October 1883 from a man named George B. Thomas and that she had paid $100 for them. Under oath, Thomas corroborated her story and later that day after court the police trailed Thomas. After obtaining arrest warrants for the pair on charges of perjury and grand larceny, they were arrested separately in September. Thomas made a full confession. According to Thomas he had known Peck for a long time and had frequently borrowed money from her. Just before her suit for the recovery of the jewels he had asked her for a loan of $20. She then told him her story and that if he would swear in court as she would instruct him he would receive the $20 to keep as well as another $50. He agreed.[7]

Released on bail on the perjury and larceny charge involving Bough, around November 23, Peck remained free only until December 6 when she was arrested on a charge of larceny made against her by Mrs. Ann McConnell of New York. McConnell advertised in the newspaper that she had money to loan on good security. On September 20, 1884, McConnell received a visit from a Mrs. Crosby (possibly Peck's maiden name) who said she had seen the advertisement and wished to borrow $250. McConnell was favorably impressed by the appearance, "innocent bearing" and mild manner of her visitor and the loan was made, with a chattel mortgage executed on her furniture as security. Crosby gave her real address, 307 Putnam Avenue, Brooklyn and agreed that at the end of the loan's 30-day period she would repay the $250 plus $75 in interest. Just two weeks later McConnell read of the arrest of Peck on the perjury and larceny charge and was alarmed to read that Peck lived at 307 Putnam Avenue. She called at the Tombs and saw Peck, confirming her worst fears. Straightaway McConnell went to the Tombs Police Court and asked for a warrant for Peck's arrest on a charge of larceny. However she was told she would have to wait until the 30 day loan period expired and Ellen was in default. While she waited she learned there were at least half a dozen other chattel mortgages all executed on the same furniture. Finally the warrant was issued and Peck arrested in this case. At her examination her successful defense was that she had simply defaulted on a loan agreement and that was a civil matter that could not be construed as a larceny. The judge agreed. In spite of all the dubious transactions she had been involved in, and despite the number of times she had been arrested, Ellen Peck had still never in her life been convicted of any crime or misdemeanor.[8]

The next arrest of Peck took place on January 5, 1885, on a warrant procured on the complaint of Mrs. Emily P. Bissell of New York. Bissell alleged Peck obtained a loan of $574 from her the previous September, payable in two months. As security Bissell received a chattel mortgage on the furniture at 307 Putnam Avenue. That mortgage instrument also contained the signature of Richard K. Peck, her husband. After the two months, of course, the money was not repaid and Bissell foreclosed the mortgage held on the household items. Deputy Sheriff H. A. Middleton, of Kings County, was sent to seize the furniture but he was prevented by Richard Peck, who said the furniture was his property and not that of his wife. When the Sheriff showed him the mortgage instrument with his signature affixed to it, Richard declared his signature was a forgery and that he knew nothing about it. Then he showed Middleton everything in the house that was owned by his wife. Middleton seized those items but when they were sold at auction they brought only $34 in total. Bissell then swore out a warrant for Peck's arrest with Detective Timothy Golden taking her into custody. She was held at the Tombs Prison when she was unable to raise $1,000 bail. Ellen remained there until a conviction, on another charge, was registered against her for the first time.[9]

When Peck was convicted of forgery in the third degree by a jury on May 28, 1885, a reporter commented, "After defiantly tramping around the borders of State prison for more than seven years, slipping again and again from the clutches of the law through good luck and legal technicalities Mrs. Ellen Peck was yesterday found guilty...." Eleven indictments were then pending against her in the District Attorney's office. This case represented only her second appearance in front of a jury, having been acquitted on the earlier occasion. Besides the indictments, she then also had 17 civil suits pending against her, all growing out of her confidence game operations. According to a reporter, "Her remarkable police record has made her notorious. All the jurors summoned knew of her, and singularly enough, most of them in connection with some different charge than the one on which she was being tried." A news account described her as follows: "She is a sharp-looking little woman, with a composed, absolutely colorless countenance and a cynical smile. Modestly dressed and moderately perfumed, she looked altogether more like a well-to-do country schoolmistress than a woman acquainted with the devious paths of crime in a great city. Her husband did not come near the court room all day."[10]

She was convicted of executing and uttering a forged bond to secure a $3,000 mortgage obtained from the Mutual Life Insurance Company, and represented to be on real estate in the name of herself and her husband Richard at 307 Putnam Avenue. That was in September 1882. The man Peck induced to sign as her husband was convict George Burnett (serving time in Sing Sing prison on unrelated matters at the time of Ellen's trial). Subsequent to the Mutual Life transaction Peck procured another mortgage (for $4,000) on the Putnam Avenue property from the executors of the estate of Francis Mangan, late of Brooklyn. Burnett had lived for years in Peck's home on Putnam Avenue under the name of Dr. Lawrence. He used to sit at the table every day with Richard Peck and was said to be on "quite intimate" terms with him. While her lawyer was summing up, said a reporter, "Mrs. Peck did some good, quiet acting while her lawyer was talking. She sobbed a little and buried her face in her handkerchief, but the well spring of her emotions failed to respond with tears." Jurors returned with a guilty verdict "inside of three minutes." Detective Timothy Golden, who had personally arrested her 11 times over the years, was in court to hear the verdict and later told a reporter, "She is a dangerous little woman and the community is much safer with her behind bars." Ellen Peck was sentenced to the penitentiary at Blackwell's Island for a term of 4.5 years.[11]

Appearing before Judge Cowing in court in New York in November 1897, Peck was sentenced to five years in prison after being convicted of the larceny of $1,200 worth of jewelry from Christopher Gini of New York. As security for the items she gave the jeweler a $1,000 bond that proved to be worthless.[12]

"A little gray-haired woman, dressed all in decent black and wearing the bonnet of our grandmothers," was locked up by the police on November 28, 1908, on the charge of getting $2,000 on false pretenses from the property development firm of Normand & Wilson of New York. Only a few of the older members of the New York police force recognized the "quiet-mannered" old woman as Ellen Peck, "the confidence queen" of some 20 years earlier. She admitted then to the age of 70.[13]

Two weeks previously Assistant District Attorneys Kresel and Bosler were assigned to investigate an alleged swindling scheme that had been worked on the firm of Normand & Wilson by a woman calling herself Eliza Knight. It was a story that had its beginnings in 1795 when James Monroe, later U.S. President, was Governor of Virginia. In that year Governor Monroe granted to Alexander Walcott 650,000 acres of land that supposedly belonged to the state of Virginia. It became subject to a border dispute between Virginia and Kentucky and in 1850 the courts declared the land belonged to Kentucky. That meant Walcott's title to the land was invalid and persons to whom Walcott and his heirs sold portions of the tract had no title. In spite of that fact deeds to parts of the Walcott tract continued to pass through the hands of many people. One came to Amelia O. Schelling, who conveyed her right to Eliza Knight in 1892. That deed was registered in Kentucky by Knight. Between 1892 and 1908, Knight made conveyances of parts of that land to various people and in September 1908 she went to Normand & Wilson and proposed they develop a portion of her land. Peck agreed to turn over title to them and to take the purchase price in the form of stock to be issued by a to-be formed company to develop it. The developers agreed. On the following day, though, Peck returned to the firm's office to say she was in urgent need of money and offered to mortgage her property for $2,000. Normand & Wilson advanced her the money only to subsequently find her title to be worthless. When Peck was arrested and confronted with the evidence, said a reporter, "She confessed at once. She admitted she knew that the supposed title to the Walcott tract was worthless." Peck was sentenced to Auburn prison for swindling for a term of 10 years.[14]

Governor John A. Dix of New York commuted Peck's sentence in December 1911 after she had served about two years, saying he thought Ellen was then too old (said to be 82) to any longer be a menace to society. Lawyer Robert J. Haire, and others in New York, had been seeking a commutation of sentence since her committal. When a petition for her release reached Governor Hughes in 1909 he refused to grant it, declaring, "Old age is no excuse for crime." Seemingly coming to crime only when she was about 50 years old, next to nothing was ever reported of this woman's first half century of life. One account said she was born

Nellie Crosby in Woodville, New Hampshire in 1829 and as a young schoolteacher in New York and Connecticut she was once described as "demure in manner and faultless in face and form." She married Richard W. Peck of New York City and was the mother of three children. Inspector Byrnes of the New York police once estimated Peck's swindles brought her $1 million in total. Some earlier swindles not previously mentioned included an 1887 allegation of her swindling Dr. Jason Marks of New York City out of $20,000 in money and jewels. In 1894 she was said to have posed as Mrs. Mary Hansen, wife of Admiral Johann Carll Hansen of the Danish Navy, and to have lived luxuriously in Brooklyn by borrowing money freely on the unsuspecting Admiral's good name. Shortly after that, using a similar method, she was alleged to have scammed Dr. Christopher Lott, a Brooklyn physician, out of $10,000 over time. Another victim was said to have been a nurse by the name of Miss Nellie Shea.[15]

Time proved Peck was not as harmless as Dix surmised. She was accused in June 1914 (when she was around 84) of swindling a Central American out of $1,000. When A. A. Garcia, Consul from Guatemala in New York, tried to recover the money of his compatriot, she turned her wits on him and tried to relieve him of $2,000 of his money. Some months earlier Peck had been a passenger on a steamer leaving Vera Cruz, Mexico, as was Jose Menendez of Guatemala, who was carrying $10,000. After making his acquaintance Peck spoke of her mining interests in Mexico and her land holdings in Kentucky (the Walcott tract again) as well as the problems of being a lone woman with no one to help her manage her affairs. Menendez finally handed over $1,000 to Ellen for an "interest in the mines" with the understanding that he would contribute more money when they arrived in New York. Garcia saved the man from further financial losses by telling him who she really was. But it was found the only way to try and retrieve Menendez's money was through civil action as Peck had been careful to give only her personal note for the $1,000. Through an attorney a civil judgment for the money was entered against Peck but when it came to trying to collect it was found to be difficult to access her property. Peck declared she had no money with which to pay the claim and any real estate she owned was mortgaged to the hilt. As a result Garcia gave up hope of every regaining Menendez's money. Ellen Peck died in 1915.[16]

Chapter Notes

Chapter 1

1. "Spirit photos." *Los Angeles Times*, March 30, 1880, p. 5.
2. *Ibid.*
3. "Exposed." *Los Angeles Times*, April 23, 1887, p. 1.
4. *Ibid.*
5. *Ibid.*
6. "Tricky Elsie." *Los Angeles Times*, April 25, 1887, p. 1.
7. "Elsie Reynolds." *Los Angeles Times*, October 1, 1888, p. 5.
8. "Elsie escapes." *Los Angeles Times*, October 24, 1888, p. 5.
9. "Ghost Elsie." *Los Angeles Times*, November 19, 1888, p. 1.
10. "Spooks." *Los Angeles Times*, January 10, 1889, p. 5; "Airy Elsie's spook fight." *Los Angeles Times*, August 30, 1901, p. 9; "Elsie kissed congregation." *Los Angeles Times*, October 6, 1903, p. 7.
11. "Exposes fake of spookess." *Los Angeles Times*, March 23, 1906, sec 2, p. 4.
12. "Bogus spiritualists exposed." *Washington Post*, April 28, 1888, p. 6.
13. "Chicago's bogus spiritualists." *Washington Post*, April 17, 1888, p. 6.
14. *Ibid.*
15. Wilford Kyrke. "Spook pictures. *Los Angeles Times*, February 15, 1891, p. 15.
16. "Spook tells of fraud." *New York Times*, November 26, 1895, p. 8.
17. "Bares mediums' past." *Washington Post*, June 12, 1907, p. 5.
18. *Ibid.*
19. *Ibid.*
20. "Spook knew finances." *Washington Post*, June 14, 1907, p. 3.
21. "May Pepper appears." *Washington Post*, September 6, 1907, p. 3.
22. "Returns Vanderbilt house." *Washington Post*, November 13, 1907, p. 15; "Fail to find spook bishop." *Washington Post*, November 10, 1908, p. 11.
23. "To drive spiritualist swindlers out of town." *Los Angeles Times*, April 5, 1912, sec 2, p. 1.
24. *Ibid.*
25. *Ibid.*
26. "Spiritist cases are dismissed." *Los Angeles Times*, May 9, 1912, sec 2, p. 11.

Chapter 2

1. "Personal intelligence." *Washington Post*, April 1, 1888, p. 4.
2. "Mme. Diss Debar arraigned." *Washington Post*, April 13, 1888, p. 6.
3. "Dr. Lawrence speaks." *New York Times*, May 14, 1888, p. 5.
4. Frank M. White. "Master crooks and criminals deluxe." *Washington Post*, November 16, 1913, p. MT5.
5. "The madame as witness." *Washington Post*, June 14, 1888, p. 4.
6. "The Diss Debars sentenced." *Washington Post*, June 19, 1888, p. 6.
7. "Madame Diss Debar's plans." *Washington Post*, July 8, 1888, p. 7.
8. *Ibid.*
9. *Ibid.*
10. "Madame Diss Debar released." *Washington Post*, December 19, 1888, p. 3.

11. "Mme. Diss Debar's debts." *Washington Post*, July 15, 1889, p. 2.
12. "A receiver for Mme. Diss Debar." *Washington Post*, July 21, 1889, p. 7.
13. Frank M. White, op. cit.
14. "Believe she is Diss Debar." *Washington Post*, September 19, 1891, p. 6; "Diss Debar under arrest." *Washington Post*, October 22, 1892, p. 7.
15. Frank M. White, op. cit.; "Ann O'D. Diss Debar again out of prison." *Washington Post*, August 14, 1906, p. 4.
16. "Tales of the town." *Washington Post*, December 9, 1900, p. 26.
17. Frank M. White, op. cit.; "Ann O'D. Diss Debar again out of prison," op. cit.
18. "Swindlers are hypnotists." *Washington Post*, October 6, 1901, p. 3.
19. "Diss Debar raves in court." *Washington Post*, October 19, 1901, p. 4.
20. "Ann O'Delia held for trial." *Washington Post*, November 24, 1901, p. 3.
21. Frank M. White, op. cit., p. MT4.
22. *Ibid.*
23. *Ibid.*
24. *Ibid.*
25. *Ibid.*
26. *Ibid.*
27. *Ibid.*
28. *Ibid.*
29. *Ibid.*; "Ann O'D. Diss Debar again out of prison." *Washington Post*, August 14, 1906, p. 4.
30. "Defend their queen." *Washington Post*, March 30, 1907, p. 2.
31. Frank M. White, op. cit., p. MT5; "Third degree for Ann." *Washington Post*, August 29, 1909, p. 11.
32. "Diss Debar is fired." *Washington Post*, August 26, 1909, p. 4.
33. "Look for Diss Debar." *Washington Post*, August 27, 1909, p. 3.
34. "Third degree for Ann." *Washington Post*, August 29, 1909, p. 11.
35. "Chance for Mme. Diss Debarr." *Variety*, September 4, 1909, p. 4; "Mme. Ann Diss DeBar." *Variety*, September 11, 1909, p. 15.
36. Frank M. White, op. cit.

Chapter 3

1. "A matrimonial swindle." *Washington Post*, August 5, 1889, p. 7.
2. "Schemes of a woman." *Washington Post*, August 22, 1889, p. 2.
3. *Ibid.*
4. "Charges with fraud." *Los Angeles Times*, April 24, 1899, p. 11.
5. "Woman indicted for fraud." *Los Angeles Times*, May 3, 1899, p. 7; "Mrs. Ponder sentenced." *Los Angeles Times*, May 4, 1899, p. 10.
6. "Thiebaud Bauer's defense." *Los Angeles Times*, March 11, 1900, sec 4, p. 1.
7. *Ibid.*; "Thiebaud Bauer's story." *Los Angeles Times*, March 13, 1900, p. 10.
8. "Bauer trial concluded." *Los Angeles Times*, March 14, 1900, p. 10.
9. "Matrimonial bunco game." *Los Angeles Times*, October 27, 1901, p. 3.
10. "Profit in mad woman's plan." *Washington Post*, May 21, 1905, p. E3.
11. "Insane woman's idea." *Washington Post*, March 31, 1906, p. 2.
12. "Mrs. Young indicted." *Washington Post*, March 26, 1910, p. 11.
13. "Widow hated beards." *Washington Post*, April 5, 1910, p. 16.
14. "Victim's note to lady love." *Los Angeles Times*, February 2, 1909, sec 2, p. 3.
15. *Ibid.*
16. "Matrimonial agency fraud." *Los Angeles Times*, December 16, 1909, p. 9.
17. "Seeks to put bride in jail." *Los Angeles Times*, October 13, 1912, p. 1.
18. "Suspect four of bunco game." *Los Angeles Times*, May 21, 1913, p. 3.

Chapter 4

1. "A singular case — the exploit of an aged female imposter." *New York Times*, August 24, 1865, p. 8.
2. *Ibid.*
3. "General city news." *New York Times*, November 17, 1867, p. 5.
4. "Birds of prey." *New York Times*, April 10, 1870, p. 3.
5. "Not a beggar on horseback." *New York Times*, October 30, 1878, p. 5.
6. *Ibid.*
7. "A female imposter in Paterson." *New York Times*, August 4, 1881, p. 8.
8. "An imposter on her rounds." *New York Times*, February 23, 1883, p. 1.
9. "The Queen beggar arrested." *New York Times*, August 20, 1884, p. 8.
10. "A female swindler arrested." *New York Times*, September 29, 1888, p. 5.
11. "Fair-weather fakirs." *Washington Post*, March 7, 1892, p. 2.

12. "Aged imposter identified." *Washington Post*, January 9, 1897, p. 2.
13. *Ibid.*
14. "New York City beggars." *New York Times*, July 17, 1898, p. 12.
15. *Ibid.*
16. *Ibid.*
17. *Ibid.*
18. "Cherry Hill's pride gone." *New York Times*, December 26, 1898, p. 4.
19. "Arrest of a beggar." *Washington Post*, March 15, 1899, p. 11; "Charged with false pretenses." *Washington Post*, March 18, 1899, p. 8.
20. "Woman held as a swindler." *Washington Post*, September 27, 1907, p. 2.
21. "Tells tale of crime." *Washington Post*, June 23, 1919, p. 12.
22. "Borrows rail fares of eleven housewives." *Washington Post*, February 8, 1922, p. 10.
23. "Mother of 13, declared fraud, gets 360 days." *Washington Post*, March 18, 1923, p. 2.
24. "Mrs. Redmond convicted." *New York Times*, June 2, 1900, p. 16.
25. "Accuse begging woman of fraud." *Washington Post*, April 3, 1901, p. 2.
26. "Wanted burial in Alexandria." *Washington Post*, March 23, 1899, p. 10.
27. "Her dupes are many." *Washington Post*, August 2, 1901, p. 2.
28. *Ibid.*
29. *Ibid.*
30. *Ibid.*
31. "Warned to leave District." *Washington Post*, August 4, 1901, p. 10.
32. "Beggar spat upon her." *New York Times*, December 11, 1901, p. 10.
33. "Well-dressed beggar girl fined $10." *New York Times*, December 12, 1901, p. 7.
34. *Ibid.*
35. *Ibid.*
36. "Ways of a woman beggar." *Washington Post*, October 18, 1903, p. 2.
37. *Ibid.*
38. "Woman in black sentenced." *New York Times*, February 15, 1903, p. 12.
39. *Ibid.*
40. "Widow gets easy money." *Los Angeles Times*, September 21, 1904, p. A1.
41. *Ibid.*
42. "Mrs. Estel is yet grafting." *Los Angeles Times*, October 23, 1904, p. 16.
43. *Ibid.*
44. "Beggars make babies cry." *New York Times*, February 1, 1904, p. 12.
45. "The ancient profession of street begging." *New York Times*, June 19, 1904, p. MS2.
46. "Beggar of 70 years is worth $27,000." *New York Times*, April 6, 1905, p. 13.
47. "Women in nuns' garb in jail as imposters." *New York Times*, July 2, 1905, p. 12.
48. "Waters tale with tears." *Los Angeles Times*, February 13, 1907, sec 2, p. 11.
49. "Found profit in evictions." *New York Times*, September 22, 1911, p. 7.
50. "A female fraud." *Los Angeles Times*, July 14, 1888, p. 3.
51. *Ibid.*
52. *Ibid.*
53. "Mrs. Hall's scheme of fraud." *Washington Post*, May 28, 1891, p. 7.
54. "Beware of these frauds." *New York Times*, December 10, 1894, p. 9.
55. "Imposters denied use of mails." *Washington Post*, August 30, 1897, p. 8.
56. "New York City's beggars." *New York Times*, April 18, 1897, p. 28.
57. "Mrs. Taylor imposter." *New York Times*, March 19, 1900, p. 8.
58. *Ibid.*
59. "Weepy papers gold-bricked." *Los Angeles Times*, June 26, 1904, p. B12.
60. "Fakers multiply after Bush fraud." *Los Angeles Times*, May 22, 1904, p. A6.
61. *Ibid.*

Chapter 5

1. "A girl's triple crime." *New York Times*, June 16, 1872, p. 3.
2. "The check forgery." *New York Times*, April 19, 1875, p. 3.
3. "Law reports." *New York Times*, September 25, 1875, p. 2.
4. *Ibid.*
5. "Forgeries by a woman." *New York Times*, February 5, 1876, p. 3.
6. "Mrs. Trau found guilty." *New York Times*, April 9, 1881, p. 2; "Seeking a release from jail." *New York Times*, August 23, 1881, p. 8.
7. "A female forger." *Washington Post*, November 14, 1881, p. 4.
8. "Piano robbers trapped." *New York Times*, January 24, 1882, p. 2.
9. *Ibid.*
10. "The piano swindler in custody." *New York Times*, January 29, 1882, p. 5.
11. "A female swindler." *New York Times*, September 16, 1883, p. 10.
12. *Ibid.*

13. *Ibid.*
14. "Fine chance for gossip." *New York Times*, November 17, 1886, p. 2.
15. "Vermont's social scandal." *New York Times*, November 21, 1886, p. 2.
16. "Charged with fraud." *New York Times*, November 18, 1886, p. 5.
17. *Ibid.*
18. "Spendthrift widow's fall." *New York Times*, October 14, 1888, p. 5.
19. "Forgery of a young woman." *New York Times*, April 7, 1889, p. 8.
20. The woman forgers held in bail." *New York Times*, May 28, 1889, p. 5; "The female forgers." *New York Times*, May 29, 1889, p. 5.
21. "Too ready with a pen." *Washington Post*, February 17, 1890, p. 7.
22. *Ibid.*
23. *Ibid.*
24. "She gambled in stocks." *Washington Post*, February 23, 1890, p. 16.
25. *Ibid.*
26. "Mrs. Lippincott free." *New York Times*, December 14, 1890, p. 3.
27. "Bogus bank drafts." *Washington Post*, November 12, 1892, p. 4.
28. "Mrs. Annie Murphy in Montreal." *Washington Post*, November 13, 1892, p. 7; "Industrious Mrs. Murphy checked." *Washington Post*, December 16, 1892, p. 10.
29. "Female forger in jail." *Washington Post*, July 24, 1894, p. 6.
30. "Check game worked by a woman." *Washington Post*, July 28, 1895, p. 3.
31. "Mrs. Davis believed innocent." *New York Times*, June 16, 1895, p. 13.
32. "She's a fraud." *Los Angeles Times*, January 18, 1895, p. 2.
33. "Rogue or chump." *Los Angeles Times*, April 5, 1895, p. 10.
34. *Ibid.*
35. *Ibid.*
36. "All a mistake." *Los Angeles Times*, April 11, 1895, p. 6.
37. "Her Uncle Sam." *Los Angeles Times*, April 26, 1895, p. 8.
38. "Forged check swindlers." *New York Times*, December 26, 1897, p. 2.
39. "May Kellard on trial." *New York Times*, November 19, 1897, p. 10.
40. "Accused juror of flirting." *New York Times*, November 20, 1897, p. 12.
41. "May Kellard on trial." *New York Times*, November 24, 1897, p. 5; "Kellard jury disagrees." *New York Times*, November 27, 1897, p. 3.
42. "May Kellard on trial again." *New York Times*, February 25, 1898, p. 12.
43. "Forgery and false pretenses." *Washington Post*, March 26, 1898, p. 3.
44. "Female check swindler." *Washington Post*, March 22, 1900, p. 9.
45. *Ibid.*
46. "Woman dupes a messenger." *New York Times*, December 22, 1900, p. 3.
47. "Woman forger kept out of prison by mother's sacrifices." *Washington Post*, December 4, 1904, p. B7.
48. "Mrs. Bolch under bond." *Washington Post*, December 5, 1906, p. 3.
49. "Five years for Mrs. Bolch." *Washington Post*, December 15, 1906, p. 3.
50. "Count's daughter swindler." *Washington Post*, January 10, 1907, p. 3.
51. "Black hand was a girl." *New York Times*, December 14, 1907, p. 16.
52. "Lay worthless checks to her." *Los Angeles Times*, December 25, 1910, p. 5.
53. "Bonifaces bled." *Los Angeles Times*, September 14, 1911, sec 2, p. 7.
54. "Jail for colored forger." *New York Times*, June 10, 1911, p. 6.
55. "Mrs. Harris in court." *Washington Post*, January 26, 1911, p. 3.
56. "Convicted as forger." *Washington Post*, May 18, 1911, p. 14.
57. "Hold woman for forgery." *New York Times*, August 15, 1912, p. 18.
58. "Miss Zindel in a frenzy." *New York Times*, September 7, 1912, p. 22.
59. "Rosa Zindel asks clemency." *New York Times* October 11, 1912, p. 8.
60. "Mrs. Burkett tells of Roosevelt note." *New York Times*, June 23, 1921, p. 16.
61. "Woman once in jail in Roosevelt case." *New York Times*, June 24, 1921, p. 14.
62. "Accuse woman of Roosevelt forgery." *New York Times*, July 13, 1921, pp. 1, 5,
63. "Fraud letter read in Burkett case." *New York Times*, October 12, 1921, p. 13.
64. "Mrs. Burkett held guilty of forgery." *New York Times*, October 14, 1921, p. 36; "Three-year sentence for Mrs. Burkett." *New York Times*, October 25, 1921, p. 16.
65. "Actress arrested in theatre chase." *New York Times*, August 11, 1914, p. 13.
66. "Woman forger captured." *New York Times*, August 5, 1903, p. 5.
67. *Ibid.*
68. "Admits she is forger." *Washington Post*, November 18, 1916, p. 4.
69. "Woman arrested on bogus check

charge." *Los Angeles Times*, March 22, 1919, sec 2, p. 9.
70. "Mystery woman nabbed at jail." *Los Angeles Times*, November 1, 1919, sec 2, p. 12.

Chapter 6

1. "Mabel Parker remanded." *New York Times*, August 17, 1903, p. 10.
2. "Smiles over forgeries." *New York Times*, August 18, 1903, p. 3.
3. *Ibid.*
4. "Woman denies forgery." *New York Times*, December 16, 1903, p. 16.
5. "Says Mabel Parker forged check names." *New York Times*, January 27, 1904, p. 5.
6. *Ibid.*
7. "Mabel Parker's trial." *New York Times*, January 28, 1904, p. 7.
8. "Mabel Parker denies all." *New York Times*, January 29, 1904, p. 6.
9. "Mabel Parker sentenced." *New York Times*, January 30, 1904, p. 1.

Chapter 7

1. "Police reports." *New York Times*, November 15, 1860, p. 8.
2. "Local intelligence." *New York Times*, May 20, 1865, p. 2.
3. "A swindler on her rounds." *New York Times*, January 26, 1883, p. 2.
4. "A charitable fraud." *New York Times*, January 12, 1887, p. 5.
5. *Ibid.*
6. *Ibid.*
7. *Ibid.*
8. "Bicycle swindler gets off." *Washington Post*, April 29, 1894, p. 14.
9. "Clever swindlers caught." *New York Times*, March 16, 1899, p. 2.
10. "Mrs. Ruth Howard a victim." *New York Times*, March 18, 1899, p. 4.
11. "Held as a swindler." *Washington Post*, May 15, 1899, p. 2.
12. "Her project checked." *Washington Post*, July 7, 1901, p. 2.
13. *Ibid.*
14. "Nab alleged crooks." *Washington Post*, July 4, 1904, p. 2.
15. "Pretty thief driven away." *Los Angeles Times*, December 12, 1903, p. 10.
16. *Ibid.*
17. "Held her for mail frauds." *New York Times*, April 27, 1905, p. 7.
18. "Society folk victimized." *New York Times*, October 29, 1906, p. 3.
19. "Young poetess is held as swindler." *New York Times*, August 19, 1907, p. 14.
20. "Held for theatre frauds." *New York Times*, July 21, 1910, p. 7.
21. "Alleged women swindlers." *Los Angeles Times*, January 29, 1911, p. 8.
22. "Can you speak in pot-hooks?" *Los Angeles Times*, June 26, 1913, sec 2, pp. 1, 5.
23. *Ibid.*
24. "Court clears Mrs. White." *Los Angeles Times*, June 27, 1913, sec 2, p. 6.
25. "Woman pleads guilty." *Los Angeles Times*, July 4, 1916, sec 2, p. 8.
26. "She got $54,000 in 116 days." *Washington Post*, November 17, 1918, p. 11.

Chapter 8

1. "A female broker arrested." *New York Times*, December 8, 1887, p. 2.
2. *Ibid.*
3. "A woman's poor speculation." *New York Times*, October 18, 1882, p. 8.
4. *Ibid.*
5. "Mrs. Carrie Morse's victims." *New York Times*, April 6, 1884, p. 7.
6. "The female stock broker." *New York Times*, April 8, 1884, p. 8.
7. "A commonplace swindler." *New York Times*, December 9, 1887, p. 2.
8. *Ibid.*
9. "How the trick is done." *New York Times*, December 10, 1887, p. 2.
10. *Ibid.*
11. "Woman, 85, faces life prison term." *New York Times*, August 4, 1931, p. 23.
12. "Mrs. La Touche held in big bail for theft." *New York Times*, August 4, 1917, p. 14.
13. *Ibid.*
14. "Woman, 85, faces life prison term." *New York Times*, August 4, 1931, p. 23.
15. "Woman, 85, in court fights a life term." *New York Times*, August 7, 1931, p. 19.
16. "Woman, 85, is indicted." *New York Times*, August 20, 1931, p. 4.
17. "Woman, 85, escapes life term as thief." *New York Times*, September 1, 1931, p. 17.
18. "Woman, 85, is freed." *New York Times*, September 10, 1931, p. 27.

Chapter 9

1. "Local miscellany." *New York Times*, March 14, 1876, p. 10.

2. "A clever swindler." *New York Times*, November 7, 1876, p. 2.
3. Thomas Byrnes. *1886 Professional Criminals of America*. New York: Chelsea House, 1969, pp 314–316.
4. "Mrs. Hansen surrendered." *New York Times*, July 21, 1897, p. 3.
5. "A clever female swindler." *New York Times*, December 12, 1876, p. 5.
6. *Ibid*.
7. "Living on the hotels." *New York Times*, May 21, 1884, p. 2.
8. *Ibid*.
9. "A girl of many names." *New York Times*, May 25, 1884, p. 14; "Complaints against Kate Laird." *New York Times*, May 27, 1884, p. 8.
10. "Big Bertha." *Los Angeles Times*, April 27, 1888, p. 4.
11. "Big Bertha." *Los Angeles Times*, June 13, 1888, p. 5.
12. "Big Bertha." *Los Angeles Times*, November 29, 1888, p. 5; "Big Bertha acquitted." *Los Angeles Times*, February 2, 1889, p. 5.
13. "Her bonds were bogus." *Washington Post*, November 2, 1892, p. 7.
14. *Ibid*.
15. "Accused son released." *Washington Post*, January 20, 1906, p. 3.
16. "Mrs. Smith must answer." *New York Times*, November 5, 1895, p. 9.
17. *Ibid*.
18. "How Mrs. Giddings jollied the town." *Los Angeles Times*, June 1, 1901, p. 11.
19. *Ibid*.
20. *Ibid*.
21. "Mrs. Giddings gets there." *Los Angeles Times*, June 18, 1901, p. 10.
22. "Tragedy reveals life of woman swindler." *Los Angeles Times*, November 27, 1907, p. 15.
23. "Vanderbilt name aids alleged fraud." *New York Times*, November 6, 1915, p. 4.
24. "Many were fooled by Vanderbilt name." *New York Times*, November 11, 1915, p. 18.

Chapter 10

1. "Arrest of Mrs. Casselman." *New York Times*, November 21, 1876, p. 8.
2. *Ibid*.
3. *Ibid*.
4. "The arrest of Mrs. Casselman." *New York Times*, November 22, 1876, p. 5.
5. "The boarding-house ravager." *New York Times*, November 23, 1876, p. 4.
6. *Ibid*.
7. "Local miscellany." *New York Times*, November 23, 1876, p. 8.
8. "Local miscellany." *New York Times*, November 24, 1876, p. 2.
9. "The criminal record." *New York Times*, November 25, 1876, p. 10.
10. *Ibid*.
11. "Law reports." *New York Times*, November 26, 1876, p. 5.
12. *Ibid*.

Chapter 11

1. "Altogether too confiding." *New York Times*, September 11, 1880, p. 8.
2. *Ibid*.
3. "An inflated estate." *New York Times*, October 26, 1880, p. 3.
4. Thomas Byrnes. *1886 Professional Criminals of America*. New York Chelsea House, 1969, p. 200.
5. "A confidence woman's arrest." *New York Times*, July 1, 1881, p. 8.
6. "Miscellaneous city news." *New York Times*, October 27, 1881, p. 3.
7. "A confidence woman's arrest." *New York Times*, July 1, 1881, p. 8.
8. "Miscellaneous city news." *New York Times*, October 27, 1881, p. 3.
9. "Lying to suit herself." *New York Times*, January 24, 1883, p. 8.
10. *Ibid*.
11. "Bertha Heyman's pride." *New York Times*, July 11, 1883, p. 5.
12. "Bertha Heyman found guilty." *New York Times*, august 23, 1881, p. 8.
13. "Big Bertha in trouble again." *New York Times*, April 1, 1888, p. 16.
14. Thomas Byrnes, op. cit., p. 201.

Chapter 12

1. "Mrs. Chadwick's luxury." *New York Times*, November 30, 1904, p. 2.
2. *Ibid*.
3. "Amazing career of graft." *Washington Post*, December 25, 1904, p. A6.
4. *Ibid*.
5. *Ibid*.
6. *Ibid*.
7. *Ibid*.

8. *Ibid.*
9. *Ibid.*
10. *Ibid.*
11. "Mrs. Chadwick's luxury." *New York Times*, November 30, 1904, p.2.
12. "Mrs. Chadwick's life story." *Washington Post*, December 9, 1904, p. 5; "Says she is her sister." *New York Times*, December 9, 1904, p. 2.
13. "Identify Mrs. Chadwick as Mme Devere, forger." *New York Times*, December 16, 1904, p. 2.
14. "Beckwith's amazing story." *New York Times*, December 11, 1904, p. 2.
15. *Ibid.*
16. *Ibid.*
17. *Ibid.*
18. "Amazing career of graft." *Washington Post*, December 25, 1904, p. A6.
19. "The story of Mrs. Chadwick, the high priestess of fraudulent finance." *Washington Post*, December 25, 1904, p. A6.
20. "Mrs. Chadwick got big sums easily." *New York Times*, November 5, 1907, p. 14.
21. "The story of Mrs. Chadwick....." op. cit.
22. "Eccentric and extravagant." *Washington Post*, December 25, 1904, p. A6.
23. *Ibid.*
24. "Mrs. Chadwick dead." *Washington Post*, October 11, 1907, p. 1.
25. "Behind prison doors." *Washington Post*, January 13, 1906, p. 3.
26. "Cassie Chadwick." *Washington Post*, January 14, 1907, p. 6.
27. "Mrs. Chadwick ready to die." *Los Angeles Times*, October 10, 1907, p. 2.
28. "Fair frauds made history." *Washington Post*, April 10, 1910, p. MS4.

Chapter 13

1. "Pension frauds." *New York Times*, September 9, 1869, p. 2.
2. *Ibid.*
3. "Pension fraud." *New York Times*, March 6, 1876, p. 8.
4. *Ibid.*
5. "Mrs. Kingsbury's alleged forgery." *New York Times*, January 23, 1880, p. 3.
6. "Mrs. Sadler an imposter." *Washington Post*, November 1, 1890, p. 6.
7. "Pension fraud by an aged woman." *New York Times*, June 5, 1895, p. 13.
8. "Fined for pension fraud." *New York Times*, October 28, 1901, p. 2.

9. "A female swindler." *New York Times*, December 29, 1872, p. 8.
10. "The female swindler." *New York Times*, December 30, 1872, p. 5.
11. "A clever woman swindler." *New York Times*, February 19, 1899, p. 9.
12. "Daughter of Lincoln's cabinet officer charged." *New York Times*, May 25, 1904, p. 2.
13. "Foxy female fooled them." *Los Angeles Times*, November 17, 1905, sec 2, p. 1.
14. "Woman waltzes her way to jail." *New York Times*, October 4, 1909, p. 20.
15. *Ibid.*
16. "Baby stare helped." *Washington Post*, September 28, 1912, p. 3.
17. "Love of man and finery make trouble for girl." *Los Angeles Times*, October 10, 1912, p. 11.
18. "An aged imposter." *Los Angeles Times*, May 22, 1913, sec 2, p. 10.
19. "Took son-in-law's name." *New York Times*, July 23, 1915, p. 9.

Chapter 14

1. "Arrest of a clever female swindler." *New York Times*, March 2, 1873, p. 8; "Business in the Court of General Sessions." *New York Times*, March 11, 1873, p. 2.
2. "A dress for Mrs. Davis." *Washington Post*, August 26, 1883, p. 5.
3. "A brace of female swindlers." *New York Times*, February 16, 1885, p. 5.
4. "An accusation of theft." *New York Times*, March 25, 1885, p. 8.
5. "A she fakir." *Los Angeles Times*, June 27, 1888, p. 6.
6. "Fakir Clark." *Los Angeles Times*, February 13, 1890, p. 6.
7. "Those fakirs." *Los Angeles Times*, May 11, 1890, p. 3.
8. "She was a winning woman." *New York Times*, May 13, 1894, p. 18.
9. "Brooklyn." *New York Times*, November 2, 1894, p. 8.
10. "A female fakir." *Los Angeles Times*, January 29, 1895, p. 9.
11. "Secured goods by false orders." *Washington Post*, September 25, 1899, p. 2.
12. "Bunco woman caught." *Los Angeles Times*, December 1, 1907, p. 6.
13. "The capture of Mrs. Rowland." *Washington Post*, August 26, 1889, p. 2.
14. "Did the matron steal." *Washington Post*, September 20, 1889, p. 6.

15. "Mrs. Rowland's bail." *Washington Post*, September 21, 1889, p. 7.
16. "Dr. Hammond's bills." *Washington Post*, September 26, 1889, p. 8.
17. "Mrs. Rowland sues for damages." *Washington Post*, November 20, 1890, p. 6.
18. "Woman held for forgery." *New York Times*, March 11, 1911, p. 22.
19. "Woman forger took $14,000 in a year." *New York Times*, March 12, 1911, p. 57.
20. "Arrest woman, fraud charged." *Los Angeles Times*, September 6, 1911, sec 2, p. 6.
21. "Suspect band of swindlers." *Los Angeles Times*, September 7, 1911, sec 2, p. 3.
22. "David Harum in petticoats." *Los Angeles Times*, November 10, 1905, sec 2, p. 5.
23. "Wants scalp of she Harum." *Los Angeles Times*, November 17, 1905, p. 17.
24. "Think she's a fraud." *New York Times*, March 14, 1893, p. 8.
25. "Adroit woman swindler." *Washington Post*, October 21, 1897, p. 3.
26. "Say woman is an imposter." *Los Angeles Times*, December 16, 1909, p. 9.
27. "Queen of the fakers lands in Oregon jail." *Variety*, June 2, 1922, pp. 1–2.
28. "Says her falls are frauds." *New York Times*, June 7, 1910, p. 7.
29. "Came back from the dead." *Washington Post*, June 22, 1901, p. 4.
30. "Ellis Glenn, free, still a mystery." *Washington Post*, June 25, 1905, p. A2.
31. *Ibid.*
32. *Ibid.*
33. *Ibid.*
34. "Came back from the dead." *Washington Post*, June 22, 1901, p. 4.
35. "Women's garments in room." *Washington Post*, July 12, 1901, p. 4; "Ellis Glenn, free, still a mystery." *Washington Post*, June 25, 1905, p. A2.
36. "Ellis Glenn's false teeth." *Washington Post*, July 14, 1901, p. 6; "Ellis Glenn freed." *Washington Post*, June 4, 1905, p. 9.
37. "The mysterious Ellis Glenn." *Washington Post*, December 27, 1908, p. M2.
38. "A female swindler trapped." *New York Times*, November 25, 1882, p. 3.
39. *Ibid.*
40. "A mystery cleared up." *New York Times*, June 1, 1885, p. 8.
41. *Ibid.*
42. *Ibid.*
43. "Fines Mrs. Wiborg $1,750." *New York Times*, October 24, 1913, p. 6.
44. "Mrs Warren faces duty fraud charge." *New York Times*, December 11, 1915, p. 22.
45. *Ibid.*
46. "Authoress charged with stock frauds." *New York Times*, October 3, 1915, p. 25.

Chapter 15

1. Thomas Byrnes. *1886 Professional Criminals of America*. New York: Chelsea House, 1969, p. 317.
2. *Ibid.*, pp. 317–318.
3. "A notorious confidence woman." *New York Times*, December 4, 1881, p. 10.
4. *Ibid.*
5. "Mrs. Peck caught at last." *New York Times*, September 30, 1884, p. 4.
6. *Ibid.*
7. *Ibid.*
8. "The confidence queen again." *New York Times*, December 7, 1884, p. 14.
9. "Back in the Tombs again." *New York Times*, January 6, 1895, p. 2.
10. "Behind the prison bars." *New York Times*, May 29, 1885, p. 8.
11. *Ibid.*
12. "Queen of confidence women." *Washington Post*, November 6, 1897, p. 4.
13. "She swindles at 80." *New York Times*, November 28, 1908, p. 1.
14. *Ibid.*
15. "Confidence queen to be free at 82." *New York Times*, December 7, 1911, p. 8.
16. "Confidence queen, at 84, is busy again." *New York Times*, June 2, 1914, p. 20.

Bibliography

"An accusation of theft." *New York Times*, March 25, 1885, p. 8.
"Accuse begging woman of fraud." *Washington Post*, April 3, 1901, p. 2.
"Accuse woman of Roosevelt forgery." *New York Times*, July 13, 1921, pp. 1, 5.
"Accused juror of flirting." *New York Times*, November 20, 1897, p. 12.
"Accused son released." *Washington Post*, January 20, 1906, p. 3.
"Actress arrested in theatre chase." *New York Times*, August 11, 1914, p. 13.
"Admits she is a forger." *Washington Post*, November 18, 1916, p. 4.
"Adroit woman swindler." *Washington Post*, October 21, 1897, p. 3.
"An aged imposter." *Los Angeles Times*, May 22, 1913, sec 2, p. 10.
"Aged imposter identified." *Washington Post*, January 9, 1897, p. 2.
"Airy Elsie's spook fight." *Los Angeles Times*, August 30, 1901, p. 9.
"All a mistake." *Los Angeles Times*, April 11, 1895, p. 6.
"Alleged women swindlers." *Los Angeles Times*, January 29, 1911, p. 8.
"Altogether too confiding." *New York Times*, September 11, 1880, p. 8.
"Amazing career of graft." *Washington Post*, December 25, 1904, p. A6.
"The ancient profession of street begging." *New York Times*, June 19, 1904, p. MS2.
"Ann O'D. Diss Debar again out of prison." *Washington Post*, August 14, 1906, p. 4.
"Ann O'Delia held for trial." *Washington Post*, November 24, 1901, p. 3.
"Arrest of a beggar." *Washington Post*, March 15, 1899, p. 11.
"Arrest of a clever female swindler." *New York Times*, March 2, 1873, p. 8.
"Arrest of Mrs. Casselman." *New York Times*, November 21, 1876, p. 8.
"The arrest of Mrs. Casselman." *New York Times*, November 22, 1876, p. 5.
"Arrest woman, fraud charged." *Los Angeles Times*, September 6, 1911, sec 2, p. 6.
"Authoress charged with stock frauds." *New York Times*, October 3, 1915, p. 25.
"Baby stare helped." *Washington Post*, September 28, 1912, p. 3.
"Back in the Tombs again." *New York Times*, January 6, 1885, p. 2.
"Bares medium's past." *Washington Post*, June 12, 1907, p. 5.
"Bauer trial concluded." *Los Angeles Times*, March 14, 1900, p. 10.
"Beckwith's amazing story." *New York Times*, December 11, 1904, p. 2.
"Beggar of 70 years is worth $27,000." *New York Times*, April 6, 1905, p. 13.
"Beggar spat upon her." *New York Times*, December 11, 1901, p. 10.
"Beggars make babies cry." *New York Times*, February 1, 1904, p. 12.
"Behind prison doors." *Washington Post*, January 13, 1906, p. 3.

"Behind the prison bars." *New York Times*, May 29, 1885, p. 8.
"Believe she is Diss Debar." *Washington Post*, September 19, 1891, p. 6.
"Bertha Heyman found guilty." *New York Times*, August 23, 1881, p. 8.
"Bertha Heyman's pride." *New York Times*, July 11, 1883, p. 5.
"Beware of these frauds." *New York Times*, December 10, 1894, p. 9.
"Bicycle swindler gets off." *Washington Post*, April 29, 1894, p. 14.
"Big Bertha." *Los Angeles Times*, April 27, 1888, p. 4.
"Big Bertha." *Los Angeles Times*, June 13, 1888, p. 5.
"Big Bertha." *Los Angeles Times*, November 29, 1888, p. 5.
"Big Bertha acquitted." *Los Angeles Times*, February 2, 1889, p. 5.
"Big Bertha in trouble again." *New York Times*, April 1, 1888, p. 16.
"Birds of prey." *New York Times*, April 10, 1870, p. 3.
"Black hand was a girl." *New York Times*, December 14, 1907, p. 16.
"The boarding-house ravager." *New York Times*, November 23, 1876, p. 4.
"Bogus bank drafts." *Washington Post*, November 12, 1892, p. 4.
"Bogus spiritualists exposed." *Washington Post*, April 28, 1888, p. 6.
"Bonifaces bled." *Los Angeles Times*, September 14, 1911, sec 2, p. 7.
"Borrows rail fares of eleven housewives." *Washington Post*, February 8, 1922, p. 10.
"A brace of female swindlers." *New York Times*, February 16, 1885, p. 5.
"Brooklyn." *New York Times*, November 2, 1894, p. 8.
"Bunco woman caught." *Los Angeles Times*, December 1, 1907, p. 6.
"Business in the Court of General Sessions." *New York Times*, April 19, 1875, p. 3.
Byrnes, Thomas. *1886 Professional Criminals of America*. New York: Chelsea House, 1969.
"Came back from dead." *Washington Post*, June 22, 1901, p. 4.
"Can you speak in pot-hooks?" *Los Angeles Times*, June 26, 1913, sec 2, pp. 1, 5.
"The capture of Mrs. Rowland." *Washington Post*, August 26, 1889, p. 2.
"Cassie Chadwick." *Washington Post*, January 14, 1907, p. 6.
"Chance for Mme. Diss Debarr." *Variety*, September 4, 1909, p. 4.
"Charged with false pretenses." *Washington Post*, March 18, 1899, p. 8.
"Charged with fraud." *New York Times*, November 18, 1886, p. 5.
"Charged with fraud." *Los Angeles Times*, April 24, 1899, p. 11.
"A charitable fraud." *New York Times*, January 12, 1887, p. 5.
"Check game worked by a woman." *Washington Post*, July 28, 1895, p. 3.
"Cherry Hill's pride gone." *New York Times*, December 26, 1898, p. 4.
"Chicago's bogus spiritualists." *Washington Post*, April 17, 1888, p. 6.
"A clever female swindler." *New York Times*, December 12, 1876, p. 5.
"A clever swindler." *New York Times*, November 7, 1876, p. 2.
"Clever swindlers caught." *New York Times*, March 16, 1899, p. 2.
"A clever woman swindler." *New York Times*, February 19, 1899, p. 9.
"Complaints against Kate Laird." *New York Times*, May 27, 1884, p. 8.
"The confidence queen again." *New York Times*, December 7, 1884, p. 14.
"Confidence queen, at 84, is busy again." *New York Times*, June 2, 1914, p. 20.
"Confidence queen to be free at 82." *New York Times*, December 7, 1911, p. 8.
"A confidence woman's arrest." *New York Times*, July 1, 1881, p. 8.
"A commonplace swindler." *New York Times*, December 9, 1887, p. 2.
"Convicted as forger." *Washington Post*, May 18, 1911, p. 14.
"Count's daughter swindler." *Washington Post*, January 10, 1907, p. 3.
"Court clears Mrs. White." *Los Angeles Times*, June 27, 1913, sec 2, p. 6.
"The criminal record." *New York Times*, November 25, 1876, p. 10.

Bibliography

"Daughter of Lincoln's cabinet officer charged." *New York Times*, May 25, 1904, p. 2.
"David Harum in petticoats." *Los Angeles Times*, November 10, 1905, sec 2, p. 5.
"Defend their queen." *Washington Post*, March 30, 1907, p. 2.
"Did the matron steal." *Washington Post*, September 20, 1889, p. 6.
"Diss Debar is fired." *Washington Post*, August 26, 1909, p. 4.
"Diss Debar raves in court." *Washington Post*, October 19, 1901, p. 4.
"Diss Debar under arrest." *Washington Post*, October 22, 1892, p. 7.
"The Diss Debars sentenced." *Washington Post*, June 19, 1888, p. 6.
"Dr. Hammond's bills." *Washington Post*, September 26, 1889, p. 8.
"Dr. Laurence speaks." *New York Times*, May 14, 1888, p. 5.
"A dress for Mrs. Davis." *Washington Post*, August 26, 1883, p. 5.
"Eccentric and extravagant." *Washington Post*, December 25, 1904, p. A6.
"Ellis Glenn, free, still a mystery." *Washington Post*, June 25, 1905, p. A2.
"Ellis Glenn freed." *Washington Post*, June 4, 1905, p. 9.
"Ellis Glenn's false teeth." *Washington Post*, July 14, 1901, p. 6.
"Elsie escapes." *Los Angeles Times*, October 24, 1888, p. 5.
"Elsie kissed congregation." *Los Angeles Times*, October 6, 1903, p. 7.
"Elsie Reynolds." *Los Angeles Times*, October 1, 1888, p. 5.
"Exposed." *Los Angeles Times*, April 23, 1887, p. 1.
"Exposes fake of spookess." *Los Angeles Times*, March 23, 1906, sec 2, p. 4.
"Fail to find spook bishop." *Washington Post*, November 10, 1908, p. 11.
"Fair frauds made history." *Washington Post*, April 10, 1910, p. MS4.
"Fair-weather fakirs." *Washington Post*, March 7, 1892, p. 2.
"Fakers multiply after Bush fraud." *Los Angeles Times*, May 22, 1904, p. A6.
"Fakir Clark." *Los Angeles Times*, February 13, 1890, p. 6.
"A female broker arrested." *New York Times*, December 8, 1887, p. 2.
"Female check swindler." *Washington Post*, March 22, 1900, p. 9.
"A female fakir." *Los Angeles Times*, January 29, 1895, p. 9.
"A female forger." *Washington Post*, November 14, 1881, p. 4.
"Female forger in jail." *Washington Post*, July 24, 1894, p. 6.
"The female forgers." *New York Times*, May 29, 1889, p. 5.
"A female fraud." *Los Angeles Times*, July 14, 1888, p. 3.
"A female imposter in Paterson." *New York Times*, August 4, 1881, p. 8.
"The female stock broker." *New York Times*, April 8, 1884, p. 8.
"A female swindler." *New York Times*, December 29, 1872, p. 8.
"The female swindler." *New York Times*, December 30, 1872, p. 5.
"A female swindler." *New York Times*, September 16, 1883, p. 10.
"A female swindler arrested." *New York Times*, September 29, 1888, p. 5.
"A female swindler trapped." *New York Times*, November 25, 1882, p. 3.
"Find chance for gossip." *New York Times*, November 17, 1886, p. 2.
"Fined for pension fraud." *New York Times*, October 28, 1901, p. 2.
"Fines Mrs. Wiborg $1,750." *New York Times*, October 24, 1913, p. 6.
"Five years for Mrs. Bolch." *Washington Post*, December 15, 1906, p. 3.
"Forged check swindlers." *New York Times*, December 26, 1897, p. 2.
"Forgeries by a woman." *New York Times*, February 5, 1876, p. 3.
"Forgery and false pretenses." *Washington Post*, March 26, 1898, p. 3.
"Forgery by a young woman." *New York Times*, April 7, 1889, p. 8.
"Found profit in evictions." *New York Times*, September 22, 1911, p. 7.
"Foxy female fooled them." *Los Angeles Times*, November 17, 1905, sec 2, p. 1.
"Fraud letter read in Burkett case." *New York Times*, October 12, 1921, p. 13.

"General city news." *New York Times*, November 17, 1867, p. 5.
"Ghost Elsie." *Los Angeles Times*, November 19, 1888, p. 1.
"A girl of many names." *New York Times*, May 25, 1884, p. 14.
"A girl's triple crime." *New York Times*, June 16, 1872, p. 3.
"Held as a swindler." *Washington Post*, May 15, 1899, p. 2.
"Held for theatre frauds." *New York Times*, July 21, 1910, p. 7.
"Held her for mail frauds." *New York Times*, April 27, 1905, p. 7.
"Her bonds were bogus." *Washington Post*, November 2, 1892, p. 7.
"Her dupes are many." *Washington Post*, August 2, 1901, p. 2.
"Her project checked." *Washington Post*, July 7, 1901, p. 2.
"Her Uncle Sam." *Los Angeles Times*, April 26, 1895, p. 8.
"Hold woman for forgery." *New York Times*, August 15, 1912, p. 18.
"How the trick is done." *New York Times*, December 10, 1887, p. 2.
"How Mrs. Giddings jollied the town." *Los Angeles Times*, June 1, 1901, p. 11.
"Identify Mrs. Chadwick as Mme Devere, forger." *New York Times*, December 16, 1904, p. 2.
"Industrious Mrs. Murphy checked." *Washington Post*, December 16, 1892, p. 10.
"An inflated estate." *New York Times*, October 26, 1880, p. 3.
"Insane woman's idea." *Washington Post*, March 31, 1906, p. 2.
"An imposter on her rounds." *New York Times*, February 23, 1883, p. 5.
"Imposters denied use of mails." *Washington Post*, August 30, 1897, p. 8.
"Jail for colored forger." *New York Times*, June 10, 1911, p. 6.
"Kellard jury disagrees" *New York Times*, November 27, 1897, p. 3.
Kyrke, Wilford. "Spook pictures." *Los Angeles Times*, February 15, 1891, p. 15.
"Law reports." *New York Times*, September 25, 1875, p. 2.
"Law reports." *New York Times*, November 26, 1876, p. 5.
"Lay worthless checks to her." *Los Angeles Times*, December 25, 1910, p. 5.
"Living on the hotels." *New York Times*, May 21, 1884, p. 2.
"Local intelligence." *New York Times*, May 20, 1865, p. 2.
"Local miscellany." *New York Times*, March 14, 1876, p. 10.
"Local miscellany." *New York Times*, November 23, 1876, p. 8.
"Local miscellany." *New York Times*, November 24, 1876, p. 2.
"Look for Diss Debar." *Washington Post*, August 27, 1909, p. 3.
"Love of man and finery make trouble for girl." *Los Angeles Times*, October 10, 1912, p. 11.
"Lying to suit herself." *New York Times*, January 24, 1883, p. 8.
"Mabel Parker denies all." *New York Times*, January 29, 1904, p. 6.
"Mabel Parker remanded." *New York Times*, August 17, 1903, p. 10.
"Mabel Parker sentenced." *New York Times*, January 30, 1904, p. 1.
"Mabel Parker's trial." *New York Times*, January 28, 1904, p. 7.
"The madame as witness." *Washington Post*, June 14, 1888, p. 4.
"Madame Diss DeBar released." *Washington Post*, December 19, 1888, p. 3.
"Madame Diss Debar's plans." *Washington Post*, July 8, 1888, p. 7.
"Many were fooled by Vanderbilt name." *New York Times*, November 11, 1915, p. 18.
"Matrimonial agency fraud." *Los Angeles Times*, December 16, 1909, p. 9.
"Matrimonial bunco game." *Los Angeles Times*, October 27, 1901, p. 3.
"A matrimonial swindle." *Washington Post*, August 5, 1889, p. 7.
"May Kellard on trial." *New York Times*, November 19, 1897, p.10.
"May Kellard on trial." *New York Times*, November 24, 1897, p. 5.
"May Kellard on trial again." *New York Times*, February 25, 1898, p. 12.

"May Pepper appears." *Washington Post*, September 6, 1907, p. 3.
"Miscellaneous city news." *New York Times*, October 27, 1881, p. 3.
"Miss Zindel in a frenzy." *New York Times*, September 7, 1912, p. 22.
"Mme Ann Diss DeBar." *Variety*, September 11, 1909, p. 15.
"Mme. Diss Debar's debts." *Washington Post*, July 15, 1889, p. 2.
"Mother of 13, declared fraud, gets 360 days." *Washington Post*, March 18, 1923, p. 2.
"Mrs. Annie Murphy in Montreal." *Washington Post*, November 13, 1892, p. 7.
"Mrs. Bolch under bond." *Washington Post*, December 5, 1906, p. 3.
"Mrs. Burkett held guilty of forgery." *New York Times*, October 14, 1921, p. 36.
"Mrs. Burkett tells of Roosevelt note." *New York Times*, June 23, 1921, p. 16.
"Mrs. Carrie Morse's victims." *New York Times*, April 6, 1884, p. 7.
"Mrs. Chadwick dead." *Washington Post*, October 11, 1907, p. 1.
"Mrs. Chadwick got big sums easily." *New York Times*, November 5, 1907, p. 14.
"Mrs. Chadwick ready to die." *Los Angeles Times*, October 10, 1907, p. 2.
"Mrs. Chadwick's life story." *Washington Post*, December 9, 1904, p. 5.
"Mrs. Chadwick's luxury." *New York Times*, November 30 1904, p. 2.
"Mrs. Davis believed innocent." *New York Times*, June 16, 1895, p. 13.
"Mrs. Diss De Bar arraigned." *Washington Post*, April 13, 1888, p. 6.
"Mrs. Estel is yet grafting." *Los Angeles Times*, October 23, 1904, p. 16.
"Mrs. Giddings gets there." *Los Angeles Times*, June 18, 1901, p. 10.
"Mrs. Hall's scheme of fraud." *Washington Post*, May 28, 1891, p. 7.
"Mrs. Hansen surrendered." *New York Times*, July 21, 1897, p. 3.
"Mrs. Harris in court." *Washington Post*, January 26, 1911, p. 3.
"Mrs. Kingsbury's alleged forgery." *New York Times*, January 23, 1880, p. 3.
"Mrs. La Touche held in big bail for theft." *New York Times*, August 4, 1917, p. 14.
"Mrs. Lippincott free." *New York Times*, December 14, 1890, p. 3.
"Mrs. Peck caught at last." *New York Times*, September 30, 1884, p. 4.
"Mrs. Ponder sentenced." *Los Angeles Times*, May 4, 1899, p. 10.
"Mrs. Redmond convicted." *New York Times*, June 2, 1900, p. 16.
"Mrs. Rowland sues for damages." *Washington Post*, November 20, 1890, p. 6.
"Mrs. Rowland's bail." *Washington Post*, September 21, 1889, p. 7.
"Mrs. Ruth Howard a victim." *New York Times*, March 18, 1899, p. 4.
"Mrs. Sadler an imposter." *Washington Post*, November 1, 1890, p. 6.
"Mrs. Smith must answer." *New York Times*, November 5, 1895, p. 9.
"Mrs. Taylor imposter." *New York Times*, March 19, 1900, p. 8.
"Mrs. Trau found guilty." *New York Times*, April 9, 1881, p. 2.
"Mrs. Warren faces duty fraud charge." *New York Times*, December 11, 1915, p. 22.
"Mrs. Young indicted." *Washington Post*, March 26, 1910, p. 11.
"The mysterious Ellis Glenn." *Washington Post*, December 27, 1908, p. M2.
"A mystery cleared up." *New York Times*, June 1, 1885, p. 8.
"Mystery woman nabbed at jail." *Los Angeles Times*, November 1, 1919, sec 2, p. 12.
"Nab alleged crooks." *Washington Post*, July 4, 1904, p. 2.
"New York City beggars." *New York Times*, July 17, 1898, p. 12.
"New York City's beggars." *New York Times*, April 18, 1897, p. 28.
"Not a beggar on horseback." *New York Times*, October 30, 1878, p. 5.
"A notorious confidence woman." *New York Times*, December 4, 1881, p. 10.
"Pension fraud by an aged woman." *New York Times*, June 6, 1895, p. 13.
"Pension frauds." *New York Times*, September 9, 1869, p. 2.
"Pension frauds." *New York Times*, March 6, 1876, p. 8.
"Personal intelligence." *Washington Post*, April 1, 1888, p. 4.

"Piano robbers trapped." *New York Times*, January 24, 1882, p. 2.
"The piano swindler in custody." *New York Times*, January 29, 1882, p. 5.
"Police reports." *New York Times*, November 15, 1860, p. 8.
"Pretty thief driven away." *Los Angeles Times*, December 12, 1903, p. 10.
"Profit in mad woman's plan." *Washington Post*, May 21, 1905, p. E3.
"The queen beggar arrested." *New York Times*, August 20, 1884, p. 8.
"Queen of confidence women." *Washington Post*, November 6, 1897, p. 4.
"Queen of fakers lands in Oregon jail." *Variety*, June 2, 1922, pp. 1–2.
"A receiver for Mme. Diss Debar." *Washington Post*, July 21, 1889, p. 7.
"Returns Vanderbilt house." *Washington Post*, November 13, 1907, p. 15.
"Rogue or chump." *Los Angeles Times*, April 5, 1895, p. 10.
"Rosa Zindel asks clemency." *New York Times*, October 11, 1912, p. 8.
"Say woman is an imposter." *Los Angeles Times*, December 16, 1909, p.9.
"Says her falls are frauds." *New York Times*, June 7, 1910, p. 7.
"Says Mabel Parker forged check name." *New York Times*, January 27, 1904, p. 5.
"Says she is her sister." *New York Times*, December 9, 1904, p. 2.
"Schemes of a woman." *Washington Post*, August 22, 1889, p. 2.
"Secured goods by false orders." *Washington Post*, September 25, 1899, p. 2.
"Seeking a release from jail." *New York Times*, August 23, 1881, p. 8.
"Seeks to put bride in jail." *Los Angeles Times*, October 3, 1912, sec 2, p. 1.
"A she fakir." *Los Angeles Times*, June 22, 1888, p. 6.
"She gambled in stocks." *Washington Post*, February 23, 1890, p. 16.
"She got $54,000 in 116 days." *Washington Post*, November 17, 1918, p. 11.
"She swindles at 80." *New York Times*, November 28, 1908, p. 1.
"She was a winning woman." *New York Times*, May 13, 1894, p. 18.
"She's a fraud." *Los Angeles Times*, January 18, 1895, p. 2.
"A singular case — the exploit of an aged female imposter." *New York Times*, August 24, 1865, p. 8.
"Smiles over forgeries." *New York Times*, August 18, 1903, p. 3.
"Society folk victimized." *New York Times*, October 29, 1906, p. 3.
"Spendthrift widow's fall." *New York Times*, October 14, 1888, p. 5.
"Spirit photos." *Los Angeles Times*, March 30, 1880, p. 5.
"Spiritist cases are dismissed." *Los Angeles Times*, May 9, 1912, sec 2, p. 11.
"Spook knew finances." *Washington Post*, June 14, 1907, p. 3.
"Spook tells of fraud." *New York Times*, November 26, 1895, p. 8.
"Spooks." *Los Angeles Times*, January 10, 1889, p. 5.
"The story of Mrs. Chadwick, the high priestess of fraudulent finance." *Washington Post*, December 25, 1904, p. A6.
"Suspect band of swindlers." *Los Angeles Times*, September 7, 1911, sec 2, p. 3.
"Suspect four of bunco game." *Los Angeles Times*, May 21, 1913, p. 3.
"Swindled by a woman." *New York Times*, October 10, 1883, p. 5.
"A swindler on her rounds." *New York Times*, January 26, 1883, p. 2.
"Swindlers are hypnotists." *Washington Post*, October 6, 1901, p. 3.
"Tales of the town." *Washington Post*, December 9, 1900, p. 26.
"Tells tales of crime." *Washington Post*, June 23, 1919, p. 12.
"Thiebaud Bauer's defense." *Los Angeles Times*, March 11, 1900, sec 4, p. 1.
"Thiebaud Bauer's story." *Los Angeles Times*, March 13, 1900, p. 10.
"Think she's a fraud." *New York Times*, March 14, 1893, p. 8.
"Third degree for Ann." *Washington Post*, August 29, 1909, p. 11.
"Those fakirs." *Los Angeles Times*, May 11, 1890, p. 3.

"Three-year sentence for Mrs. Burkett." *New York Times*, October 25, 1921, p. 16.
"To drive spiritualist swindlers out of town." *Los Angeles Times*, April 5, 1912, sec 2, p. 1.
"Too ready with a pen." *Washington Post*, February 17, 1890, p. 7.
"Took son-in-law's name." *New York Times*, July 23, 1915, p. 9.
"Tragedy reveals life of woman swindler." *Los Angeles Times*, November 27, 907, p. 15.
"Tricky Elsie." *Los Angeles Times*, April 25, 1887, p.1.
"Vanderbilt name aids alleged fraud." *New York Times*, November 6, 1915, p. 4.
"Vermont's social scandal." *New York Times*, November 21, 1886, p. 2.
"Victim's note to lady love." *Los Angeles Times*, February 2, 1909, sec 2, p. 3.
"Wanted burial in Alexandria." *Washington Post*, March 23, 1899, p. 10.
"Wants scalp of she Harum." *Los Angeles Times*, November 17, 1905, p. 17.
"Warned to leave District." *Washington Post*, August 4, 1901, p. 10
"Waters tale with tears." *Los Angeles Times*, February 13, 1907, sec 2, p. 11.
"Ways of a beggar woman." *Washington Post*, October 18, 1903, p. 2.
"Weepy papers gold-bricked." *Los Angeles Times*, June 26, 1904, p. B12.
"Well-dressed beggar girl fined $10." *New York Times*, December 12, 1901, p. 7.
White, Frank M. "Master crooks and criminals deluxe." *Washington Post*, November 16, 1913, pp. MT4-MT5.
"Widow gets easy money." *Los Angeles Times*, September 21, 1904, p. A1.
"Widow hated beards." *Washington Post*, April 5, 1910, p. 1.
"Woman arrested on bogus check charge." *Los Angeles Times*, March 22, 1919, sec 2, p. 9.
"Woman denies forgery." *New York Times*, December 16, 1903, p. 16.
"Woman dupes a messenger." *New York Times*, December 22, 1900, p. 3.
"Woman, 85, escapes life term as thief." *New York Times*, September 1, 1931, p. 17.
"Woman, 85, faces life prison term." *New York Times*, August 4, 1931, p. 23.
"Woman, 85, in court fights a life term." *New York Times*, August 7, 1931, p. 19.
"Woman, 85, is freed." *New York Times*, September 10, 1931, p. 27.
"Woman, 85, is indicted." *New York Times*, August 20, 1931, p. 4.
"Woman forger captured." *New York Times*, August 5, 1903, p. 5.
"Woman forger kept out of prison by mother's sacrifices." *Washington Post*, December 4, 1904, p. B7.
"Woman forger took $14,000 in a year." *New York Times*, March 12, 1911, p. 57.
"Woman held as swindler." *Washington Post*, September 27, 1907, p. 2.
"Woman held for forgery." *New York Times*, March 11, 1911, p. 22.
"Woman in black sentenced." *New York Times*, February 15, 1903, p. 12.
"Woman indicted for fraud." *Los Angeles Times*, May 3, 1899, p. 7.
"Woman once in jail in Roosevelt case." *New York Times*, June 24, 1921, p. 14.
"Woman pleads guilty." *Los Angeles Times*, July 4, 1916, sec 2, p. 8.
"Woman waltzes her way to jail." *New York Times*, October 4, 1909, p. 20.
"Woman's garments in room." *Washington Post*, July 12, 1901, p. 4.
"A woman's poor speculation." *New York Times*, October 18, 1882, p. 8.
"The women forgers held in bail." *New York Times*, May 28, 1889, p. 5.
"Women in nuns' garb in jail as imposters." *New York Times*, July 2, 1905, p. 12.
"Young poetess is held as swindler." *New York Times*, August 19, 1907, p. 14.

Index

Adams, Daisy 27
Associated Charities 58, 61–62
Associated Charities of Los Angeles 73–74
asylums, insane 39–40

Babbitt, B.T. 210
babies, abuse of 47, 65–66
Balderson, V.M. 191
Bangs, Bessie 96
Bangs, Lizzie 12–13
Bangs, May 12–13
banking fraud 163–175
banks 85
Barling, Elizabeth 198
Barris, Antoinette 100
Bauer, Thiebaud 37–38
Baynes, P.J. 94
Beattie, Elinor 182–183
Beck, Mary 86
Beckwith, C.G. 168, 169, 170, 171, 174
begging 46–47, 49–51, 52–53, 60–61, 66, 68–75
Bellah, Anna 91–92
Bessie, Adolph 79
Bishop, Eleanor 155
Bissell, Emily P. 214
Biszant, J.J. 18
blackmail 26
Blackstone, Mrs. T.B. 108
Blannon, Mabel 191–192
Blighton, Ida Miller 208–209
boarding-house scam 152–153
Boaz, B.L. 10
Bolch, Catherine 98–99

Botty, Henry C. 158
Bough, John 212–213
Bowers, Rose E. 195–196
Bowman, Bessie 96
Bradford, Kate 190
Bradford, W.H. 190
Brady, Elizabeth 54
Brandt, Charles 159–160
Brayfield, Matilda 179
Brekes, David 153
Brice, Harriet 117
Brink, Mary A. 130
buggy rentals 188
burial scams 46, 49, 50, 58
Burkett, Emma Richardson 104–105
Burleigh, George W. 38
Burnett, George 215
Bush, Mrs. 74–75
business partnerships 41–42
businesses, home-based 115–116, 120–121, 122–123, 126
Byers, Ernie 203
Byrnes, Thomas 162, 210

calling cards 62
Cameron, Mary 105–106
Campbell, Elizabeth C. 123–124
Capetown, South Africa 26
Cardinal McCloskey 136–137
Carey, Mary D. 60–61
Carfare scam 53
Carnahan, Adella 17–19
Carnegie, Andrew 164, 167, 170, 172
Carter, Mrs L. 7–8

Casselman, Sarah 151–156
Cayce, Ethel J. 126–127
Chadwick, Cassie 163–175; background 164–165; lifestyle 173–174; prison and death 174–175
Chadwick, Leroy 166
Chadwick, Matilda 14–15
Charity Organization Society 49, 52–53, 62–63, 67, 70–71, 72, 116
charity scams 116–117
cheques, bad 76–114
children, use of 46–47, 50
Christy, Mrs. Francis A. 101
Clark, Mrs. Andrew 71
Clark, Belle 188–190
Clark, F.K. 188–190
Clark, May 42–43
Clifford, Kate 186
Clogg, Harriet T. 96–97
Cohen, Herman 108, 118–119
commercial scams 115–127
costumes, religious 67
Couch, George 146–147
Cowan, Amanda 12
Crandall, Elsie 9–10
Crandall, Harry 10
Crane, David W. 22
credit 181, 189, 191, 193
Creighton, Florence 113
Crocker, Edwin R. 126–127
Crocker, Harry 127
Croysdale, Vera 27–31
Cunningham, Cora Alice 200–204

235

Index

Daly Elizabeth 49–50
Daly, James 82
Davidson, Mary 84
Davis, Caroline 186–187
Davis, Maud Craig Burke 90–91
Dentel, Julius 38
Deppe, Bernard 42
De Witt, Mary 130
Diaz, Mrs. 179–181
diplomats, Spanish 143–144
Diss Debar, Ann O'Delia 20–34; appearance 28, 31; background 24–25; bankruptcy 24–25; in London, England 26–32; in prison 22–23; in vaudeville 34
Diss Debar, Joseph 20
Dix, John A. 216
Domestic Utilities Manufacturing Company (L.A.) 127
Dooley, Kate 85
door-to-door soliciting 46–47, 56, 63–64
Doyle, F.R. 196
drugged and robbed scam 45–46
Ducat, Florence 80
Duke, Ella 201–202
Dunbar, John D. 12
Dungan, Etna 39
Dunn, Kate 66
Durand, Catherine 37–39
Durand, Paul 41–42
duties, customs, avoidance 207–208

Eaton, Charles A. 167
Ennis, Mary 176–177
entertainment scams 123–124
Ernshaw, Mrs. E. 192
Estel, Helen 63–65
eviction, fake 68
extortion 100

faking wealth 27–30, 136–175
Fay, Anna Eva 14
Field, Ellen 191
financial fraud 128–134, 210–217
financial instruments, bad 76–114
Fishel, Charles 197
Fitzgerald, Anna 133

Fitzgerald Music Company 195–196
Flood, Bernard 182
Flynn, Sarah 179
Foote, Jane Eliza 116–118
forgeries 76–114, 201–204
fortune telling 26–27

Garcia, A.A. 217
Gardiner, Henry B. 40
Gerke, Herman 80–81
Gerry Society 72–73
Giddings, Mrs. H.J. 146–148
Giles, Mary 99
Given, Ralph 56
Glenn, Ellis 200–204
Gold, Jennie 60–61
Golden, Timothy 214
Gordon, Mrs. 68
Gorham Manufacturing Company 182–183
Grady, John D. 212–213
Gray, Mrs Stoddard 14
Grenier, Emma 132
Gruhn, William 142–143

Haines, Minnie A. 87–89
Hall, F.M. 17–18
Hall, Lillian 70
Hammer, Aloise 77
Hammond, William 192–194
Hanfent, Mary Ann 115
Hansen, Mary 136–139
Harmer, George 41
Harris, Josephine 102
Hartley, Margaret 45–46
Hayes, Carrie E. 119–120
Hayward, Claire 125–126
Heinze, F. Augustus 32–33
Hennery, Elizabeth 62–63
Herder, Hattie 130
Hewes, M.S. 189
Heyman, Bertha 157–162
Higgins, Nellie 126
Hill, Mrs. 188
Hitchcock, Sarah 35–36
Hitchcock, Seymour 35–36
Hobart, Lillian 32
Hocke, Mary 133
Hoffman, Mrs. Earl 57–58
Hoffman, Gottlieb 78
Hoffstott, Frank N. 172
Hogan, Elizabeth 66–67
Hollander, Frances 183–184
Hoover, Mrs. George 203
hotels 101, 106, 140–142, 179–180, 181, 188
Howard, Laura 115

Howard, Ruth 118–119
Howe, William F. 20–21
Hubbard, Sadie 92–94
Hudson, Mrs. E.S. 187–188
Huntington, Mrs. Collis P. 144–145
Hurst, Emil 43
Hurst, Olga 43–44
Hutchinson, Alice 133
hypnotism 27, 95, 168

impersonations 144–145
imposters 179–185
injuries, fake 66–67, 74–75, 165, 197–200
investment scams 128–134

Jackson, Theodore 27–31
Jenkins, Wilson 89
Jerome, Sophie 84–85
John Lane Publishing Company 194–195
Johnson, Anita 43–44
Johnson, Clara 131
Johnson, John J. 211
Johnson, Maude Myrtle 198–199
Joslyn, Mrs. 69
Jutte, W.C. 172

Karpe, Charles 160–161
Kellard, May 94–95
Kelly, J.T. 42
Kennefick, Joannah 177–178
Kett, Edward B. 48
Kingsbury, Harriet N. 178
Kley, Annie C. 136
Klink, Julius 137

Laine, Charles 43
Laird, Kate 140–142
Lamb, George 76
Lamb, Joseph 166
land scams 216–217
Langdon, Florence 108–109
Langdon, Mary 97–98
Langer, Loyance 211
La Touche, Marion 128–134
Lawrence, Benjamin 20–21
Lawrence, Felice 65–66
Lawrence, Frank 20–21
League of Justice (L.A.) 17–18
lectures 21, 24
Leonard, Ann 176–177
letters, theft of 112
Levitan, Benjamin 149
Lewis, Doc 188
Lewis, Elizabeth 98

Index

Lincoln, Lemuel 91
Linton, Annie L. 129
Lippincott, Edwin 86–89
Lippincott, Julia 86–89
Livingstone, Euniez 121–122
Lloyd, D. Frank 95
Loewenherz, Samuel 21–22
Los Angeles 7, 17–18
Low, David B. 196–197
Lowenstein, Fay 41–42
Luchs, Norman 56–57

Mack, Mamie 101–102
Mackay, David Livingstone 32–33
Macomber, Susan 194–195
Macumber, Ida Grace 39–40
Mahatma Institute 32–33
Mahoney, Frank J. 185
mail solicitations 68–75
Malone, Dudley 207–208
marriage ceremonies 42
Marsh, Luther 20–21
Martin, George B. 119
Martin, H.T. 42
Martin, Joseph 81–82
Mason, John L. 82–83
materialization 11
matrimonial agencies and scams 35–44, 104
Mattke, Edna 133
Mayer, Mary 197–198
Mayers, Anna 71–72
McConnell, Ann 213
McCrimmon, Gertrude 196–197
McGowan, William J. 25
McKenzie, Jennie 132
McLean, Minnie D. 108
McMurrow, Anita de Bettincourt 143–144
McSweeney, Wallace B. 112
Menendez, Jose 217
Mesam, Mary 137–138
Meyers, Mrs. 50
Miller, Mary A. 94
Minuth, Anna 148–150
money orders, postal 106–107
Monroe, James 216
Monroe, Mrs. J.P. 16
Monte Vista Mission Association 120
Morgan, M.A. 97
Morris, Theodore 159
motion picture scams 124
Much, Ada 57–60

Murphy, Annie 89
Murphy, Roger P. 40

Newland, Tom 122
newspaper ads 121
newspapers 73–74
Newton, Herbert 163, 166
Nutson, Andrew 39

organs, musical 54
Oster, Mrs. N. 100–101

Page, Jennie 56–57
paintings, spirit 21–22
Parker, James 110–114
Parker, Mabel 110–114
Parmenter, Harry 139
Parsons, Henry 142
Patterson, Jacob M. 177
Payne, A.L. 120
Peck, Ellen 210–217
Peck, Richard 214
Pells, Caroline 77–78
pension fraud 176–179
Pepper, George William 16
Perrin, Edward 157–158
Perrin, Tilly 157–158
Phelan, George 139
photographs, spirit 7–8, 14
Pinzer, Samuel W. 211
Ponder, Dora 36–37
Ponzi scheme 102, 128–134, 190
posing as a man 201–204
Pratt, Mrs. 61–62
Preece, Mrs. T.J. 111
Price, Sophia 115
prostitution 115, 122

Rammage, Walter H. 125–126
Redmond, Bridget 56
rental scam 139–140
retailers 186, 189
Reynolds, Elsie 8–12
Reynolds, Ira 163, 166–167, 169
Richmond, Cora 13
Rogers, Henry R. 14–15
Roosevelt, Theodore 104–105
Ross, Samuel 51
Rowland, A.T. 99
Rowland, Annie 192–194
Ryan, Bridget 98–99

Sadler, Sarah C. 178–179
Sagendorph, A. 39
sales, door-to-door 124–125

Salvation Army 134
Sanders, Edward 161
Sawyer, Carrie 17–19
Saxton, Jennie 82–83
Scannell, Mary Ann 15–17
Schenke, Louise 51
Schlarbaum, Pauline 159
schools, stenographer scam 125–126
Scott, Florence 99
Seaman, P.M. 188–190
séances 8–12, 14–19
Seymour, Mrs. Don 124
Sharpley, Annie 106–108
Shaw, Louise 202–207
shorthand scam 125–126
Simons, Mrs. M.L. 208–209
Siskind, Rifka 68
Smith, Anna D. 181–182
Smith, Henry 43
Smith, Hester 54–56
Smith, Samuel 141
Smith, Sophia Caroline 144–146
Smith, W.F. 37
sob stories 45–75
solicitations, mail 35–44
Spear, A.B. 168, 170, 174
spirits 15–16
spiritualism 7–34
Spragins, Mrs. G.N. 147
Stafford, Mary 68–70
Stanford, Leland 20
Stanley, Bertha 142–143
Stebbins, Sarah E. 92–93
Sterling, Frederick W. 127
store-to-store soliciting 46–47, 56–57, 66–67
Stryker, Mrs. Tobias 14
Sturia, Anna A. 199–200

Taylor, Harriet 72–73
Taylor, R.B. 147–148
theatrical scams 123–124
Thomas, Edward George 165
Thomas, George B. 213
Thomas, W.F. 92–94
Thompson, Martha 117
Trau, Josephine 79
Tupper, Ellen 78–79
Turner, George 43

United States Postal Service 35, 39, 40, 71, 120, 123

Valentine, Mrs. 116
Vandarstain, Jeannette 206

Vanderbilt, Edward Ward 15–17
Vanderbilt, Elsie French 149
Vanderbilt, Minerva 16
Van Rensselaer, Bella 113
Vanschaack-Smith, Grace Anton 148
vaudeville 34
Vernon, Dolly 86

Wade, Adelle Winifred 102
Wahre, Joseph 141
Walker, Hiram 115
Walker, John 145–146
Waltham, W.T. 194
Ward, James 149–150
Warren, Elizabeth 109
Warren, Mrs. Whitney 207–208
Waters, Catharine 139–140
Waters, T. Leeds 80–81
Watson, Louise 81–82
Webster, Alice 118
Weiss, Margaret 80–81
White, Edna 89–90
White, Frank 28–29
White, Lena A. 125–126
White, Mary 48–49
Whitford, Elizabeth 49
Wiborg, Mrs. Frank 207
Wills, Eliza A. 14
Wilson, Mrs. Andrew 57
Wilson, Belle 122–123
Wilson, Caroline 47–48
Wilson, Francis K. 121
Wilson, Helen 130
Wilson, May H. 120–121
Wilson Sign Company 122–123
Wolter, A. 42
Wood, William D. 95
writings, spirit 13

York, Alice M. 164, 169
Young, Elizabeth 40–41

Zindel, Rosa 102–104
Zobrist, Mrs. 73–74